An Essay on the Trinity

On the Discrepancy between the Sabellian
and Athanasian Method of Representing the
Doctrine of the Trinity

by Friedrich D. E. Schleiermacher

Translated, with notes and illustrations,
by M. Stuart in 1835

Printed in the United States of America
Columbus, OH
ISBN: 978-1-63174-170-8

Contents

Part I

(April, 1835. The Biblical Repository and Quarterly Observer)

Part II

(July, 1835. The Biblical Repository and Quarterly Observer)

THE

BIBLICAL REPOSITORY

AND

𝕼𝖚𝖆𝖗𝖙𝖊𝖗𝖑𝖞 𝕺𝖇𝖘𝖊𝖗𝖛𝖊𝖗.

No. XVIII.

APRIL, 1835.

ARTICLE I.

On the discrepancy between the Sabellian and Athanasian method of representing the doctrine of the Trinity.

By Dr. Frederic Schleiermacher, late Professor in the University of Berlin. Translated, with Notes and Illustrations, by M. Stuart, Prof. Sacred Lit. in the Theol. Sem. Andover.

INTRODUCTION BY THE TRANSLATOR.

[The individual above named as the author of a comparison between the Sabellian and Athanasian Creeds, was beyond all doubt one of the most distinguished men in the walks of theological and philosophical literature, which Germany has of late years, or even perhaps at any time, presented to the notice of the public. His acquisitions, although exceedingly varied, and extending not only to the science and history of Christian doctrine, but also to the whole round of ancient philosophy, particularly the Platonic, as well as to much of the wide circle of Latin and Greek philology, were, in every department where he extended them, original and profound. He was one of the few men, who always thought and was able to think for himself; and consequently he was never a mere copyist or retailer of other men's opinions. Yet, as a general thing, he does not appear to have given way to the temptations which naturally beset a mind of this cast, and solicit it to indulge in singular and ex-

1

cessive speculations, at the expense of sober reason and sound judgment; a characteristic which may, with much justice, be predicated of many distinguished writers in Germany, especially of many who have been conversant with philosophy and sacred criticism.

That the cast of Schleiermacher's mind was philosophic and speculative, will be admitted fully by his warmest admirers, and is indeed plain enough. That he undertook, in his leisure hours, to translate and briefly to comment upon Plato's works; and this from pure love of such study as the works of this distinguished philosopher invited him to engage in; of itself evinces a cast of mind in love with tenuous and refined speculation. The masterly version which he produced, in the course of his Platonic studies, has scarcely a parallel among modern translations of the ancient writers; so deeply did he drink in of the spirit of his favourite author, so thoroughly did he penetrate the deepest recesses of his meaning, and such an admirable power did he possess of transferring the original, body and soul, into his own vernacular language—a language which, of all those now spoken in Europe, seems to be the most capable of fully expressing the force of Plato's original diction. How weak, how diluted, how *petit maitre* like, for example, does the prince of Grecian philosophers appear, in the hands and in the vernacular of the French philosopher Cousin! How contemptible even, in those of the English Taylor! which, however, is more the fault of the translator than of the language.

The printed works of Schleiermacher, with the exception of his version of Plato, are not numerous. His principal one is his *Glaubenslehre* or *Christliche Glaube*, i. e. *System of Christian Faith* or *Doctrine,* to which he adverts in the commencement of the following Essay. There, from beginning to end, the intelligent and critical reader will find striking and original thoughts; worthy in general at least of being examined and weighed, if they are not entitled to reception. If however I might venture a single remark upon this book as a whole, I should say, that the author has aimed too much at system and theoretical perfection of orderly and logical analysis and development. That he is consistent with himself; that he carries through what he begins; and that his mind, granting him his premises, never falters as to logical deduction; will be conceded, I think, by all who read and well understand him. That he pursues his own way, independent of every preceding discussion, and of every authority except what he deems to be reason and Scripture, will be doubted by no impartial reader. That his thoughts are powerful, acute, deep, learned, striking, worthy of much examination and reflection, will be as little doubted by any except hasty and superficial readers. Every where the grasp of a mighty mind, in search of a resting place among the simple and systematic elements of truth, appears upon the very face of his disquisitions. If he has failed, and in some respects it is my full conviction that he has, it seems to be owing, at least in part, to his too great love of perfect philosophical and theoretical system. In attaining to this, he appears occasionally to have left out of sight some of the plain and practical declarations of the Scriptures. This we shall have occasion hereafter to notice, in respect to some of his speculations with regard to the doctrines of the Trinity.

As a whole, his *System of Christian Faith* can hardly be said to be adapted to common use. The speculative parts of it, which every where abound, are beyond the reach of common readers, who can attain only to an imperfect understanding of the views which he means to present. One reason of this is, that he supposes a great deal of *Vorkenntnisse* (preparatory knowledge) in his readers; and this, in respect to a great variety of subjects. Indeed the reading of his System in an intelligent way requires so much of this, that it can scarcely be supposed his book will ever become popular, in the usual sense of this word.

When I read a book of this cast, I feel myself spontaneously moved to ask the question : Can this be Christianity in its simple elements—a religion beyond all doubt designed for " every kindred and tongue and people and nation ?" I am constrained to answer this question in the negative. A religion designed by Heaven for *all*, must be intelligible to all, so far as it is to profit them. They cannot be profited by what they cannot understand. Does the System of Schleiermacher develope such a religion ? I cannot think it does. I do not mean to say, that the elements, the great and essential truths, of religion are not contained in his system. On the contrary, I fully believe that they are. But what I mean to say is, that the world at large are shut out from them, by reason of their being removed to a region so elevated and speculative that but few minds can attain to them.

I will not say, that it is of no use to write such books. I am far from believing this. But thus much we may say, viz. that it is of little *direct* use for the great mass of readers. Still, as philosophy so named has endeavoured, in a thousand ways, to embarrass religious truth, and to represent it as unreasonable and indefensible on the ground of argument and logic, it is of serious moment, at times, to shew that philosophy, in its legitimate and proper use, can never be made to bear witness against Christianity. In this respect such efforts as those of Schleiermacher may find a satisfactory apology.

The influence which some of his expositions and defences of divine truth may have, on those intelligent readers who peruse and understand them, may be *indirectly* of great use even to the multitude. If the teachers of religion are rendered more enlightened by this perusal, and become better instructed as to some highly important points of Christian doctrine, then may those committed to their care and instruction as to things pertaining to religion, reap the benefit, though in an indirect way, of such works as those which Schleiermacher has left behind him. One may say of him: *Ubi bene nemo melius;* and even where we feel compelled to dissent from him, we are almost sure to get the best arguments that can be adduced against the opinions which we espouse; a privilege which all are not willing to accept with any thankfulness, and of which, it may truly be said, only a moderate number are skilled in making a right use.

With regard to Schleiermacher's views as a Trinitarian, I can truly say, that I have met with scarcely any writer, ancient or modern, who appears to have a deeper conviction of, or more hearty belief in, the doctrine of the real Godhead of Father, Son, and Holy Spirit. This is the basis, on which the whole superstructure of his Christian system rests. No where can be found a writer more entirely alien from the views and speculations of Arians and Socinians; no where one who appears to contend more with his whole heart and soul for the proper, true, supreme Divinity of his Lord and Saviour. *God manifest in the flesh* seems to be inscribed, in his view, on every great truth of the gospel, and to enter as a necessary ingredient into the composition of its essential nature.

Yet Schleiermacher was not made a Trinitarian by Creeds and Confessions. Neither the Nicene or Athanasian Symbol, nor any succeeding formula of Trinitarian doctrine built on this, appears to have had any influence in the formation of his views.

4

From the Scriptures, and from arguments flowing, as he believed, out of Scriptural premises, he became, and lived, and died, a hearty and constant believer in the one living and true God, revealed to us as Father, Son, and Holy Ghost. Not content with receiving the formulas of ancient or of modern times, as the dictates of inspiration in regard to this awful and important subject; and unwilling to occupy his time merely in arranging, illustrating, and defending the *dicta* of Councils, assembled in the heat of controversy to put down one party and set up another; he ventured to tread the same ground that such Councils themselves claimed the right of treating, and to survey it anew with his own eyes, and inquire, whether, in the vehemence of dispute and in the midst of philosophical mists, the former survey had been in all respects made with thorough and exact skill and care, and whether a report of it in all respects intelligible and consistent had been made out.

The result of such a survey on his part—of an examination conducted by a mind so powerful; a mind also deeply imbued with reverence to its Saviour and its God, gifted with the highest degree of acuteness, and enlightened by almost all the radiance which ancient or modern luminaries have shed abroad; by a mind so independent and fearless, yet connected with a demeanor that was remarkably unassuming—such a result the readers of this work will surely be curious to see. And this is what I propose to present them with, on the present occasion.

The author himself states, near the beginning of the following Essay, that it is to be considered as a sequel of what he had before published in § 190 of his *Glaubenslehre*, on the subject of the Trinity. It is necessary, therefore, in order to give the reader a view in any good measure complete of Schleiermacher's sentiments on the subject of the Trinity, that he should first be presented with those views, to which the following principal piece is intended as a sequel, and also as a vindication. This can in no way be done so well, as by translating the original section to which he refers, as the ground-work on which he builds the superstructure exhibited in the comparative view that follows.

After defending in various places, in the most explicit manner and with great ability, the doctrine of the Godhead of the Son and Spirit, and shewing that such a development of the Deity is demanded by our moral wants as sinners, in order that we may obtain peace and sanctification; he concludes his book by the following remarkable proposition, and still more remarkable illustration and confirmation of it.

§ 190. (*Glaubenslehre*).

" *That the doctrine* [of the Trinity] *may entirely correspond with that pious feeling of which Christians are conscious and which acknowledges a higher nature,* EVEN THAT WHICH IS TRULY AND PROPERLY DIVINE, *in Christ and the Holy Spirit, the three Persons of the Godhead* MUST BE PLACED ON A PERFECT EQUALITY. *This, although every where and at all times demanded, has not been done by any of the* [public] *formulas of the churches.*"

Illustration and Confirmation.

" (1) It is quite plain, that the declaration which asserts that ' the three persons of the Godhead are equal in substance, power, and glory,' is of itself an unsatisfactory and insufficient explanation. In its origin it was designed only to oppose, in a polemic way, those representations in which the super-human in Christ and the Holy Spirit was attributed to some being subordinate to the Godhead ; and so far as this opposition to such view goes, it is sufficiently definitive. But after all, nothing more is done by this than to repel the idea of inequality.

"If now, on the other hand, something *positive* is to be taught by any particular declaration, this rule may be safely laid down in respect to such declaration, viz., that in representing the distinction between the three persons, nothing is admissible which will convey the idea of an *inequality* between them. This requisition can never be fulfilled, unless the distinction between the persons is so defined, as not in any way to infringe upon their perfect equality ; which is what has not hitherto been accomplished by any of the Symbols in common use.

" Let us examine the fundamental points in the representations of the Athanasian Symbol. The Father and the Son are said to be distinguished by the fact, that the Father is eternally unbegotten, [i. e. has eternal ἀγεννησία] ; the Son is from all eternity begotten, but never begets.

" Now one may represent *eternal generation* to be as remote as possible from all temporary and organic generation, yet there remains one idea, after all, which never can be removed from this view of the subject ; and this is, that the *relation of depen-*

dence is of necessity conveyed by such modes of expression. Now if the Father has from eternity exerted his power to beget the Son; and the Son has never exerted a power to beget any person of the Godhead, (which of itself seems to make a great dissimilarity between the first and second persons of the Godhead); and moreover, if there is no relation of dependence between the Son and another person of the Godhead, which can serve as an equivalent for the relation of dependence that exists between the Father and Son; then does it seem plainly to follow, that the power of the Father is greater than that of the Son, and the glory which the Father has in respect to the Son, must be greater than the glory which the Son has in respect to the Father.

"The same must be true, also, in respect to the Spirit; and this, whether we assume (with the Greek church), that he proceeds from the Father only, or (with the Latin one) that he proceeds both from the Father and the Son.   In the last case, the Son is supposed to have only *one* incapacity, compared with the Father, [viz. that of *not begetting*]; in the former [i. e. where the Spirit is said to proceed from the Father only], he has a double incapacity, [viz. that of not begetting, and that of not causing the procession of the Spirit], in case nothing proceeds from him and he begets nothing.   At all events, the Spirit must be supposed to have this two-fold incapacity, [for he neither begets nor causes procession]; and he is moreover in a relation of dependence, for the proceeding from, or the being breathed forth, necessarily implies a relation of dependence, as well as the being begotten.   It is moreover a dependence different from that which belongs to the first and second persons of the Godhead; although no one indeed can tell what it is in itself, or *how* it differs from the being begotten.

"On the ground of the Latin church, the Spirit is dependent on the Father and the Son; and in this case the Son has one capacity in common with the Father, [viz. that of causing procession of the Spirit]; and in this respect he has a pre-eminence over the Holy Ghost.   On the ground of the Greek church, the Spirit depends only on the Father, and is then in this respect like to the Son, inasmuch as the one is begotten by the Father, and the other proceeds from him.

"On each and every ground of this kind, the Father has preeminence over the other two persons; and the only question disputable is, whether the second and third persons are altogether alike and equal in their common subordination to the **Father**, or whether there is subordination also between the second and the third.

" The canon then which requires such a representation of the persons in the Trinity, *as will not make them in any respect unequal*, is not answered by such modes of representation as these.

(2) " The same proposition, [viz. that the common modes of representation have hitherto been imperfect], may be made out in another way, by a consideration of the usual manner in which the subject of the Trinity has been treated. When proof has been required in particular, with respect either to the attributes or the active powers of any particular person of the Trinity, the matter is almost exclusively managed in the following way ; viz., nearly every one of the strictly dogmatic theologians produces his proofs respecting the Son and the Spirit; but in respect to the Father, the whole matter is taken for granted, and the production of proof is deemed superfluous. If now the idea of a *perfect equality* among the persons of the Godhead lay at the basis of their scheme of doctrine, and a dependence of the Son upon the Father were not regarded as really implied by the very nature of their respective designations ; then the proof respecting the first person would be felt to be as necessary as that respecting the other persons ; and it would no more be *assumed* in the one case, than in the other. Nay, one might as well begin with the second or third person, in the argument, as with the first, and say : Because this or this is clear and certain respecting the second or third person, therefore it must be true of the first, inasmuch as they stand on the relative footing of perfect equality.

" Such a course, however, no dogmatic theologian takes ; and by this uniformity of procedure, as to the method of treating this subject, it becomes perfectly plain that a *preference* is tacitly conceded to the first person.

" But further; it is usual to treat of the being and attributes of God in and by themselves, before the *Trinity* is taken into consideration ; and having so done, writers appeal to what they have said of God simply considered, as self-evidently belonging to the Father, while at the same time they enter into a course of argument in order to prove that the same being and attributes belong to the Son and Spirit. Thus they tacitly and of course admit, that all which belongs to the Godhead simply considered,

belongs of course to the Father; and in so treating the matter
they shew, that (as they consider the subject) the Father does
himself constitute the Unity or *Μονὰς* of the Godhead, and the
expressions *Μονὰς* or *Μοναρχία* and Father, are altogether
equivalent.

"This method of representation, though not in the way of
intention yet in reality, falls back upon and altogether accords
with Origen's avowal, that the Father only is really and simply
God; while the Son and Spirit are God merely because they
participate in the divine Being.* I am aware that this mode
of representation was spurned at by the orthodox party in general of theologians in after times. Yet after all, the very same
sentiment did secretly insinuate itself into all their modes of
representation, and lies at the very basis of them.

"To the like result should we come, if we should now make
comparison of, and should subject to thorough criticism, the philosophical modes of representing the Trinity in ancient and in
later times; or if we should attentively examine the distinction
made between *God concealed and God revealed*, a distinction
often attempted, but not always in the same way. But this
could be accomplished only by a full and detailed illustration of
the whole history and state of the doctrine under consideration;
which present circumstances do not permit me to give."

Additional Considerations.

"If the remarks already made are well founded, then does it
follow, that the true method of representing the doctrine of the
Trinity has not yet been hit upon or achieved in the common
Symbols. It still remains, according to the tenor of these Symbols and the books of theology, in a state of oscillation between
subordination and equality on the one hand, and on the other
between Tritheism and such a Unitarian view as is inconsistent
with the appropriate honours due to the Redeemer, or with confident trust in the eternal efficacy of his redemption.

"It may appear strange indeed, while so many other doc-

---

* *Αὐτόθεος ὁ θεός ἐστι . . . πᾶν δὲ τὸ παρὰ τὸ αὐτόθεος μετοχῇ τῆς
ἐκείνου θεότητος θεοποιούμενον, κ. τ. λ.* [God (the Father) is very God;
but every thing else besides this very God is made divine by becoming partaker of his Divinity]. Comm. in Johan. IV. p. 50. ed. Ruell.
Here the connection sets it beyond doubt, that by *αὐτόθεος* is meant
the Father. Comp. Princip. 1. p. 62, ed. Ruell.

trines of religion which came later under discussion than the doctrine of the Trinity should have been fully and satisfactorily developed and defined, that the doctrine of the Trinity, which was one of the very earliest that was brought into discussion, should still remain invested with an imperfect and unsatisfactory costume. In the mean time it should be remarked, that in the consideration and representation of this doctrine, the wants of our moral nature have not been duly regarded; nor have they been made a basis to build upon, in respect to this doctrine, as they for the most part were in respect to other Christian doctrines in general; which was greatly to their advantage. The importance of the doctrine in itself, and also as compared with other doctrines, seems to have contributed to prevent a different view of it from being taken.

"Here moreover was abundant room for polemic zeal and party spirit, in respect to the *externals* of doctrine, to put forth their full exercise ; and how easy it is to fall into mistakes in such circumstances, every one must know. In such a state of things, moreover, every new oscillation would create a new excitement, which could not be very likely to lead to any happy results.

"It does not follow from all this, however, that no new effort to make a more consistent and unexceptionable representation of the doctrine of the Trinity, may not now be attended with better success. Christianity has become fully established, and all temptation to polytheism among us is removed ; and thus a multitude of excitements to vehement polemics, which operated on the Christians of ancient times, have now lost their power. We also now more fully admit than the ancients did, the necessity of employing *tropical* expressions in regard to the Godhead, and we better understand their true nature.

"If now I may give some hints how our future efforts ought to be conducted, I should say, that we must go back in our inquiries to ancient times, when the ground-work of our *symbolic* expressions respecting the Trinity was commenced, and which still remains for substance unaltered, and we must endeavour to find, in the history of these early efforts, the misconceptions which led astray, or occasioned a failure as to a more complete representation of the doctrine of the Trinity.

"The first supposition to be examined would be, whether, in order to escape the so-called Sabellian heresy, *too much* had not been done by the opposing party ; inasmuch as (for so the Nicene Creed represents the matter) in order to establish the union of the divine nature with the human, a twofold nature was assumed in the Godhead itself.   And although such views as those of the Nicene Fathers, were professedly in strong opposition to Arius and to all those who deny or degrade the divine nature that is in Christ and in the Spirit, yet there is room still to inquire, whether the modes of representation employed do not exhibit something which at least is of a doubtful nature, yea something which must be necessarily and substantially altered, if we would preserve the true doctrine of the Trinity.

"Such an inquiry would probably result in the conviction, that we must not in any way represent the Most High as a *mutable* being; nor the exertion of his active powers (on which his union with the human nature depends), in any other way than as having respect to what is done in time; for *causality* in the Godhead may indeed be conceived of as eternal, so far as decree or design is concerned; but so far as the actual exertion of this power is concerned, we must always consider it as taking place in time.

"The second preparatory step would be this.   If it should appear to be impossible to represent the relations of Father and Son as existing in the divine nature itself, without thereby introducing the idea of dependence and inequality, then should we inquire, whether it is correct to name the *divine* nature, as it is in itself in Christ, *Son of God;* inasmuch as the Scripture plainly calls the *whole person* of Christ only by this appellation, and makes use of *Logos* or *Word* to designate the divine nature in itself considered.   And in cases where no specific appellation is employed, it describes the union of the two natures only as *the indwelling of the fullness of the Godhead.*

"Should the expression *Son* be used only in this scriptural way, then the signification of *dependence* necessarily connected with it would not designate the internal relation in the Godhead itself, but only the relation of the same to its union with the human nature.

"In respect to the Holy Ghost, moreover, it must in like manner be investigated, whether there is any good ground for admitting any other relation of him to the Son, than that the Son, i. e. the whole Christ, sends him.

"It must also be investigated, in order to avoid the idea of dependence, how, when the Son is so designated, the Father is also admitted as a member of the Trinity.

"Only a full and protracted critical investigation of these points can afford the requisite light respecting them. This, however, belongs not to the present disquisition; and I have already proceeded as far as propriety will admit."

The deeply interesting investigations thus proposed, Dr. S. pursues in the Essay which is presented below. It is impossible that the intelligent and serious reader, after such an exhibition of critical power and analysis as the above remarks exhibit, should not feel a lively interest in pursuing the inquiries which are here proposed. To pursue them under the guidance of such a highly intelligent and learned leader, is indeed a rare privilege—one which has not often occurred in any country or at any time. Dr. S. himself states, near the commencement of his Essay, that while Arianism in all its details has been investigated and exhibited to the religious public, a comparison between the Athanasian views of the Trinity and those which have usually been denominated Sabellian, has not, to his knowledge, hitherto been fully and fairly made. Such a comparison he has undertaken; and whatever may be the opinion of the reader as to the results, or as to the correctness of the opinions of Sabellius or of Dr. S. himself, he will not fail at least to perceive, that much light is thrown, by the mighty power of acute and impartial criticism, on what was before dark and very imperfectly known, or at least very imperfectly represented. The reader, I take occasion expressly to say, is not obliged to follow Dr. S. or Sabellius in their views; but he will feel himself, as I think, obliged to say, that Sabellianism had not before been fully and fairly represented to the Christian public. What has been called Sabellianism hitherto, has been little more than the doctrine of the *Patripassians*, viz. the assumption that the Father himself is the same person that was united to Christ and who is developed in the operations of the Holy Spirit; and therefore that the distinction in the Godhead is nothing more than merely a *name*, without any corresponding reality. Such, it would appear, was after all *not* the opinion of Sabellius; but on the contrary, that he made a more definite, intelligible, and strenuous distinction between Father, Son, and Holy Ghost, than even his opponents; or at least than that part of them who did not go over into a species of occult Tritheism.

At all events, Schleiermacher himself is a strenuous and uncompromising advocate for the distinction, and full equality in all essential respects, of Father, Son, and Spirit; while the Unity or *Μονάς* of the Godhead is no where and in no measure infringed by him. Of his view of the Trinity we may at least say, that it is *intelligible.* But who will venture to say, that any of the definitions heretofore given of personality in the Godhead in itself considered, I mean such definitions as have their basis in the Nicene or Athanasian creed, are intelligible and satisfactory to the mind? At least I can truly say that I have not been able to find them, if they do in fact exist. Nor, so far as I know, has any one been able by any commentary on them to render them clear and satisfactory.

In saying all this, however, I must not by any means be understood as subscribing to all of Dr. S.'s views. I shall take occasion at the close of his Essay, to present some of the difficulties that force themselves upon my mind, in respect to his opinions concerning the Trinity. I say only, at present, that his views are, in most respects, palpable and intelligible. I can go with him, in most cases, as far as he goes; but I do not find an ultimate *resting-place* where he does. I feel obliged, by Scripture and the nature of the case, to go further, and to approximate somewhat nearer to that which I suppose to have been the real opinion of the Nicene Fathers and the advocates of the Athanasian Creed; although I cannot possibly subscribe to all the *formulas of expression* which they have employed, nor probably to *all* the views which they really entertained. If I understand their views, they do, in an occult manner indeed, but yet really and effectually, interfere with the true equality in substance, power, and glory, of the three persons or distinctions in the Godhead. This seems to be taking away with the left hand, what we have given with the right. If I say in words, that Christ and the Spirit are God, and very God; and say this ever so strongly and ever so often; and yet assign to them attributes or a condition which after all makes them *dependent* and represents them as *derived* and *originated;* then I am in fact no real believer in the doctrine of *true equality* among the persons of the Godhead; or else I use expressions out of their lawful and accustomed sense, and lose myself amid the sound of *words*, while *things* are not examined and defined with scrupulous care and accuracy.

It is not my present object to examine in full detail and in an ample manner, the diction and sentiments of the Nicene or Athanasian Creeds. But something should be said respecting the nature and import of this Symbol, in order to prepare the reader fully to appreciate the comparison of Dr. S. which is to follow.

Athanasius was himself a member of the Nicene Council, being then a deacon in the church of Alexandria in Egypt. This Council was assembled at Nice in A. D. 325, by order of the emperor Constantine, who had sought in vain to heal by other means the divisions in the church occasioned by the Arian disputes. Two hundred and fifty bishops are said by Eusebius to have been present; Socrates states them at 318; of whom the Arian party constituted but a small number. Athanasius and Marcellus, bishop of Ancyra, appear to have been the two principal speakers in behalf of the orthodox party, and to have been the agents on whom most of the doings of the Council depended.

The subsequent life of Athanasius was almost entirely devoted to a defence of the principles avowed by the Council of Nice; in which avowal he had himself been a leading if not the principal agent.

The Nicene Creed, so far as pertains to our present design, runs thus : " We believe in one God, the Father Almighty, the Maker of all things visible and invisible; and in one Lord, Jesus Christ, the Son of God, γεννηθέντα ἐκ τοῦ πατρὸς μονογενῆ, τουτέστιν, ἐκ τῆς οὐσίας τοῦ πατρός, θεὸν ἐκ θεοῦ, φῶς ἐκ φωτός, θεὸν ἀληθινὸν ἐκ θεοῦ ἀληθινοῦ, γεννηθέντα οὐ ποιηθέντα, ὁμοούσιον τῷ πατρί, by whom all things were made in heaven and earth. . . . And in the Holy Spirit. Καὶ τοὺς δὲ λέγοντας, ὅτι ἦν ποτε οὐκ ἦν, καὶ πρὶν γεννηθῆναι οὐκ ἦν, καὶ ὅτι ἐξ οὐκ ὄντων ἐγένετο, ἢ ἐξ ἑτέρας ὑποστάσεως ἢ οὐσίας φάσκοντας εἶναι, ἢ κτιστόν, ἢ τρεπτόν, ἢ ἀλλοιωτὸν τὸν υἱὸν τοῦ θεοῦ, ἀναθεματίζει, κ. τ. λ.; i. e. and those who say that there was [a time] when he [Christ] was not, that before he was born he was not, and that he came into existence from nothing [was made from nothing], or affirm that he is of a different substance or essence [different from that of the Father], or that the Son of God was created, or is mutable, or susceptible of change; them the whole church anathematizes, etc."

Such is the famous Creed of the Nicene Council. The creed

or formula of faith, long supposed to have been drawn up by Athanasius, and sometimes specifically called the *Athanasian Creed*, is now generally allowed not to have been his, but to have been· deduced from his works.   Dr. Waterland in his *Critical History* of it, ascribes it to Hilary, bishop of Arles. It is not to this, then, but to the *principles* of the *Nicene* Creed, as avowed and defended by Athanasius in a peculiarly zealous and earnest manner, that Schleiermacher is to be considered as referring, in the title of the Essay which is given at the head of this article.   The views set forth in the Nicene Creed, I suppose to be more usually styled *Athanasian*, because Athanasius was the great champion, if not the peculiar author of them.   Be this as it may in respect to Dr. S., it makes no difference of any consequence in the present instance, inasmuch as the views called in question are the same in both cases.

By reverting to the Nicene Creed, as exhibited above, the careful reader will perceive, that the doctrine of the Trinity is not developed in such a manner as to satisfy the demands of the rule which Schleiermacher lays down as required by the pious feelings of Christians, or the demands made by strict principles respecting the doctrine of the Trinity, such as are now more generally held.

The Westminster Confession of Faith declares the persons of the Godhead to be " *the same in substance, and equal in power and glory.*"   I understand by this, a NUMERICAL UNITY of substance to be asserted ; while in respect to persons or distinctions in the Godhead, an *equality of power and glory* is assigned to each.

So Turretin also.   He puts the question : An non sit *unus numero* Deus, quoad *essentiam?*   To which he answers : Quod . . . tuemur. I. p. 199.   So again, p. 282, Unica *numero* essentia ; and elsewhere often.   And thus, as it doubtless will be conceded, the greater part of modern intelligent and orthodox divines have held and do still hold.

Short of this, the *Μονάς* or divine Unity on the one side, and the *Οἰκονομία* or divine *Πρόσωπα* as revealed in the Gospel on the other, must be infringed upon.   Not that *design* of infringing on the Unity or the Trinity, is to be charged on all the representations that have been made, which. seem to present a view that differs from this.   To affirm this, would be to affirm more than can be proved, or than can be rationally supposed to be true.   But still, whatever may have been the ·*design* of those who have made representations that seem to come short of preserving the Unity, or which infringe upon the true idea of equality in the Trinity, the consistency of the representations themselves with the great and fundamental principles of Unity and Trinity, may, without any presumption, be submitted to a close and candid examination.

In order to prevent all misunderstanding of my views and feelings, I would here explicitly state, that I fully admit and believe, that the Nicene Fathers in general, and the great body of intelligent theologians in ancient times, who, subsequent to the Council of Nice advocated the Symbol which was published by them, intended truly and *bonâ fide* to recognize the doctrine of the real Godhead of Christ. Their views of what constituted, or at least what might constitute, real and proper Godhead, were doubtless affected, as it was natural they should be, by the philosophy of the day; and they were unquestionably different in some respects from those which pervade the more intelligent part of Christian theologians at the present time. Many of the Nicene Fathers and of their followers had been nurtured, in early youth, in the bosom of heathenism; and of course in the doctrines of a polytheism which admits a community of gods who are ὁμοφυεῖς, i. e. of the same nature generically considered. In other words, a divine nature, in the view of the heathen, was common to all the *Dii majores;* although these gods were admitted to be individually diverse. In addition to this, the *emanation-philosophy* had long and widely pervaded the East; where in fact it still remains, and spreads over all the eastern parts of Asia. According to this, θεοὶ δεύτεροι were not only admissible, but they were even regarded as the creators and governors of the world. Then as to the West, the New Platonics had spread far and wide their tenets, from the famous schools which existed at Alexandria, the central point of learning at this period both among heathen and Christians. This *eclectic* philosophy admitted the Logos of their system to a place secondary only to that of the original τὸ ὄντως Ὄν. It gave to this Logos a hypostatic or personal and separate existence, and exalted him to the rank of creator and governor of the world. On all sides, then, the possibility that various beings existed, which were truly divine although of secondary rank, was admitted. In this respect, the most celebrated philosophy of the West harmonized with that of the East.

It was impossible but that circumstances like these should

diminish the repugnance of the Nicene Fathers, to the admission of a being to a truly divine rank or order, who was considered by them as a substantial emanation from God, or substantial communication of God, and was therefore a partaker of his substance. Both of these points in fact stand out, in the Nicene Confession, as things most prominent. Why should those Fathers hesitate to admit Christ to a rank truly divine, inasmuch as in their view he was ὁμοούσιος with the Father and sprung immediately from him? They did not hesitate; and with the views which most of them cherished, they could not hesitate at their time, when notions respecting the Godhead prevailed, like those which Lactantius for example defends; notions moreover which did not expose them to be called in question as to their belief in the true divinity of Christ, provided only they represented him as ὁμοούσιος with the Father and as begotten by him. How could we rationally expect them to stop and ask, as we are now prone to do: ' Are *self-existence* and *independence* essentially requisite to true divinity?' One can scarcely meet with a passage among all the writers of that day, which implies that they felt compelled to urge this question as all important in respect to Christ and the Holy Spirit. Enough, in their view, that the Father possessed the attributes in question. The Son and Spirit were divine, because they were derived immediately from him, and partook of his substance.

I cannot think it to be a question, whether candour requires us to admit that they did worship, and did mean to worship, the second and third persons of the Trinity as *really divine.* Neither Unitarianism (now so called), nor Arianism, were regarded by them as compatible with true Christianity. Theodotus and Paul of Samosata on the one side, and Arius and his friends on the other, were both opposed and rejected.

But while we cheerfully and fully admit all this, it does not follow that the Nicene *exposition* of the great doctrine of the Trinity is not in itself liable to some grave and appalling objections. Dr. Schleiermacher has presented, as we have seen above, some objections apparently unanswerable, which must ever lie against making the second and third persons of the Godhead (as divine) DEPENDENT on the first. In whatever shape we present the idea of *derivation;* whether we call it by the name of *generation, procession, emanation,* or by any other like appellation; still the idea remains of *dependence.*

A *derived* God, if words are allowed to have their appropriate meaning, cannot be a self-existent God; a *dependent* God cannot be an independent one. We may assert what we please, respecting the indescribable, unspeakable, wonderful manner of generation or procession; we may disclaim all similitudes among created things ever so much or so strongly; yet all this goes only to the *manner* and not to the *matter* of the thing. The latter still remains. The idea of *dependence* and *derivation* is inseparably and by absolute necessity connected with the idea of generation and procession.

Accordingly we find that all the fathers before, at, and after the council of Nice, who harmonize with the sentiments there avowed, do with one consent, declare the Father only to be αὐτόθεος or *self-existent* God. So says Bishop Bull: "Pater solus naturam illam divinam *a se* habet, sive a nullo alio; Filius, autem, a Patre; proinde Pater divinitatis quae in Filio est, *fons, origo*, et *principium* est;" Defensio Fid. Nic. p. 251. This position he fortifies with abundant quotations from the ancient Fathers. The Greek ones speak of the Father as αἴτιον τοῦ εἶναι, i. e. *the cause* of the *being* of the Son; they call him αἴτιος and αἰτία τοῦ υἱοῦ; the ancient Latin theologians name the Father *auctor, radix, fons, caput*, in respect to the Son. The Greek Fathers again ascribe to him ὑπεροχήν; they speak of him as μείζων; but of the Son, as δεύτερος θεός. The Father they style ἀναρχής, i. e. *without beginning*, and they speak of the Son as springing from him. No one versed at all in that patristic lore which has respect to the Logos, can fail to acknowledge, that Bishop Bull in this respect has not misrepresented the ancient advocates of the Nicene Symbol.

It lies, moreover, on the very face of the Nicene Creed, that it acknowledges the Father only as the Μονάς of the Godhead. "We beleive in ONE GOD, *the Father almighty, maker of all things visible and invisible;* and in one Lord Jesus Christ, the Son of God, the only begotten of the Father, etc." Jesus Christ as here presented to us, is not the *one God*, but the *one Lord* who was begotten of the substance of the one God or the Father, etc.

The Father, then, as presented in this Creed, is not merely a distinct person, i. e. not merely one of the three persons, and on an equality with the other two; but he is the original, independent, self-existent Μονάς or Unity, who constitutes the *Fons* et *Principium* (as the Latin Fathers express it) of all true Godhead.

The ancient advocates of the Nicene Symbol were accustomed familiarly and usually to style the Father αὐτόθεος, i. e. *self-existent God;* and although this appellation was not introduced into the Nicene Creed, yet the language respecting the Son abundantly proves, that the members of the Nicene Council regarded αὐτόθειον and ἀγεννησία as belonging *exclusively* to the Father; which, indeed, is what their advocates often and every where assert.   The Son, according to them, is in his *divine* nature (for this is what they mean) γεννηθείς... ἐκ τῆς οὐσίας τοῦ πατρός, he is θεὸς ἐκ θεοῦ, φῶς ἐκ φωτός, θεὸς ἀληθινὸς ἐκ θεοῦ ἀληθινοῦ, γεννηθεὶς οὐ ποιηθείς, ὁμοούσιος τῷ πατρί. This indeed puts it past all fair question, that the Nicene Fathers meant not by any explantions which they gave, to deny the true and real divinity of the Son.   But it also makes it equally plain, that they did not regard *derivation*, (which is so assumed that it lies upon the face of the whole representation), as interfering with his real divinity.   Such were their views of philosophy and the nature of things, that *derived* divinity presented nothing incongruous or impossible to their apprehension.

But how shall we of the present day, educated out of the circle of Emanation-philosophy and Eclecticism, and taught from the cradle to believe, and led by reflection in riper years to maintain, that *self-existence* and *independence* are essential to a nature truly divine—how shall we, how can we, force ourselves to believe, that a *derived* God can be the only living and true God?   All the favourite images of Tertullian, Athanasius, Basil, Chrysostom, Gregory Nazianzen, or Gregory of Nyssa, will not help to quiet our minds and settle them down in this view.   They tell us indeed, often and seriously, of the radiance of the sun which flows always from it, is coeval with it, and must always co-exist with it; while the sun himself is still unchanged and undiminished by this radiance.   They bid us go to the fountain that sends forth a living stream, and has ever done so, and always will, and yet it is undivided and undiminished by the stream.   They call on us to observe how one torch kindles another, and yet the light of the first remains unimpared and undivided.   They tell us that the tree is not diminished by the fruit it bears; and finally they remind us that a son is ὁμοούσιος with his father, even according to human and imperfect generation, having in all respects the same nature with his father. And having passed before our eyes this splendid and striking phantasmagoria of images, they ask: ' What have you now to object to the derivation, yet perfect equality of the Son with the Father ?'

For one I can say, that I am dazzled, but not satisfied, with this splendid exhibition. I have difficulties concerning it— questions to ask, for which I should be glad to obtain some satisfactory answer. Does not radiance *depend*, then, on the sun ? Does not the stream depend on the fountain? Or the light of the second torch, on the light of the first? The fruit, on the tree? The human son, on the human father? To answer these questions, let us suppose the body of the sun to be annihilated; the fountain to be dried up; the first torch extinguished when the second comes to be applied to it ; the tree withered ; and the human father extinct before the production of the son ; will any of these *effects* or *productions* continue or come into being, independently of their cause, i. e. their *fons* or *principium ?* Plainly not. Then are all these effects, or productions, or derivations, *dependent ;* they must be and are originated by a cause *ab extra ;* they are *not* self-existent.

How can *created* objects, perishable, mutable, bound together by uniform and unceasing concatenations of causes and effects—afford any just image of the uncreated, invisible, self-existent, independent, and everlasting God? The imagination that they can, is an illusion. It may dazzle, or in some cases even charm—but *satisfy* the mind of a man, who demands reason and argument rather than splendid imagery or eloquent declamation, it cannot. *A God in verity and reality*—can not now be regarded as a derived and a dependent being.

But this is not all which may be said, in regard to the imperfect mode in which the doctrine of the Trinity is stated in the Nicene Creed. To my mind nothing can be plainer, than that the ancient advocates of that Creed differed, as to one important point, pretty widely from most of the distinguished orthodox theologians of modern and recent times, in their method of viewing and stating the doctrine of generation, derivation, or personality, in respect to the Son and Holy Spirit. The importance of this subject, (which however seems but seldom to have attracted very serious notice in modern times, and still more rarely to have been fully and explicitly discussed), reasonably demands that a few explanations and remarks should be made in relation to it. I will speak as briefly as the highly difficult and important nature of the subject will permit.

1. The great body of modern theologians admit the *numerical unity* of the divine essence or substance. They deny that there are three οὐσίαι or substances in the Godhead; they admit only that there are three ὑποστάσεις or persons. They deny that there are three οὐσίαι, because the admission of this, as they concede, would inevitably lead at least to real *theoretical* Tritheism.

2. The great body of the more acute and discerning theologians admit that the *substance* or *essence* of the second and third persons of the Trinity is not derived from the Father, but is self-existent, inasmuch as it is numerically one with his substance. The older divines of modern times take much pains to distinguish between *essence* or *substance* and *subsistence.* Essence or substance (οὐσία, φύσις, *essentia, substantia, natura,* and sometimes ὑπόστασις) are two different names of the same thing, given in consequence of apprehending it in a somewhat different light or point of view. Essence, (if we may trust that great master of definitions—that truly original thinker and powerful reasoner, as well as distinguished Christian, F. Turretin), is the *quidditas rei,* i. e. that which constitutes the very nature of a thing and is indispensable in order to make it such a thing as it is. Substance means, as theologically employed, *that which exists in and by itself.* In reference to the Divinity, both terms would mean the same thing which we mean by *essence* or *substance,* in the language of philosophy or even of common parlance at the present day. Quaest. 23. § 3 seq. Tom I.

Subsistence (ὑπόστασις, ὕπαρξις, ὑφιστάμενον, τρόπος ὑπάρξεως, *subsistentia, suppositum*) Turretin defines by *modus existendi proprius substantiis.* Subsistence moreover, as he says, is divided into two kinds; "alia quâ constituitur subtantia in *esse substantiae,* alia quâ constituitur substantia in *esse suppositi ;*" which I must leave the reader to explain. From the whole of what he says, however, on the words *subsistence* and *hypostasis,* it is plain that he refers the sense of these to designating the *modus* of existence, in distinction from existence itself, i. e. substance or essence in itself considered. And in much the same way do most of the theologians of the metaphysical school define *substance* and *subsistence* in respect to the Godhead.

We come now to our main object. *Personality,* (ὑπόστασις

ς

persona, τρόπος ὑπάρξεως) is the point to which, according to most modern representations of the doctrine of the Trinity, we are to direct our attention, when we think of the generation of the Son, or of the procession or *ἐκπεμπσις* of the Holy Spirit. Not the *essence* of the second and third persons of the Trinity is to be considered as being derived from the Father; but their *modus existendi*, their *hypostasis*, their *personality*, is what we must consider to be derived. To the Father belong *paternitas* and *ἀγεννησία;* to the Son, *filiatio* or *generatio passiva;* and to the Spirit, *processio* or *ἐκπεμπσις.*

3. Some difficulties that attend this view will be noticed in the sequel. My object under the present head, is more fully to state, how widely this mode of representation differs from that which the ancient advocates of the Nicene Council usually employed. For this purpose I might appeal to the Nicene Creed itself as stated above, where *ἐκ τῆς οὐσίας τοῦ πατρός* is evidently designed to convey the idea, that the *substance* (not merely the *modus existendi* or *subsistence*) of the Father is communicated to and produces the Son, in his divine nature. I will however select a passage from one of the most orthodox, able, consistent, and eloquent, of all the ancient fathers who have written upon the doctrine of the Trinity, in order to illustrate the ancient views. It is found in Hilary de Trinitate, Lib. II. § 6 seq.

" It is the Father, from whom every thing that exists came into being. He, in Christ and by Christ, was the origin of all things. His it is to exist in and of himself; not deriving from any other source that which he is, but obtaining it in and of himself. Infinite, because he is contained in nothing else, and all things are in him; not confined to any space, because he can have no limits ; eternally existing before all time, for time is derived from him . . . This is the truth of the mystery of God, this is the name of the incomprehensible nature in the Father. God is invisible, indescribable, infinite ; speech is reduced to silence in speaking of him ; reason becomes confounded in searching him out ; the understanding is straitened in endeavouring to comprehend him. He has, as we have said, the name of his nature in *Father;* but he alone is Father. He derives it from no source, nor in a human manner, that he is Father. He is unbegotten, eternal, having in himself the ground of perpetual existence. He is known to the Son only ; because no one knows the Father except the Son, and he to whom the

Son shall reveal him.   Nor does any one know the Son, except the Father; they have a mutual knowledge; each has a
perfect cognizance of the other.   And because no one knows
the Father except the Son, we embrace in our thoughts the
Father together with the Son who reveals him, who is the only
faithful witness.

" These things, however, I think rather than describe, respecting the Father; for I know well that all language is inadequate to the description.   He is to be thought of as invisible, incomprehensible, eternal.   But this very thing, that he
is in and of himself and by himself; that he is invisible and
incomprehensible and immortal; in all this, indeed, there is a
profession of honour, and a designation which has some meaning, and a certain circumscription of opinion; but still language
is not competent for the designation of his nature, and words
cannot explain the matter as it is.   For when we say, that *he
is in himself,* an explanation can not be given by human reason; for there is a difference between containing and being
contained, and that is one thing which is, and that another in
which it is.   If we say again, that *he is of himself,* no one is at
the same time his own giver and also the gift.   If we say that
he is immortal; then it seems to be implied that there is something besides himself, to which thing he is not exposed; * nor
can he be the sole being, who by the word [immortalis] is declared to be free from the power of another, [viz. from the
power of death].   If we say *he is incomprehensible;* then how
can he be any where, of whom it is denied that he is accessible?
if we say that *he is invisible;* whatever cannot be seen, must
be wanting in itself.

" Our confession respecting him, therefore, is deficient as to
appropriate language; and all words that may be adapted to
this purpose, will not describe God as he is, nor his greatness.
The perfection of knowledge is, so to know God, that you may
know you are not to be ignorant of him, although you can never describe him.   He is to be believed in, to be conceived of
by the mind, to be adored; and by the performance of these
duties he is to be described.

" We have launched forth from places where there is no har-
bour upon the swelling ocean, and can neither return nor go

---

* The meaning seems to be, that there is an implication that death
exists, independently of God; to which, however, he is not liable.

forward. There is more difficulty, however, as to our future than our past course. The Father is as he is; and as he is, he is to be believed in. As to the Son, the mind is in consternation when it undertakes to describe him, and speech trembles at disclosing itself. For he is the offspring of him who is unbegotten; one of one; the true one of the true one; living of the living; perfect of the perfect; the virtue of virtue; the wisdom of wisdom; the glory of glory; the image of the invisible God; the form of the unbegotten Father. What shall we think of the generation of the only begotten from the unbegotten? For the Father often says from heaven: 'This is my beloved Son, in whom I am well pleased.' Here is no abscission or division; for he is impassible who begets, and he is the image of the invisible God who is begotten; and he testifies that the Father is in him, and he in the Father. There is no adoption; for he is the true Son of God, and he says that he who has seen him has seen the Father. Neither was he ordered to exist, like other things; for the only begotten is of one, and has life in himself, as he has who begat him; for he says: 'As the Father hath life in himself, so hath he given to the Son to have life in himself.' Nor is it that a *part* of the Father is in the Son; for the Son testifies, that all which the Father hath is his; and again, All mine are thine, and thine are mine; and whatsoever the Father hath, he hath given to the Son. The apostle also declares, that in him dwelleth *all* the fullness of the Godhead bodily.... He is the perfect one of the perfect one; for he who has all things, gave all things. Nor is it to be supposed that he has not given, because he still possesses; nor that he does not possess, because he has given.

"Both understand the secret of this nativity. But if any one should impute it to his own understanding, that he cannot attain to the mystery of this generation, when the Father is perfectly understood and the Son [mutually or by each other], he will be the more grieved to hear that I also am ignorant of it. I do not know; I do not seek to know; and still I console myself. Archangels are ignorant of it; angels do not understand it; ages and generations have not disclosed it; the prophet did not comprehend it; the apostle did not inquire after it; the Son himself did not declare it. Let all complaint be hushed. Whoever thou art, I do not call upon thee to ascend the height above; nor to traverse immeasurable space; nor will I lead thee down into the abyss. While thou art ignorant of the ori-

gin of a creature, canst thou not bear it with equanimity to be
ignorant of the nativity of the Creator? I ask this of you;
You perceive that you are begotten, but do you understand how
any thing is begotten by thee? I do not ask whence you derived your reason, how you obtained your life, whence you acquired your understanding, what that is in thee which is smell,
feeling, sight, hearing. Certainly no one is ignorant of what he
does. I ask how you communicate these things to those whom
you beget? How do you engraft the reason? How do you light
up the eyes? How do you fix the heart in its station? Tell me
these things, if you can. You possess, therefore, what you do
not understand; and you give what you cannot comprehend.
You bear it with equanimity that you are ignorant of your own
matters, and behave with assuming insolence because you are
unacquainted with the things of God.

" Hear, then, that the Father is unbegotten; hear that the
Son is the only begotten; hear the declaration, The Father is
greater than I; hear again, I and my Father are one; hear also, He who hath seen me, hath seen the Father; listen to this,
I am in the Father and the Father in me; and to this, I came
out from the Father; and this, Who is in the bosom of the Father; and this, All that the Father hath, he hath given to the
Son; and this, The Son hath life in himself, even as the Father hath in himself. Hear again, that the Son is the image,
wisdom, power, glory of God; and mark well the Spirit proclaiming, His generation who will declare? Then reprove the
Lord himself who testifies, No one hath known the Father but
the Son, and he to whom the Son shall reveal him. Thrust
yourself now into this secret concerning the one God unbegotten,
and the one God only begotten; plunge yourself into this mystery which surpasses all conception. Begin, go forward, per-
severe; although I am certain you will never come to the end
of your course, yet I will rejoice that you are about to make
some progress in it. For he who pursues objects that are infinite, although he can never fully attain them, yet he will be a
gainer by making some progress. The true understanding of
words on this subject will be brought about by such a course.*

" The Son is from that Father who is; only begotten from
unbegotten; progeny from parent; living one from living one.
As the Father hath life in himself, so is it given to the Son to

* Stat in hoc intelligentia fine verborum. I am not sure that I
have caught the sense. Qui rectius intelligit, corrigat.

have life in himself. The perfect one from the perfect one, because *the whole is from the whole* (totus a toto); without division or abscission,—because the one is in the other, and the fulness of the Godhead is in the Son. The incomprehensible from the incomprehensible; for no one knows them, and only they have mutual knowledge. The invisible from the invisible; for he is the image of the invisible God, and moreover he who hath seen the Son hath seen the Father. One person from another one; for there is Father and Son. The nature [*natura*=οὐσία] of the Godhead is not one and another, for both are one. God of God; the only begotten God of the unbegotten God. There are not two Gods, but one of one; there are not two unbegotten, for there is one born of him who was unborn; the one differs in nothing from the other, because the life of the living One is in the living One.

"These things have we touched upon respecting the nature of the Godhead, not professing to comprehend even the sum of intelligence respecting it, but knowing that we speak of things incomprehensible.

"You will say, then, 'There is no duty for faith to perform here, if there is nothing that may be comprehended.' But it is not so; faith acknowledges it to be a duty, to know that what she is inquiring into, is incomprehensible."

If there be any one now, who can read this with indifference, or turn away from it with a kind of disgust because he looks upon it as a declamatory production of enthusiastic feeling, I acknowledge that I have no sympathies with him in this respect. I cannot refrain from looking upon the whole strain, and on many others of the like nature in the same author, as the result of high and intense effort to express some of the most sacred and reverential feelings that the soul can have in its present imperfect state, toward the glorious Godhead which is revealed in the gospel. That the author of the views just recited has failed in consistency and perspicuity of representation, we may attribute to the extreme difficulties in which the subject was involved, as it came before his mind; difficulties belonging to the age rather than to him.

But that he has not done as well in the expression of his thoughts—at all events as eloquently and forcibly—as has been done by any writer of antiquity, or by most in modern times, candour will hardly deny. I feel myself constrained to reverence such an attitude of soul as he manifests, wherever I meet

with it; and this, even if the speculative views which the writer
cherishes should not bear the light of critical and logical examination.   But—to our present purpose.

The whole tenor of the above extract leaves no room for
doubt, that Hilary regarded the doctrine of eternal generation,
as implying a conveyance of the essence or substance of the Father to the Son; yet without abscission or division.   It is certain
that nearly all divine attributes are particularized by him, one after another.   If there could be any doubt as to this in the minds
of any candid reader, that doubt, it would seem, must be removed by the phrase *totus a toto*, near the close of the extract;
which I have distinctly marked.   Indeed the whole tenor of the
writings of the ancient Fathers, who defend the principles of
the Nicene Creed, puts it beyond reasonable doubt, that they
held a communication *of the substance* (ἐκ τῆς οὐσίας) of the
Father to the Son; on which account the Son was and is God,
and the object of divine worship.   The modern view of Trinitarians, viz., that the Father begets only the *personality* (ὑπόστασις, *persona*, πρόσωπον) of the Son and Spirit, is a nicety in
philosophical discussion, from which the ancient Fathers were
at a great remove.   That the Father communicated the whole
of himself to the Son, οὐσιωδῶς, *substantialiter*, is what they
assert so often and in so many ways, that doubt concerning it
would seem to be impossible.

Indeed the Nicene Creed itself speaks so plainly on this
point, that I must confess it to be a matter of wonder with me,
that modern theologians have so little noticed the great difference there is, between the real doctrine of that Creed and the
modern view of personality in the Godhead which is general
among the most intelligent writers.   Even in those Christian
communities who have adopted the Nicene Symbol into their
formula of belief, the leading theologians hold to *numerical unity of substance* in the Godhead; and of course, that the substance or essence of the Godhead in the Son and Spirit was
not begotten; and consequently, that only the *personality* of the
second and third persons in the Trinity is of a derived nature.

But here I shall doubtless be asked: ' And did not the Nicene Fathers and their adherents believe also in the *numerical*
unity of the substance of the Godhead?'   And before I proceed
any further in my remarks on the Nicene Creed, I must crave
the liberty of stopping for a few moments in order to pursue this
inquiry.   I do this merely because it has so important and ex-

tensive a bearing on most that has been or will be said, in relation to the present topic.

The great contest in respect to the meaning of this Creed, and particularly in relation to the point now before us, has turned upon the words ὁμοούσιος τῷ πατρί. Did the Nicene fathers mean, that the Son is *numerically* of the same substance with the Father? Or did they mean merely that there is a *specific* unity of substance in both Father and Son, i. e. that the species of substance is of the same nature in both, or (in other words) that the kind of substance in both is the same; in like manner as Adam and Seth, both having a human nature in common, were ὁμοούσιοι? These are questions that have been often disputed; and yet, as the subject appears to my mind, they are questions that may be satisfactorily answered in a brief way.

There can be no doubt, that the word ὁμοούσιος is usually appropriated to designate a unity, which is predicated of things belonging to the same species or having a common nature. If it ever has a different meaning, (as some of the Fathers do occasionally assert), it is merely because it is *catachrestically* employed, i. e. in a sense different from that of common usage.

In order now to answer the questions proposed above, we must survey the current of opinion in relation to the point of inquiry, both before and after the publication of the Nicene Creed; *before this*, because we cannot suppose that there was a sudden leap made by the Nicene fathers, and a wide chasm in opinion between them and their immediate predecessors; *after this*, because the friends and advocates of the Nicene Symbol, who were cotemporary with it, or nearly so, must be supposed best to have understood the meaning of ὁμοούσιος τῷ πατρί.

In presenting the opinions of the fathers who preceded the Council of Nice, I can refer only to the most distinguished of them; and this, in a brief manner. The nature of my present design does not allow me to do any thing more.*

---

* I quote the opinions of the Fathers by giving a translation merely: because the room cannot be spared here for the original, inasmuch as so many notes containing this must necessarily be subjoined to the Essay of Schleiermacher. Once for all, and to save time and trouble as to any references, or as to doubts about correctness, I refer the reader to Münscher's Dogmengeschichte, I. § 91 seq. whose consummate skill in patristical learning is not called in ques-

Justin Martyr names the Son δύναμις θεοῦ; by which however, he does not mean an attribute, but an intelligent agent,
springing from God.   In his Dialogue with Trypho the Jew
(pp. 221, 222, edit. Colon.), he labours at large to prove from
Gen. 19: 26, that the Father, who is God invisible, must be
a different person from the God which appeared to Abraham,
whom he holds to have been the Son.   In p. 152 of the same
work, he says in so many words, that the Logos is different
from the Father, and ἕτερον ἀριθμῷ, οὐ γνώμῃ; where unity
of number or numerical unity is very explicitly denied, while
the oneness of the Logos with the Godhead is explained as a
oneness of will or *sentiment.*

That such must have been the opinion of Justin, as well as
of Theophilus and Tatian, must be evident from the fact, that
all three of these early teachers, held to the doctrine of a Logos
ἐνδιάθετος and Logos προφορικός.   That is, according to
them, the Logos was not from eternity a hypostasis or existing agent, separate from the Father; but was *in* God as his
reason or understanding.   When the world was created; when
God said : Let there be light, and there was light ; then the
Logos, which before had been *in* God merely as his reason or
understanding, became a Logos προφορικός, i. e. reason or
thought was uttered in words ; and these words became a
substance, a hypostasis, a separate and animate and rational
Being, the Creator of the world, the Son of the Father.   His
Word, which had from everlasting been reposing in him as
reason, now became visible, or was presented to the perception
of intelligent beings.

Such is the Logos of Justin, Theophilus, and Tatian.   All

---

tion ; and whose almost universal fairness of representation stands
unimpeached.   There, and in a masterly discussion of the same
author, on the sense of the Nicene Creed relative to the very point
now in question, which is printed in Henke's Neu. Magazin, VI. p. 334
seq., the reader may find ample illustration and confirmation of all
that is now to be said, in relation to the views of the Fathers, with
quotations for the most part from the originals.   The same thing
for substance he may find in Martini's Geschichte des Logos, with
ample quotations; and in Keilii Opuscula, de Doctoribus, etc.
Comm. IV.   But besides these general references, in order that the
reader may guard against mistakes that I might make, I give him,
for the most part, the particular places in each father, where the
sentiment quoted is to be found.

these agree, moreover, that the personality of the Logos, i. e. his becoming *prophoric*, depended on the will of the Father, and not on any necessity in his own nature ; see Münscher, Dogmengesch. I. § 93. Nothing can be plainer or more certain, then, than that a *numerical* unity of substance in the Godhead, could form no part of the system of doctrine which these fathers embraced respecting the Trinity.

The views of Athenagoras are not capable, perhaps, of being definitely ascertained. There is no doubt, however, that he adopted the idea of Logos *ἐνδιάθετος* and *προφορικός*. But whether the latter was hypostatized by him or not, is still disputed among adepts in patristical lore. Münsch. ubi sup. p. 409 seq.

Irenaeus has occasionally given the most noble example in all antiquity, of aversion to speculative and philosophical disquisitions, in order to explain the origin or generation of the Word or Son of God. " He," says this excellent Father, " who speaks of the Logos (reason) of God, and maintains that this came forth out of him—he makes God a *composite* being ; just as if God was one thing, and his original reason another. . . . The prophet says : *His generation—who will narrate it ?* [Is. 53: 8]. But you [i. e. those who make the explanations in question about a Logos prophoric, etc.] indulge in conjectures respecting his generation, and compare the utterance of human words with the generation of the Logos ; whereby you only shew, that you understand neither things human nor divine ;" Adv. Haer. I. 10.

This is laying a heavy hand upon some of the speculating theologians of his time. But this is not all.

" When any one inquires of us," says he, " *how* the Son was produced from the Father ? Our answer is, that no one knows. Since his generation is inexplicable, they do not know what they pretend to know, who undertake to explain it. . . . A word which proceeds from our understanding we can comprehend. How then can they lay claim to having made great discoveries, who apply these well known matters to the only begotten Logos of God, and represent his inexplicable birth in a way as definite, quasi ipsi obstetricaverint ;" Adv. Haeres. II. c. 28. § 6.

This is caustic irony, to be sure ; yet one can hardly say that it was not in a good measure deserved, by some of the *prophoric* and *endiathetic* speculations of the day.

In accordance with these enlightened views, Irenaeus casts

away the expression that the Son is a προβολή (emanation)
from the Father ; he rejects the comparison of the sun's radiance with the body of the sun, and also of the production of
human words by human reason. In a word, he abandons all
created analogies, as inevitably and necessarily leading to error ;
II. c. 13.

This father was so offended at the attempts to explain the
generation of the Son, that he has avoided, for the most part,
all expressions, that would lead us to a very definite knowledge
of his views concerning *personality* and *unity* in the Godhead ;
I mean as to the relative sense of these to each other. In
Haeres. IV. c. 6. § 6 he says, that " the Father is ἀόρατον, the
invisible part of the Son, and the Son is the ὁρατόν, the visible part of the Father." This looks as if he verged toward the
views, that have been gaining ground among some Trinitarians
for the last fifty years, viz., that *the Father is God concealed,
and the Son is God revealed.* Yet in other places he seems to
speak of the Son in the usual hypostatic way, as being separate
from the Father ; but of the manner in which this separation is
to be made congruous with unity, he has not explicitly said any
thing. See Lib. 'III. c. 6. § 1. IV. c. 20. § 11, and c. 10. §
2. IV. c. 7. § 4. II. c. 28. § 8, etc.

Clement of Alexandria came nearer to the views of the Nicene Creed. He maintained, indeed, the doctrine of a λόγος
ἐνδιαθετός, respecting which that Creed is not explicit. But
the production of the Logos as a hypostasis, *before* the creation
of the world, he fully admitted. He makes the Son the copy
—the exact copy of the Father (θεὸς ἐκ θεοῦ) ; but still he represents his dignity and his nature as depending on the will of
the Father ; Münsch. § 96. Of course he could not have admitted the doctrine of a *numerical* unity in the substance of the
Godhead.

Tertullian, in the vehemence of his opposition to the views of
Praxeas, whom he regarded as denying the separate hypostasis
of the Son, has expressed himself with more warmth and eloquence than logic, in regard to this subject. His assertions appear, at least, to be irreconcileable with each other. In one
place he says of the persons in the Trinity ; " Numerum *sine
divisione* patiuntur ;" which looks like holding to a numerical
unity of substance ; Contra Prax. c. 2. In another place (cap.
9) he says " Pater enim tota substantia est, Filius vero derivatio totius et *portio.*" In one place (cap. 2) he says : " Unius

substantiae, unius status, et unius potestatis;" in another (cap. 9) : " Sic et Pater alius a filio, dum filio major." In another place (cap. 22) he shews more definitely what he means by *unity:* "Unum dicit quod . . . pertinet ad unitatem, ad similitudinem, ad conjunctionem, ad dilectionem Patris, et ad obsequium Filii . . . et ita *per opera* intelligimus unum Patrem et Filium." And in another (cap. 2) : " Quasi non sic unus sit omnia, dum ex uno omnia, per substantiae scilicet unitatem, et nihilominus custodiatur οἰκονομίας sacramentum" [the mystery of the gospel-dispensation]. In this last case, the *unity* of substance is evidently *homogeneousness* of substance, and not numerical unity. This homogeneousness he admits, because the Son is *portio* substantiae Patris, as he had before said. Accordingly he compares the Son (cap. 8) with the fruit which springs from the tree, with the stream which issues from the fountain, and with the radiance that flows from the sun.

Origen's views are well known. Son and Spirit, according to him, have their origin as hypostases, in the free will of the Father ; they are subordinate to him, although they are the exact reflection of his glory ; the unity in the Godhead is a unity of will, a harmony of design and operation ; not a numerical or substantial unity, against which he strongly protests. " The Father," says he, " is the ground-cause or original source of all. Inferior to the Father is the Son, who operates merely on rational beings ; for he is second to the Father. Still more inferior is the Holy Spirit, whose influence is limited to the church. The power of the Father, then, is greater than the power of the Son and of the Spirit. The power of the Son is greater than that of the Holy Ghost. And lastly, the power of the Holy Ghost is greater than that of all other holy beings;" De Princip. I. c. 3. The *original* is in Justinian Ep. ad Menam. The version of Rufinus has misrepresented the sense here.

Dionysius, the pupil and successor of Origen at Alexandria, wrote against Sabellius. His writings are preserved only in fragments, quoted by Athanasius and others. In his diatribe against Sabellius, he names the Son *a creation* and *work* of the Father, which has not the same nature with him, but differs in essence from him. He maintains that the relation of the Son to the Father, is like that of the vine to the vintner, or the ship to its builder ; and asserts that the Son, as such, had no existence before he was created ; Athanas. de Sentent. Dionys.

cont. Arian. I. p. 551. edit. Colon.   The excess of this diversity he afterwards corrected, and retreated back nearly to the
opinions of Clement of Alexandria ; Münsch. § 101.

Gregory Thaumaturgus not only attributes to the Son a separate hypostasis, but calls him a *creation* (κτίσις).   Basil seeks
to explain away this, (ep. 210. Opp. III. p. 316) ; but finds it
a very difficult task.

Dionysius of Rome, cotemporary with Dionysius of Alexandria, opposes the views of the latter, and seeks to shew that
the Son is not *created* but *begotten*, that he is dependent on
the Father, but yet eternal ; and therefore he comes nearest of
all to the views of the Nicene Creed.

Cyprian has presented no very explicit views in relation to
this subject.   It is probable that he agreed in the main with
Tertullian, for whom he cherished a warm attachment.   In
one place, however, he says that the Holy Ghost is inferior to
the Son, (Epist. ad Pomp. 74) ; and in another, he says that
the Father is greater than the Son, (Epist. 73, ad Jub.)

Where now can any ground be discovered here, which will
lead us to believe that the fathers of the Nicene Council were
prepared by the *preceding* state of opinion, to maintain the *numerical* unity of substance in the Godhead?   All is either
unity of counsel, will, and operation ; or else *homogeneousness*
of substance, on the ground that the Son must be of the same
nature with the Parent.

Let us now pass to the times following the period of the
Nicene Council.   (*a*) One hundred and twenty-six years after this period, an ecumenical Council was assembled at Chal-
cedon, some distance below Byzantium, and on the opposite
side of the Bosphorus near the head of the Propontis.   This
Council sanctioned anew the Nicene Symbol ; and in their declaration they state, that "Jesus Christ, as to his Godhead,
is ὁμοούσιος with the Father ; and as to his humanity, he is
ὁμοούσιος with us."   Now as it is impossible to suppose, that
they meant to assert a *numerical* unity of Christ with us ; so,
as they have here given us a clue to the meaning which they
attached to ὁμοούσιος, we cannot suppose them to have understood the word as designating any thing more than *homogeneousness* of substance with the Father.

(*b*) The main point in dispute between the Nicene Fathers
and the Arians, was not whether there was a numerical unity
in the Godhead, but whether the Son was a *created* Being,

made in time, and properly belonging the order of *created* intelligencies. In the close of their formula (ἦν ποτε οὐκ ἦν κ. τ. λ,) the Council have utterly, and to the full extent that language allows, abjured these tenets of Arius. In opposition to him they maintain, that the Son was "*begotten* of the substance of the Father," and assert his true divinity in consequence of such descent. But all this bears not on the point, whether the Godhead in both is a *numerical* unity. It simply maintains the point of *homogeneousness,* and also, (for this seems to be implied in the phrase ἐκ τῆς οὐσίας τοῦ πατρός), that his generation depended not on the *will* of the Father, as many preceding theologians had taught, but that it belonged essentially to, or proceeded from, the very nature of the Father.

(c) Eusebius, the ecclesiastical historian, who was present at the Council of Nice, tells us that he found difficulties in subscribing to the expressions ἐκ τῆς οὐσίας τοῦ πατρός and ὁμοούσιος τῷ πατρί, which were introduced into their Symbol. These difficulties he proposed to the Council; and he received for explanation the assurance, that what they meant to express by ὁμοούσιος was, that there is no likeness (ἐμφέρεια) between the Son of God and any created beings; that he alone was in all respects like to the Father, who had begotten him; and that he originated not from any other being or substance, but only from the Father. In maintaining his derivation by generation, they avowed that they did not mean to imply any thing like a corporeal generation, nothing of separation or division, and not even that any change or passion in the Father should be implied, but that the generation was indescribable and incomprehensible.

With these explanations, inclined as he was to deal very leniently with the speculations of Arius, he voluntarily subscribed the Creed. Yet none of these explanations have respect to *numerical* unity of substance. They only show, that the Council meant to deny the principal thing which Arius affirmed.

(d) But the explanations of Eusebius, who was no friend to ὁμοουσία, may not be deemed impartial and satisfactory. We will resort then, to the testimony of Athanasius; for this cannot be called in question, on any such ground.

When the Nicene Council gave their opinion that the Son was of the Father, i. e. was derived from him, the Arians admitted this. But they construed it in their own way, viz., that he was of the Father in like manner as all created beings are. To put an end to this evasion the Council inserted *ἐκ τῆς οὐσίας τοῦ πατρός* in their Creed, which could not be said in reference to the derivation of any *created* objects.

Again, the Council maintained that the Son was the *εἰκών* (image) of the Father. This the Arians conceded ; for man, said they, was made in the image of God. To meet this evasion, the Council inserted *ὁμοούσιος τῷ πατρί*, which excluded the idea of likeness merely in the way of imitation, and implied a real homogeneousness of nature. Athanas. Opp. I. p. 297. Epist. ad Afric. pp. 936, 937.

According to these explanations then, the expressions " of the substance of the Father" and " homoousian with the Father," were originally and purposely designed to be antithetic to the views of the Arians ; but not to assert the *numerical* unity of the Godhead, which was not a matter of contest between the parties.

In another passage, Athanasius proposes to those who dislike *ὁμοούσιος* because it is not a scriptural expression, to substitute for it the expression, *Son by nature.* The meaning of this, as he expounds it, is, that the Son is not a *created* being, and has no beginning of existence in time. Whoever acknowledges this, he regards as acknowledging that the Son is *ὁμοούσιος.* Ep. ad Afros. p. 940. Now such an acknowledgment would be a real and thorough renunciation of Arianism ; but it would be no recognition of the numerical unity of the Godhead.

In another passage, Athanasius considers *ὁμοούσιος* and *ὁμοφύης* as equivalent expressions ; De Synod. Arim. et Seleuc. p. 923. But *ὁμοφύης* designates *specific* unity, not numeric. In another passage he says, that the Son is *τοιοῦτος οἷος ὁ πατήρ ;* Orat. cont. Arianos, p. 326.

Athanasius rejects the expression *μονοούσιος τῷ πατρί*, and considers it as being Sabellian ; I. p. 241. In another place he says of the *οὐσία* of the Son, that it is *γέννημα υἱσίας τοῦ πατρός ;* de Synodis, p. 923. Moreover he admits of two kinds of *οὐσίαι*, viz., au *οὐσία ἀγέννητος* and an *οὐσία γεννητός.* How can these be *numerically* one and the same ?

(*e*) Gregory Nazianzen was confessedly a disbeliever in *numerical* unity and admitted only a specific unity. He places the unity of the Godhead in harmony of purposes and operations, *ὥστε κἂν ἀριθμῷ διαφέρῃ, τῇ ἐξουσίᾳ μὴ τέμνεσθαι,* ' so that although they [the persons in the Godhead] *differ in num-*

ber, they are not divided in power;' Opp. I. p. 562. He brings an example from the like natures of Adam, Eve, and Seth, who were ὁμοούσιοι, to illustrate the ὁμοουσία of the Godhead, p. 598. He even compares the Trinity to' three suns, which shine with combined light.

(*f*) Basil, the particular friend of Gregory, cherished the same views. He says, that the advocates of the Nicene Creed acknowledge a God who is one, not in a *numerical* way, but as being of one nature, ἕνα οὐκ ἀριθμῷ, ἀλλὰ τῇ φύσει; III. p. 81. Again, the Father is φῶς ἄναρχον, but the Son is φῶς γεννηθέν; and he represents the Nicene Fathers as choosing the word ὁμοούσιος in order to designate ὁμότιμον τῆς φύσεως, i. e. the same *dignity* of nature; Ep. 52. p. 145. The unity then is not *numerical*, in his view, but specific and one of like rank or elevation.

(*g*) Finally, Gregory of Nyssa, the third in this cotemporary band of very distinguished men, is more explicit still in favour of *specific* unity. He repels the charge of Tritheism, and says, that one need not aver that there are *three* Gods, because the name God is a *generic* idea, whereby the whole divine nature is designated. This he illustrates by referring to Peter, Paul, and Barnabas, who, he says, were not three οὐσίαι, but only one. If one calls them three men, he goes on to say, this is only by a *catachresis or abuse* of language, which indeed may be allowed in respect to men, but cannot be made use of in respect to the Godhead; Opp. II. p. 914. Cur non tres Dii sunt, p 447 seq.

It lies now upon the very face of this representation, that *Godhead* was in his mind only a generic idea; and that Father, Son, and Spirit were individuals under this *genus*. How this differs from theoretical Tritheism, it would be very difficult to show.

Lower down we need not go, in order to show how the ὁμοούσιος of the Nicene Symbol was understood. It were easy to appeal to Chrysostom; who not only calls Adam and Eve ὁμοούσιοι (Homil. XVI. in Gen.), but appeals to the fact that children are of the same nature (ὁμοούσιοι) with their parents, in order to show that the Son is ὁμοούσιος with the Father; Orat. advers. Anom. I. p. 359. ed. Francof. So Hilary, in explaining the unity of the Father and the Son, comes at last to the conclusion, that it consists in having the same power and glory; De Synodis, pp. 1187—1191. De Trinit. III. p. 828 seq.

In a word, that a *homogeneousness* of nature, and not a numerical unity of substance, was understood by the leading
teachers in the churches, after the Council of Nice, to constitute the unity of the Godhead, appears from the fact, that three
of them, viz. Basil, Gregory Nazianzen, and Gregory of Nyssa, one and all, unite in insisting, that there is in the Godhead,
in and by itself considered, three hypostases and one divine
substance.   Their own explanation of what they meant by
this proposition, seems to leave us no room for doubt how we are
to class their opinion.   They compare the three hypostases of
the Godhead to *individuals* among men.   They tell us that
Paul, Peter, and John are three different subjects or hypostases; and yet all belong to the same genus, i. e. to the genus
man.   So in the Godhead there are three subjects, as they
assert, which have one and the same nature, inasmuch as they
belong to the *genus divinum;* i. e. they all partake of the nature of Godhead.   Basil Opp. III. p. 115 seq. Greg. Naz.
Orat. XXIII. p. 423.   See also Theodoret, Dial. I. Opp. IV.
p. 67, ed. Halle.

But I have proceeded far enough.   All which results from
this view, lies indeed upon the very face of the Nicene Creed.
The Son is θεὸς ἐκ θεοῦ, φῶς ἐκ φωτός; then he is of course
not οὐσία ἀγέννητος, like the Father; and therefore a proper
numerical unity of substance seems to be out of all question.
The Son only belongs to the same *genus,* or (if one prefers so
expressing it) *species,* and has therefore only a *specific* unity.
Self-existent substance and independent being are entirely
out of the question.   This idea the Nicene Fathers, at least
many of them, would probably have opposed with all their
might; for, as bishop Bull affirms, *cum uno ore* they declared,
that the Father only is αὐτόθεος.

I return from this digression, (if indeed that must be named
digression, which connects itself so intimately with the inquiry
respecting the real views of the Nicene Creed), to make some
further remarks on the main position of that Symbol, viz., the
divine derivation of the Son; and also on those views of the
Trinity which are more usually presented by the leading orthodox writers of modern times, and which stand connected as to
their origin with the doctrine of the Nicene Creed.

4. Dr. S., in the extract from his *Glaubenslehre* given in the
preceding pages, has briefly suggested, but not fully illustrated,
the inconsistency of the Athanasian or Nicene views of the

Trinity, with the *equality* of the persons in the Godhead as to *power and glory.* The additional views which I wish here to suggest, may be summarily exhibited as follows.

The eternal power and Godhead of the Divinity " are clearly seen by the things that are made ;" at least we must acknowledge this, if we take the apostle for our guide. " The heavens declare his glory, and the firmament sheweth forth the works of his hands," if we are to credit the Psalmist. The view of God as creator and author of all things, is one of the most exalted which the Bible discloses. Hence when the challenge is made to compare him with all idol gods, the holy prophets appeal to the attribute of Jehovah as creator and author of all things, as the final and unquestionable decision of the matter in debate.

It is then one of the highest exhibitions of *power* made by the Godhead, that it is the efficient cause of being. Consequently the *glory* due to God, and given to him by holy beings, for and on account of this, is one among the most conspicuous features of all the glory which is ascribed to him.

But if such power and glory are his, because he is the author of inferior beings and of the natural creation, is not unspeakably more power and glory exhibited, (and therefore may be justly claimed), by the generation of the Son and procession of the Spirit? If the Father is the *fons et principium* of the second and third persons, as the Latin fathers say : or the αἰτία or αἴτιον of these, as the Greek ones affirm ; then the power and glory manifested in the production of Godhead itself is as much greater than what is manifested in the creation of inferior things, as Godhead is elevated above them. The higher we rank the second and third persons of the Trinity, then, the more in proportion do we elevate the power and glory of the first person who produced them.

I do not see that we can retreat from the consequences of such a sentiment, by saying that ἀγεννησία is the characteristic merely of the first person, *filiatio* of the second, and ἐκπεμψις of the third. The characteristic of ἀγεννησία involves in its very nature attributes fundamental and essential to Godhead itself. Be it that you allow the Son and Spirit to be the author of the natural and spiritual creation, you still place the Father immeasurably above them, when you make him the sole author of the generation of the Son as a divine nature, or (if you believe with the Greek church of ancient days) of the procession of the Spirit who is of the same nature. The *Fons et Principium of*

GODHEAD must be immeasurably and beyond all conception above any and all other beings.

Nor is this radical difficulty removed, by the modified views and more cautious statements of modern theologians. According to them, the Father is the author of only the *subsistence*, i. e. the *modus existendi* or personality of the Son and Spirit, while the substance or essence of the Godhead is *numerically* one and the same in all the three persons. But here too a difficulty arises of somewhat formidable magnitude. It is this. Father and Son and Spirit are conceded to be numerically one and the same in essence or substance. Yet, if we are to credit the views now before us, we must at least believe that the Father is the origin or author of the *modus existendi* of the Son and Spirit. The whole reduces itself then simply to this, viz., that while the substance of the Son and Spirit is self-existent and independent and the same with that of the Father, it has still no *modus existendi* but that which the Father gives it. But how, we may be allowed to ask, could the substance of the Son and Spirit be self-existent and independent, and yet be supposed to exist without any *modus existendi* necessarily attached to it? And if that modus cannot by any possibility be even imagined to be disconnected from the existence of the substance itself, and cannot possibly have ever been as it were in abeyance and waiting to be determined, how could that modus spring from the Father, and not come from, or be necessarily connected with, self-existent substance itself? Or (to put the matter in another light), how is it that the Father, being *one and the same substance* numerically with the Son and Spirit, could have the attribute of ἀγεννησία, while the Son and Spirit have it not? Do not attributes, at least according to the usual methods of thinking and reasoning, arise from the nature and essence of substances? And if the Son and Spirit possess the same substance in all respects, (which must be true if the substance of the Godhead is *numerically* one), then how can it be shewn, that the second and third persons are dependent for the *mode* of their existence on the first? The same causes produce the same effects. If the very same substance belongs to the Father which belongs to the Son and Spirit; and, as possessing this, the Father has ἀγεννησία; how can it be shewn, that the attributes attached to this substance must not in each case be the same?

But if you say again, in order to avoid the difficulty now suggested, that ',there may be a distinction in some respects in the

Godhead, which does not involve the question of *equality of power and glory*,' I concede this; but then I ask, whether it has not been shewn above, that the difference now before us cannot be deemed to be one of this nature. To be the author of the proper substance of the Godhead of Son and Spirit, according to the patristical creed; or to be the author of the *modus existendi* of the Son and Spirit, according to the modern creed; both seem to involve the idea of a power and glory in the Father, immeasurably above that of the Son and Spirit; and this, just in the ratio stated by Origen.

The venerable Ridgley, who is not wont to shrink from difficulties, and was somewhat deeply imbued with attachment to Symbols, feels obliged, for the reasons above suggested or some others, (for he does not expressly assign his reasons), thus to declare himself, (Body of Div. I. p. 123, ed. 1731): "The principal thing in which I am obliged, till I receive further conviction, to differ from many others, is, *whether the Son and Spirit have a communicated or derived personality.* This many assert, but, I think, without sufficient proof; for I cannot but conclude, that the divine personality, not only of the Father, but of the Son and Spirit, is as much independent and underived, as the divine essence." He had before repeatedly said, that Father, Son, and Spirit have the same *self-existent* divine nature.

This sensible and solid writer then goes on to shew, that all the texts which are brought to prove the doctrine of eternal generation, refer to Christ as *Mediator;* and that the name *Son of God*, has reference to the same character.

But as Ridgley is not held by some to be orthodox on this point, let us turn our attention for a moment to the more sharp-sighted and powerful Turretin. "The essence," says he (I. p. 306), "is one; the persons are three; that is absolute, these are relative; that is communicable, these are incommunicable."

But how can this last declaration be substantiated to our satisfaction? How can *self-existent* essence be communicated? The being that exists by *communication* from another, is of course dependent on that other; and what can it mean that a *self-existent essence* is communicated to him, who does not become self-existent thereby? Or if he is self-existent, then how can he exist by *communicated* substance?

These difficulties are not diminished, when the venerable writer just cited says: "[The essence] is communicable not in the way of multiplication, but *secundum identitatem*, i. e. in the way of identity. . . . For although the essence is in sum the same as the three persons taken together, yet each [person] has a somewhat larger extension (latior est), because each person has the whole Godhead; although not adequately and totally, so to speak, i. e. not exclusively in respect to the other persons, for it belongs to them all."

How *identity* can be communicated, remains as yet unexplained; and as to the allegation, that each person has the whole Godhead, and yet that this Godhead belongs in common to them all, it needs a mind of greater subtilty than I possess, to deduce an intelligible proposition out of this.

After all, Turretin, in pursuing the distinction of personality to the *ne plus ultra*, comes in the end to this conclusion : " *Person* may be said to differ from *essence*, not really and essentially, as one thing and another thing; but *modally*, i. e. as *modus* differs from the thing itself." He goes still further; for the attributes of God, such as power, wisdom, justice, etc., he makes *essential* to Godhead; but personality, he thinks, is *not* of the divine essence; " it is God in the concrete, but not in the abstract."

How all of these representations, (which are only a specimen of what many others are), can be made to consist together, is a fair question, and one of serious import. Let us pass in review the course of thought. First we have it, that only the essence of the Deity is communicable, and this in the way of *identity.* Personality or the *modus existendi* cannot be communicated. It is to be remembered in the meantime, that we have the recognition, every where, that the substance of the Godhead is *numerically one and the same,* in all the three persons, inasmuch as it is self-existent in all. Then again, although personality is only *modal,* i. e. *modus existendi* only, yet the personality of Son and Spirit Turretin holds to be *derived* from the Father. But how is this to be made out, when the same writer expressly tells us that personality is an *incommunicable* attribute? How could the Father give, what he could not communicate? I might add : How could he give that, which (according to Turretin) he did not so possess as to give? inasmuch as the *modus existendi* of the Son is necessarily attached to the substance of his Godhead, and this substance is *self-existent*, not given or communicated by the Father. To say that the Son had no personality except that which was *given*, would be to say that his substance existed without any *modus existendi ;* which does not seem to need refutation.

If then the Father communicates personality, i. e. modus existendi, to the second and third persons of the Godhead, it must be because he communicates his *substance* to them; and so the communication of the substance occasions the personality. But this view, which is the ancient Nicene one, has also difficulties enough. If the whole substance is identically communicated, then personality is bestowed of course along with it; for *modus existendi* must necessarily accompany substance in all its conditions. If this be so, and the whole substance of the Father is *identically* communicated, then why should not ἀγεν—νησία and *paternitas* belong to the second and third persons of the Godhead, as well as to the first? But if personality is given without the communication, or independently of the communication, of the substance of the Godhead, then how can personality be an *incommunicable* attribute?

Such are the difficulties that force themselves upon my mind, in relation to this scheme of Trinitarianism, so extensively received in modern times, in the room of the ancient Nicene views. Are the difficulties lessened in any good measure, by the efforts of even a Turretin to explain them? And can a simple view of the scriptural doctrine, be one fraught with such an excessive measure of subtilties as this? And indeed we may well be permitted to ask : Can the human mind reconcile views so discrepant and jarring? And where in all the Bible do we find any thing which introduces such subtile views to our notice?

I am aware of the manner in which suggestions of this nature are usually met. 'The mystery of the Trinity,' it is said, 'is high and holy and inscrutable.' True, indeed; it is and must be so. No serious mind will object to this sentiment, if it be properly defined and understood. But may we not be allowed to ask, after what has been produced above : Why have so many men, who allow in theory that the mystery of the Trinity is inscrutable, practically neglected what they have urged upon others, and undertaken to give us graphic and specific views of it, and to settle with precision the relation of the persons in the Godhead? Why did they not content themselves with adopting the simple biblical declarations, and leave the subject there if it be truly inscrutable? How can the man who believes really and truly, that in many respects the *modus existendi* of the Godhead is altogether inscrutable, when he reads many things that have been written on this subject, refrain from the conviction and feeling, that those persons are usually most prone to exclaim, *mystery! mystery!* on every occasion where close inquiry is urged, who take the greatest liberties of all in defining, or attempting to define, the mysteries of the Godhead by metaphysical propositions?

Or will it be said, (as doubtless it may be), that all the difficulties and apparent contradictions which we may seem to find in the views of the Nicene fathers, or of many modern Trinitarians, arise simply from the fact, that the divine substance and subsistence or modus existendi are altogether different from those of created things; and that such conclusions as those that have been drawn above, are drawn merely by virtue of analogical reasoning which will not hold here?

If this should be alleged, as it probably will be because it often has been, the answer is near at hand.   A sincere believer in a scriptural Trinity, who at the same time is cautious in making positive statements, might still reply and say : ' If it be indeed true, as you affirm, that the divine substance and subsistence are immeasurably above our comprehension, and that no analogies in that mode of reasoning which has its basis in truths that respect created things, will apply here, then what confidence do you, by your own averment, allow me to place in your own propositions and distinctions and minute and subtile divisions of a metaphysical nature?   Is God absolutely incomprehensible, and so infinitely superior to all perception and knowledge on our part? Is the mystery of the Trinity one that is so utterly unfathomable and beyond investigation?   Then why should you call on me to follow you through distinctions respecting the Godhead, which purport to be the result of the most complete and entire analytical knowledge ; distinctions indeed so minute, that nothing short of a full view of the whole subject, a complete analysis of the Godhead, can fairly be a ground of support for them? You urge on me the mysterious and incomprehensible and awful nature of this subject; and all this I fully believe in, as to various particulars ; and yet you seem to me, at the very moment when you are doing this, to be yourself endeavouring to enter into the *sanctum sanctorum* itself of the Godhead ; and rending the sacred veil asunder, you are anxiously striving to inspect those things which mortal eyes are not permitted to behold, and to speak those things which it is not lawful for any one to utter! If such is your case, what ground can you claim of complaint against the freedom and temerity of others in speculation on the subject of the Trinity?

Most fully do I accede to the proposition, that in many respects the being and perfections of God must be objects that are elevated far above our comprehension. I repeat this sentiment to avoid being misunderstood. But my difficulty with you is, that while you so often and audibly proclaim this, you appear to have so little of apprehension, that you are yourself becoming an offender against the very doctrine which you proclaim.'

I do not see what reply any one of the minute metaphysical definers of the Trinity could well make to this. Certainly those ought not to cry out *mystery*, in order to repress the inquiries of others, who consider and treat the whole subject as though it were within their own grasp.

The impression naturally made upon my mind by the reading of some books on the subject of the Trinity, is, that those who warn us most against reasoning *more humano* concerning it, are usually those whose reasoning will least bear the test of close examination. It is peculiar to conscious strength never to boast, and never to shrink from contest. Usually it is only when a man sees his cause to be weak, or suspects it to be so, that he cries out *procul! O procul!* to others. But in many a case of this kind, a great mistake is committed. The man who warns against all approach to the most holy place, has himself, perhaps, not only thrust aside the vail which screened it from view, but without even putting the shoes from off his feet has endeavoured to traverse the whole of the sacred enclosure. Then why does he so zealously warn us against all approach? The believer, as already mentioned above, might well say: ' Is it not lawful for me to examine what he tells me I must believe? If his mind has comprehended what he teaches, why cannot mine comprehend it too? What he has taught, I may apprehend and learn. If he has said unintelligible things, I know full truly that they must have been unintelligible to him as well as to me. Why should he attempt to hinder me from examining the consistency and propriety of his assertions, by averring that the subject of which he treats is mysterious? Be it so; yet so far as he himself can penetrate into this mystery, so far I can follow him, provided I am not much his inferior; and if I am, there are others able to follow him. What he can teach, others can learn. What is *unknowable*, he does not understand any better than I do; why then should he make propositions concerning it, as though he did understand it, and then forbid me to examine them on the ground that the subject is *mysterious*? So far as it is so, it is mysterious to him as well as to me. Why should he attempt to make the impression on me, that he understands the deep things of God, and then tell me that the place where he has taken his own stand is too holy for me to approach? This may do with minds of a certain cast, which are too indolent or too little informed to think for themselves; but every mind truly enlightened and that thinks for itself, will easily understand how inconsistent and futile all allegations of the nature in question are, when they are made rather to cover the defects of one's own reasoning, or the inconsistency of his assertions, than to distinguish the true boundaries between what is knowable and what is not. I would that all the lovers of truth might forbear making any efforts to hide the faults of their reasoning or the conscious weakness of their cause, under exclamations of such a nature as have been suggested. The men who most indulge in them, are not unfrequently those who most offend against the very rules which they prescribe to others.'

But I am digressing from my subject. Let us return, then, and inquire a little further respecting the views of the Nicene fathers.

We have seen that the *equal power and glory* of the three persons in the Godhead does not seem to be compatible with their mode of setting forth the doctrine of the Trinity. We have also seen, that the greatly modified views of leading Trinitarians in modern times, do not by any means relieve the subject from seeming incongruities and apparently insurmountable obstacles. But I must caution my readers against deducing any thing from all this, to the prejudice of the scriptural doctrine itself of the Trinity. What can be more obvious, than that writers in ancient and in modern times, who believed in the true and real divinity of Father, Son, and Holy Ghost, may have made imperfect representations of this, and such as will not bear scanning by the principles of criticism and logic, and yet the doctrine itself be true? Might I not easily bring forward analogies of this kind? Do we not know, that the great and cardinal doctrine of the atonement was for ages represented as a compensation or satisfaction made to the leader of the spirits of darkness, on account of taking men away from his dominion? Now this obscured, but did not quench, the glory of this doctrine. And so it has been with other doctrines; and that of the Trinity does not seem to form an exception.

The darkness that is in men, is not in God, nor in his truth. Clouds may eclipse the sun; but they will pass over, and sooner or later he will shine in all his strength.

Allowing then that ages and generations have failed to represent, in a satisfactory manner, the great doctrine of the Trinity, it is no proof that it is not true; nor is it even a proof, that in its *practical* bearings it had not a substantial influence upon the minds of Christians, when imperfectly represented, although not its full and proper influence. When the error noted above respecting the atonement was cherished and propagated, it did not hinder Christians from believing in the vicarious satisfaction made by the death of Christ, nor extinguish the gratitude that was felt for his redemption.

So in the case before us. When we examine, part by part, the imperfections of the Nicene Creed, we may be tempted to ask: Can the abettors of this be regarded as believers in the divinity of the Son and Spirit? Indeed we almost spontaneously ask: Shall we draw the conclusion that the Nicene fathers, and those who preceded and followed them and sympathized in their views and expressions, were Arians or Tritheists? Candour will oblige us to say, I have no doubt at all, that they had no apprehension of cherishing the errors of either the one or the other of these parties. That they meant *not* to be Arians, their rigid scrutiny, their most thorough opposition to and denunciation of their peculiar sentiments, show so plainly, that a man must shut his eyes against the light of the mid-day sun, if he does not perceive it. That they disclaimed Tritheism, every where appears in all their writings. Most abundant pains did they take to do this. In *intention* and *design*, then, or in their own estimation, they were neither Arians nor Tritheists, but believers in the real divinity of the Saviour, and probably of the Spirit; and if so, then they were worshippers of a Trinity in Unity.

The question what they supposed themselves to be and meant to be, does not indeed seem to admit of any rational doubt. The answer lies upon the face of their multiplied and most solemn and earnest asseverations and explanations. But the question, after all, whether the principles which they assumed and defended, would not, when understood in a simply logical way, lead to something not much diverse from Arianism, or else to Tritheism, is a question of a very different nature from those that have just been put. It is impossible for me in my own mind to hesitate in saying, that either what is but little better than Arianism, or else what amounts to real theoretical Tritheism, must be the legitimate and inevitable *logical* result of their principles. I readily allow that these are serious declarations, and such as involve responsibility ; and we must stop for a moment to consider them.

The essence of Arianism consisted in maintaining, that *Christ was a being in some respects inferior to God, and created in time ;* in other words, that he was a derived, dependent being, and therefore neither infinite nor eternal. The great rallying point was, that he was a *created* being. On this, by deduction, all the rest of Arius' positions depended.

This position the Nicene Fathers, in the most express and direct manner possible, often and earnestly contradicted. We ought in justice to allow their disclaimer or contradiction. But what did they substitute in the room of an origin by *creation ?* They substituted *generation*—and (by implication) *eternal* generation, inasmuch as they anathematize all who say, ἦν ποτε οὐκ ἦν. Where then are we now? We are simply in this predicament, viz., we have passed from the camp of those who maintain a beginning of the Son's existence *in time* and *by creation,* and gone over to the camp of those who declare that there is no definite time or limitation as to the beginning of the Son's existence, and that he was not created but *begotten.* It is well; but we may still inquire, How much have we gained by this transition? The Scriptures assert that Christ is *God over all,* that he is *the true God and eternal life,* that he is the *great God our Saviour ;* assigning to him the highest possible names and attributes. In possession of such inspired declarations, we are spontaneously compelled, living as we do beneath the light of the present advanced gospel-day, to attach the attributes of self-existence and independence to the Son of God; for without these, our minds can form no idea of a *God over all, the true God,* and *the great God.* Yet the Nicene Symbol tells us, that the Son is a *derived* God, θεὸς ἐκ θεοῦ, φῶς ἐκ φωτός. If so, then he has neither self-existence nor independence. To assert that the idea of *dependence* is not necessarily connected with the plain and obvious sense of the Nicene Creed, is to assert that language has no appropriate meaning, or that it may mean any thing or every thing, at the will of the interpreter. And then the very fact that the origin of the Son is expressly and designedly traced to the Father, shows that the idea of self-existence is *designedly* contradicted.

I repeat the question then: What have we gained by a transition from the camp of the Arians to that of the Nicenians? We have gained one advantage, at least, viz., the position that the existence of the Son is not of definite and temporary origin, but eternal. So far, so good; for " the Logos was *in the beginning* with God and was God"—was God even *then.* But as to the other all-important points, viz., self-existence and independence—attributes without which our minds are unable now to form any conception of true and proper Godhead—have we gained any thing here by our transition? Not in the least. All that the Nicene Symbol does, is to deny one mode of production, viz. creation as asserted by the Arians, and to put another in its stead. *Production* or *generation*—applied fully and directly to the Saviour's *divine* nature—is what the Nicene fathers meant most explicitly to declare.

As soberly contemplated by us, then, of the present day, it is really a matter of comparatively small importance, whether Nicenian or Arian views now obtain the ascendency. Neither of them in fact go any further, than an effort to explain the *manner* in which the Son originated, viz., whether it was by creation or by generation. And is this a point capable of explanation? I might appeal to Irenaeus here, and refer the reader to what is quoted from him on a preceding page, (p. 294). Indeed, if the question were fully answered in respect to either of the inquiries just suggested, I see not how it would benefit our faith or our practice. What Christ *is*, is the great question. *How* he became so, is a question of a different nature. It may be very important to remove incongruous assertions respecting this; but the mode of his existence as divine Logos, how can we expect to understand?

Both Arius and his opponents, then, virtually acknowledge the *derivation* and *dependence* of the Son. They divide, and dispute, and anathematize each other, because of different opinions about the *mode* of his derivation; and the dispute was principally concerning this; although the *time* when his rise took place, was a question that necessarily connected itself with the other.

Why should we greatly sympathize now in such a dispute; a great and bitter dispute about that which Irenaeus declares to be not only unknowable, but which it is presumptuous even to seek to know? For myself I feel compelled to say, that although I view the Nicene Creed as a nearer approach than Arianism to the Scripture doctrine concerning the Son, inasmuch as it maintains that he is *eternal,* yet on the great point of *self-existence* and *independence,* those indispensable and essential attributes of Godhead—what there is to choose between Arianism and Nicenism I wot not. I have repeatedly endeavoured, as my readers will bear me witness, to vindicate the fathers of the Nicene Symbol from all *design* to mar the divinity of the Saviour ; but what they intended and purposed to do was one thing; and what is the legitimate consequence of their unwary language, is another. And in this last respect, I know not how to make, after all their opposition to Arius, any very important distinction between him and them. The *modes* in which the Son's existence took rise, cannot well be supposed to belong to *practical* theology at least ; and disputes about it can never profit the church, except that it may be important to the interests of truth to repel erroneous declarations respecting any great subject of theology.

I must speak a word, also, on the subject of *Tritheism.* The Nicenians one and all disclaim this. They often and earnestly do so; and they do it with the strongest asseverations. Let us give full credit to their repeated and strong avowals; for honest and pious men we may well believe most of them to have been. Still, when the heat of dispute is passed away ; and emanation-philosophy, and polytheistic notions, and Eclecticism have taken their departure from our world, (an everlasting one I would hope) ; we may now look at and coolly examine the explanations and defences which the Nicenians have made of their views. It is lawful to do so ; it is also expedient.

We have seen then, in a word, that the unity of the Godhead is, in their apprehension, *homogeneousness* of nature among the persons of the Trinity ; and so in the view of the most distinguished advocates of Anti-arianism. We have seen, that some of these did not scruple to refer to individual personality among men, and to *specific* unity, as an illustration of their views of personality in the Godhead. As a general thing this cannot be charged upon the defenders of the Symbol in question. Yet there is such an oscillation among them,—such a struggling of the mind, and such a seizing hold of every kind of illustration that promises any analogy or relief amid the difficulties which charges of Tritheism threw in their way— that one must abate much from some representations to be found even in the more moderate part of them, in order to get upon safe and solid ground.

At all events, whatever disclaimer may be made as to Tritheism, the comparison of individuality in the Godhead with that among men, does essentially involve theoretical Tritheism. If not, then how could the Greeks be accused of polytheism, who believed in a common nature among the *Dii majores?* And if not, then we must come to the absurd conclusion of Gregory of Nyssa, that it is *catachresis* when we speak of Peter and Paul and Barnabas as *three* men, because in truth they have but *one* common human nature. It is impossible to put the mind upon receiving such an incongruity, without its reluctating. It instinctively revolts; and the worst of it is, that it is apt to go back, driven on by disgust, to some opposite extremity which involves other things nearly or quite as incredible or improbable, or at least as contrary to the simple views of the Scriptures.

In modern times, these particular illustrations of personality, and these modes of asserting distinction in the Godhead, have indeed been pretty generally abandoned, from an instinctive apprehension of their interference with the *unity* of the Godhead. Now and then a zealous partisan of the Nicene Symbol—a Bull, a Waterland, a Jones of Nayland, or some writer of this cast—has told us of three distinct consciousnesses, wills, and affections, in the Godhead, and of the eternal "society" which must have always been in it. But the ears of intelligent Christians in general, are not now open to these things. Yet still, the unwary and unthinking are affected by them, and led unconsciously, it may be, into real Tritheism. But such assertions are avoided with instinctive repugnance, by most of those Christians who have much examined or thought upon the subject. Even the fathers, with all their looseness of expression, did not reach the perilous point, to which the authors of such representations proceed.

Still, Tritheism is not even here *intended.* From this we may fully and cheerfully absolve most of the authors of such declarations. But whatever was the *intention,* we are entitled to ask : What does the language naturally imply? And what will the unlearned reader naturally deduce from it ?

But enough. I can only add at the close of this investigation, (protracted much beyond my original intention, in consequence of the deep interest that I have felt in the subject as it grew under my hand), that I never can be a *subordinarian* or a *Nicenian,* nor admit that a *derived* divine nature is true and proper Godhead, until I become satisfied that self-existence and independence are *not* essential to real and veritable Godhead. Until then, I must believe with John, that the Son is " true God and eternal life;" that " in the beginning he was with God, and was God, and made all things ;" and with Paul, that he is " God over all and blessed forever," and that he is " the great God and our Saviour." Is not such a being αὐτόθεος ? Then the Maker of heaven and earth is not so ; then God supreme, and great, and true, is not so. But while the New Testament asserts these predicates of the Son, I cannot exchange them—simple, intelligible, awful, delightful as they are—for the emanation-diction of the Nicene Council, and the language of dialectic subtilty which was called into being by the vagaries of Arius. With the yielding and believing Thomas, 1 can say of my Saviour : *My Lord ! and my God !* not *"God of God, light of light."* The humble and simple Christian, who goes to John and Paul for instruction, will follow them rather than the philosophizing Nicene fathers, great and good as they were; and rather than subtile and speculating modern writers. When the apostles speak, he will listen. If the anathemas of even ecumenical councils were to be fulminated in defence of the Nicene Symbol; if the thunders of the Vatican were to speak loud in its favour; yea, if seven thunders like these were to utter their voices in proclaiming θεός ἐκ θεοῦ, φῶς ἐκ φωτός, the humble believer would press the New Testament to his bosom, and say : Jesus, Saviour ! Thou art my Lord and my God ! Thee, thee I love and adore ; the great God, the true God, eternal life, God over all and blessed forever ; first and last, king eternal and immortal, only wise God my Saviour; thee, thee, I adore and love and worship forever and ever ! Let me be united here and hereafter with those who ascribe " blessing and glory and wisdom and thanksgiving and honour and power and might" to thee, God manifest in the flesh, and redeeming a world from ruin by thine own precious blood!

' But where are we now?' I shall doubtless be asked, and not without emotion on the part of some; ' where are we now? Is there then no distinction in the Godhead? Are we then to go back to the heresy of Praxeas, and Noetus, and Sabellius? or must we become Patripassians? Must we then deny that the Logos or divine nature of Christ antecedent to the incarnation, was generated by the Father or derived from him? Truly, while you urge us away from the shoals, you are endeavouring to plunge us into the whirlpool.'

But I must beg the gentle reader to use a little moderation. In such a great business, which has kept ages and generations in a state of boisterous commotion, by reason of the difficulties that men have attached to it through speculation, and philosophy so called, and efforts to unveil mysteries that God's word has not unveiled—in such an affair, we are not to expect that all doctrine is to be laid down, or all the necessary explanations made, in a single paragraph, or even in the same chapter. It is one thing to examine and expose the errors or defects of language or description in Symbols already before the world, and to shew wherein it comes short of ascribing true and real Godhead to Christ, and wherein the advocates of it have approximated now to Arianism, and anon to Tritheism, without any design indeed on their part to do either ; it is another thing to lay down and establish better, more simple, more intelligible propositions in the room of these. The first I have endeavoured to do ; the effort to accomplish the last I must defer, until I shall have first presented the views of Dr. S. in full. In his comparison of the Athanasian with the so-called Sabellian views, he has here and there partially, and at last fully, disclosed his own views of what is true in respect to the doctrine of a Trinity and of a Unity in the Godhead. Those views are at least intelligible. They appear to be self-consistent. They offer no violence to the mind, which believes that God can as well reveal himself to man, as create and preserve him. When these are fully presented, then comes the proper time for me to say, how far I adopt or reject the views of Sabellius or of Schleiermacher. I have already made my objections to the views of the Nicene Creed, and to the modern substitute for it.

The sum of Schleiermacher's opinion, (and it may be grateful to the reader here to have a hint of it), is, that the Unity is

God concealed, and the Trinity is *God revealed*.   The Unity
or *Μονάς*, as he supposes, is God *in seipso*, i. e. simply and
in and by himself considered, immutable, self-existent, eternal,
and possessed of all possible perfection and excellence.   But
as to the Trinity ; the Father is God as revealed in the works
of creation, providence, and legislation ; the Son is God in human flesh, the divine Logos incarnate ; the Holy Ghost is God
the Sanctifier, who renovates the hearts of sinners, and dwells
in the hearts of believers.   The *personality* of the Godhead
consists in these *developments*, made in time, and made to intelligent and rational beings.   Strictly considered, personality is
not in his view eternal ; and from the nature of the case (as thus
viewed) it could not be, because it consists in developments of
the Godhead to intelligent beings ; and those developments
could not be made, before those beings had existence.

As to the *number* of persons, *three* are reckoned by him, and
three only, because the Scriptures reveal no more, and because
our natural and moral woes and wants require no more for their
full alleviation and satisfaction.

Such are the main features of the portrait drawn by Dr. S. ;
or rather, such are the mere *outlines* of those features.   The
explanation and defence of his views are best left to his own efforts ; and the reader will meet with both in the sequel.   When
all that he has to say in the way of proposition, and also of illustration and confirmation, is presented, then it will be appropriate
for me to avow my own opinions, and briefly to state some reasons for them.

I cannot adopt the Nicene Creed, because I do not believe
that the natural meaning of the words is consistent with an enlightened and scriptural view of the Trinity in Unity.   Most
fully must I subscribe to the canon laid down by Schleiermacher,
viz., that the moral consciousness of Christians, and also the
Scriptures, demand such a representation of the persons of the
Godhead as will present each as *fully equal* to the other.   The
Nicene Symbol does not appear to fulfil the demands of this
canon.   It presents the Father as the *Μονάς*, the divinity or
proper Godhead in and of himself exclusively ; it represents
him as the *Fons* et *Principium* of the Son, and therefore gives
him superior power and glory.   It does not even assert the
claims of the Blessed Spirit to Godhead ; and therefore leaves
room to doubt, whether it means to recognize a *Trinity* or only
a Duality.   After a profession of belief in one God, the Father,

who is the maker of all things visible and invisible; and in one Lord, Jesus Christ, who is the only begotten ἐκ τῆς οὐσίας τοῦ πατρός; it simply adds: καὶ [πιστεύομεν] εἰς τὸ ἅγιον πνεῦμα. But *how*, or in what capacity, is he believed in? we naturally inquire.   To this no answer is given ; and we are left to gather the views of the Council from other exhibitions of their sentiments on this point than those made in their Symbol.   A Unitarian would say, that he believes in the Holy Spirit; an Arian would say the same thing; both construing the words as meaning *divine influence* merely, and not divine hypostasis.   The Nicene Symbol, then, does not appear plainly and explicitly to acknowledge, that " there are three persons in one God, the Father, the Son, and the Holy Ghost ;" nor that " these three are one God, the *same in substance*, and EQUAL *in power* and glory?" No; it comes, or seems to come, far short of this.   I reject it therefore because I do believe in a Trinity in Unity; because I believe the Bible teaches this doctrine.   I reject it for the very reason, that it seems to me to teach a different doctrine from that of the Bible, or at all events to teach such doctrine in an incongruous and imperfect manner.

Nothing can be more natural here than the question : Why should this branch of Christian theology so long have remained in so imperfect and unsatisfactory a state, while most other Christian doctrines have been advancing as to illustration, precise statement, and confirmation ?

The answer to this question may not be obvious ; at least all my readers may not, perhaps, be satisfied that it is, even if they admit the general correctness of the remarks which I have made above.   Several things may however be truly said, in the way of answer.

(1) The civil power of the Roman empire that held the world in subjection, was often employed to defend and establish the Nicene Creed.   Constantine followed the refusal to subscribe to it with deposition from ecclesiastical office, and with banishment and exile.   Other emperors did the same ; as did the Arians, on the other side, when they gained the ascendancy.   When the Roman church had finally suppressed the Arian party, by civil and ecclesiastical penalties, the Nicene Creed of course prevailed again.   It was the Symbol of the dark ages through, and mostly undiscussed and undisturbed. More illustration, accuracy of definition, and sound confirmation, one could not expect would be added, under such circumstances.

(2) When the era of the Reformation began to dawn, the great controversy between the Romish and the Reformed churches did not turn on the doctrine of the Trinity. Both churches admitted this in common. Discussion on this point, therefore, was considered as in a manner uncalled for and needless; and the minds of the religious public were too intent on other points more immediately involved in the controversy, and too deeply interested in them, to turn aside to matters in which both parties were substantially agreed. Hence the spirit of the Reformation, active, bold, unsparing as it was in respect to superstitions and much of patristical theology and schoolmen's lore, was not employed in making investigations as to the correctness of the Nicene Symbol.

(3) When the writings of Socinus and his coadjutors in Poland were directed against the doctrine of the Trinity, they contained so much that was grossly offensive to those who worshipped God in their Saviour and Redeemer, that a strong and widely diffused prejudice arose in the Christian community against all discussions of this nature, in which the reasoning and philosophy of men were so prone to raise objections and difficulties in the way of the plain and palpable declarations of the Bible. Men became timid in regard to discussing the awful mysteries of the Godhead, because free discussion had been so greatly abused.

(4) Similar causes have continued to prevent free discussion on the part of believers in the Trinity, except in the way of defence against the so-called Unitarians and Arians, or in the way of attack upon them. So long as this was the case, partial views and only such as belonged to the immediate points in controversy, would naturally continue to be taken; and such has been the fact. After some display of arms and preparatory skirmishing, the battle has pretty generally been fought on the ground of patristical opinion. What did the fathers and the ecumenical councils believe and decide? These questions have produced the *History of Early Opinions* and a multitude of other like books, the main object of which is, to take refuge, on one side or the other, under the shield of antiquity. The Bible—the simple, plain, positive, declarations of the Bible— alas! how little have they been consulted by many combatants, except to help out some claudicating position of antiquity.

(5) Other reasons might easily be given why sober, free, extensive, radical investigation with regard to the topic before

us has no oftener been pursued. An excitability in the public mind, brought down by tradition, and continued by sympathy with the disputes of early ages, has had its full share in suppressing free discussion. The proneness of those, who seek for their religious sentiments in symbols and systems sanctioned by time and by numbers, to anathematize all who venture to appeal from them to the Bible alone ; the readiness to cry: *Foenum habet in cornu,* or *Hic niger est, hunc tu, Romane, caveto,* whenever one ventures to ask the precise meaning, the *why* and the *wherefore* and the *Scripturality* of received symbols, has appalled many a heart that loved inquiry, and wished to make it, but dare not incur the suspicions that would be raised among the Symbolists. One trembled to risk his eyes, amid the clouds of dust that would be thrown into them. Add to all this, (and perhaps this is one of the most weighty of all the reasons), the reckless and irreverent manner in which the doctrine of the Trinity—a subject which is one of the most solemn and awful that the human mind can be called to contemplate—has often been treated, and is even now treated ; and then reckon into the account the proneness to speculate and theorize on this subject, and the extravagancies of many of the real friends of this doctrine ; put all these causes together, and the reader may conceive, without any wonder or astonishment, how the doctrine in question has so long continued much in the state that it was centuries ago.

After all, however, we have seen that many of the more distinguished theologians of modern times have silently, unobserved as it were, and perhaps in some cases unconsciously, adopted a mode of stating the doctrine of the Trinity, widely at variance with that of the Nicene Creed. The *numerical unity of substance* they generally admit. Personality or *modus existendi* only, they suppose to be conferred by the Father on the second and third persons of the Godhead ; distinctly avowing, that the idea of derived substance is inconsistent with the notion of real Godhead, and inconsistent with the proper unity of the Godhead. But whether any real advance has been made upon the Nicene doctrine by all this, in respect to congruity and even the well-grounded principles of metaphysical philosophy, has already been the subject of inquiry above, and need not be here again investigated.

During the period since the Reformation, there have now and then risen up individuals, who doubted or disputed the doctrine of the Nicene Creed, and who rejected most of the subtile distinctions adopted by many of the leading orthodox writers, on the ground that they were dark, and difficult, and uninstructive, and above all that they were not made any where by the sacred writers.   It were easy to name some of these, eminent for piety and learning.   Even in the days of Arminius, the younger Trelcatius ventured in his lecture-room to call in question the doctrine of *derived* divinity.   Arminius tells us with what zeal he fought against him; and that Gomer himself attacked him on this point; while still the opinion found so much favour among the Anti-remonstrants, that Trelcatius was never disturbed on account of it.   Many a Christian, and preacher too, have doubted, or in their own minds rejected this doctrine, who still have cherished their doubts in silence, because they did not wish to agitate the public mind respecting them.

In New England, in particular, it has been long a predominant opinion among the clergy, that there is something in the doctrine of eternal generation, which is not entitled to their faith, and which indeed is altogether inexplicable.   Still, the discussion has not been carried on with any considerable zeal; and we can hardly be said to have more than a kind of *negative* belief on this subject.

Thus much as to the state and condition of the doctrine, in many of the symbols still in use, and among many distinguished theologians.   A more interesting question remains.   Is this state of things always to continue?   Is no investigation—careful, sober, scriptural investigation—which admits neither symbols nor fathers at all into the place of Christ and his Apostles, ever to be made?   I hope and trust that the spirit of the Reformation and of Christianity, that the love and honour of the Saviour, that zeal for the doctrine of the Trinity in Unity, will forbid that it should not.

If I need any apology for the freedom of the preceding discussions, I have already presented one.   My reason for examining and rejecting human creeds which do not admit the *numerical unity* of substance in the Godhead, nor the *equal power and glory* of Father, Son, and Holy Ghost, is, that such creeds "take away my Lord, and I know not where they have laid him."   It is not that I am a lower Trinitarian, but because I am a *higher* one, that I reject them.   *God over all and blessed forever*, I must believe him to be, "who redeemed me by his blood." " Blessing and honour and power and glory be his—forever and ever !"

Let me add a word more as to the following Essay of Dr. S., and I have done for the present. His views respecting the opinions of Artemon, Noetus, Praxeas, Beryll, and Sabellius, will be found by the careful and well-informed reader to differ in some respects from those which are presented in the common books on Ecclesiastical History, and in the more usual accounts of the individuals named, in the particular histories of the ancient heresies. That Dr. S. has applied a more sharp-sighted and rigid criticism than usual, to the investigation of the so-called Sabellian opinions, is what I apprehend to be true. His Monogramm on this subject, to which his special and most strenuous efforts were directed, seems better adapted, *caeteris paribus*, to the discovery and development of truth in respect to it, than a general history of the church, or a general history of heretics.

At all events, if he has failed in some historical particulars, the views which he every where suggests are worthy of a most attentive perusal and consideration. The gradual development he has made of the Sabellian system, and the comparison of this all along with the opinions of its antagonists, (which were mostly like those that 'are expressed in the Nicene Creed), is full of instruction. Every man who attentively reads and considers them, must be better prepared to read and judge of the writings of the fathers, in relation to the doctrine of the Trinity as held by them.

I have found the office of a translator an exceedingly difficult one, in the present case. Dr. S. indulges in long sentences and involved constructions; after the manner so common among the recent writers of Germany who are of a philosophical cast. He writes on for several pages, at times, without a single break or paragraph in his discourse. But this is not all the difficulty. His words are so very pregnant with meaning, that in this respect one is reminded of Tacitus; although the construction of his sentences is exceedingly different from that of the Roman historian. He indulges in all the technics of philosophy and theology. He binds his sentences all together, with an *auch* or a *doch*, or a *wenn*, or a *weil*, or some other particle, very much in the manner in which his favourite Plato connects his with an οὖν, or a δέ, or a μέν, or a μενοῦν, or a καὶ δή, and the like. Add to all this, the difficult nature of the subject, the tenuous distinctions which it demands of the writer and reader, and the perplexing looseness of diction and 'definition among the fathers whose opinions are examined ; and the translator has no ordinary task before him.

I am not sure that I have in every case hit upon the exact idea of the original. The matter itself is too subtile, and the writer too terse and remote from the common methods of thought and expression, to allow me to be very confident. But I can promise the reader, that I have in no case willingly misrepresented the meaning of the author. I have given a free, in some cases even a paraphrastic, version, because I felt that the matter would not be intelligible to the religious public in general of our country, unless I did so. I am not translating the Scriptures ; and therefore I do not feel the same responsibility of holding fast, as closely as possible, to the exact diction of the original. I have in some cases added an epexegetical clause. Where this is very short, and not of much moment, I have forborne to mark it ; but in other cases of a different nature, I have inclosed my addition in brackets.

As to the Notes ; most of them are quotations from the fathers. These Dr. S. has no where translated. I have taken the pains to translate them all, for the aid of the less experienced or young reader ; who will probably thank me for this uninviting yet often thankless labour. I have included the translation in brackets, in order to signify that it does not come from any version by Dr. S. of the original. These translations I have marked with single commas ; in order that they may at once be distinguished by the reader, from the remarks with which I have sometimes accompanied them. All in the notes, not included in brackets, belongs to Dr. Schleiermacher.

If I have failed to render some of the Greek passages quoted so as to do justice to the originals, the reader is at liberty to correct me. I am sure he will find no small difficulty in making intelligible some of the assertions of the fathers on the subject of the Trinity. In some cases I had not the original works quoted at hand, and my circumstances did not permit me to hunt them up. I have used my best endeavours, in order to do justice to the authors without them.

The principal remarks that I have to make on the scheme of doctrine held by Sabellius, or proposed by Dr. S., I have purposely reserved, as before intimated, for a *sequel* to the piece. They will be read with more satisfaction, and be better understood, when the reader shall have before his mind all which the Essay presents.

After all that has been said above of Schleiermacher, it may be presumed that the reader will feel a desire to know something more of a *personal* nature respecting him. It so happens that this natural desire can, in the present case, be in some good measure gratified. From two different sources, we have accounts of the last days of Schleiermacher; and from one of these, brief sketches also of some leading particulars of his biography. These are presented in the account given by Mr. C. H. Stobwasser, a merchant in Berlin, a member of the Moravian church, and a particular and intimate friend of Dr. S. I shall transcribe a part of his account, and abridge some other parts. In addition to this, I shall interweave the account given by the wife of Dr. S., respecting his last hours, which comes through another medium. The first of these I find in the *Messenger*, a paper for the Reformed German Church, printe d at York in Pennsylvania, and dated Jan. 15, 1835; the second I take from the Boston Recorder of Dec. 5, 1834. The introductory remarks to the second, I suppose to be from my friend, Prof. E. Robinson, the late editor of the Biblical Repository. Mr. Stobwasser thus commences his account.

" He was born November 21st, 1768, and died February 12th, 1834. On the second of February, at 7 o'clock in the morning, he preached his last sermon. During the two preceding weeks he had suffered from a cough and hoarseness. Many in his situation would have spared themselves; but he thought it impossible, inasmuch as he had undertaken to complete many labours before Easter. Having gone a journey, in the preceding year, to Norway and Denmark, from which he returned only at the end of October, he had commenced his lectures later than usual, and hastened now to finish every thing before the Easter holy-days, which in this year would come very early; and when he was admonished, he referred to the urgency that arose from the shortness of the time. On this morning his wife had provided a carriage for him, and after the sermon sent her daughter to him into the sacristy with a request that he should ride home, as the morning was windy, and he usually perspired much while preaching, and he was moreover hoarse and unwell; but he would not be persuaded to deviate from his custom, and walked home. Many of his friends, among whom was the Counsellor Eichhorn, who could boast of possessing some influence over him, urged him to resign some of his offices. His reply was, " Shall I take my rest? It is what I cannot do.—My lectures are of too much importance with me to be discontinued; more important still is the religious instruction of the youth; and most of all the preaching of the gospel." The utmost that he

60

could have been persuaded to relinquish was the Secretaryship in the Academy of Sciences; and this only to gain time for the preparation of works for the press, and to put the last hand to several things in church history and an exegesis on the Acts of the Apostles, which are left among his papers, and, together with many other treatises, are now to be published by the Rev. Mr. Fonas."·

It appears that on the 6th of Feb., he delivered two lectures, and attended a catechising of the youth; and in the afternoon of the same day, he attended to his duties as Secretary in the Royal Academy at Berlin. He then attended a library meeting, being all the time very hoarse and inclining to chills. From that time his disease assumed an inflammatory aspect, the progress of which could not be stayed, and which in one week's time ended in his death. The news of his dangerous sickness occasioned great agitation and excited much interest in Berlin; and his house was so thronged with anxious inquirers, that its inmates were obliged to expose a kind of Bulletin of his state, at the door, in order that the house might be freed from noise and commotion.

"On the 11th of Feb.," continues Mr. Stobwasser, "towards evening, he requested his wife to read for him one of the hymns of his dear Baptiste von Albertini. Which of the hymns it was I am not informed. As I went daily to his house after the 9th instant, I was every time requested to put up a fervent prayer that the Lord would grant to him a truly blessed death; or if his life was preserved, that he would make him a very fervent preacher of the death of Jesus Christ upon the cross, and his meritorious sufferings for us and in our stead, as he had hitherto been a preacher of his glory.

"On the 12th I learned that he had assembled his family around him to bid them adieu. As his wife and family wished to be alone with him, acquaintances were not admitted into his bed-chamber. On receiving this information I took my departure. It was his last hour. I could not but pray for him with tears, that the Saviour might grant to him a very clear and blessed view of his vicarious sufferings."

Then follows an account of his death by Mr. Stobwasser; which I omit for the sake of inserting a better one from the hand of Dr. S.'s beloved wife. I copy nearly the whole paragraph from the Boston Recorder, because the preface to the account of Mrs. S., is a matter of interest to the reader.

'The death of this distinguished man in February last, after an inflammatory illness of a few days, is very generally known in this country; and the public have also in general terms been informed of

the triumph of his Christian faith, and of his administration of the
Lord's supper upon his dying bed. By the kindness of a friend recently from Germany, we are enabled to lay before our readers the
following deeply interesting details of the closing scene, in an extract from a letter of his wife to a female friend. This extract has
been widely circulated in Germany in manuscript, but has never, so
far as we know, been printed. We read it first with deep emotion ;
for the whole transaction, and the narration, are worthy of the man,
for they are the perfect image of his own simplicity. We give the
account to the Christian public as doing honor both to the illustrious
dead and to the living writer ; and also as the dying testimony of another great and good man to the simplicity and power of the truth as
it is in Jesus.'

" Once he called me to his bedside and said : ' My dear, I seem to
be really in a state which hovers between consciousness and uncon-
sciousness ;' (he had taken laudanum, and slumbered a good deal) ;
' but in my soul I experience the most delightful moments. I must
ever be in deep speculations, but they are united with the deepest religious feelings.'

" Once he raised his hand and said with solemnity : ' Here kindle
a flame upon the altar !' Another time : ' I leave to my children the
charge of the apostle John, Love ye one another !' Again : ' My dear,
you will have many painful duties ! friends will aid you. I could so
gladly have still remained with you and the children !' As I uttered
some hope, he replied : ' Do not deceive yourself ;' and then with the
greatest solemnity : ' My love, there is still much that will be hard
to bear.'

" On the last morning, Wednesday, Feb. 12th, his sufferings evidently became greater. He complained of a burning inward heat,
and the first and last tone of impatience broke from his lips : ' Ah,
Lord, I suffer much !'—The features of death came fully on, the eye
was glazed, the death-struggle was over! At this moment, he laid
the two fore-fingers upon his left eye, as he often did when in deep
thought, and began to speak : ' We have the atoning death of Jesus
Christ, his body, and his blood.' During this he had raised himself
up, his features began to be re-animated, his voice became clear and
strong ; he inquired with priestly solemnity : ' Are ye one with me
in this faith ?' to which we, Lommatzsch* and F.† who were present,
and myself, answered with a loud *yea.* ' Then let us receive the
Lord's supper ! but the sexton is not to be thought of ; quick, quick !
let no one stumble at the form ; I have never held to the dead letter !'

" As soon as the necessary things were brought in by my son-in-
law, during which time we had waited with him in solemn stillness,

---

* Schleiermacher's son-in-law, Professor in Berlin.
† A female friend.

he began,—with features more and more animated, and with an eye to which a strange and indescribable lustre, yea, a higher glow of love with which he looked upon us, had returned,—to pronounce some words of prayer introductory to the solemn rite. Then he gave the bread first to me, then to F., then to Lommatzsch, and lastly to himself, pronouncing aloud to each, the words of institution,*—so loud indeed, that the children and Muhlenfels,† who kneeled listening at the door of the next room, heard them plainly. So also with the wine, to us three first, and then to himself, with the full words of institution to each. Then, with his eyes directed to Lommatzsch, he said: 'Upon these words of Scripture I stand fast, as I have always taught; they are the foundation of my faith.' After he had pronounced the blessing, he turned his eye once more full of love on me, and then on each of the others, with the words: 'In this love and communion, we are and remain ONE.'

"He laid himself back upon his pillow; the animation still rested on his features. After a few minutes he said: "Now I can hold out here no longer,' and then, 'Lay me in a different posture.' We laid him on his side,—he breathed a few times,—and life stood still!

"Meanwhile the children had all come in, and kneeled around the bed; his eyes closed gradually. I had several times thought during these moments of deep interest, Had I but the children here!—Still the sublimity of the scene was so great, that I could only wait in solemn stillness, bound motionless to my place as by a spell; yea, even as entranced and incapable of any voluntary exertion.

"How widely does recollection already fall short of the reality of those moments of thrilling agitation!"

'We learn that the manuscripts of his lectures, and of some other works, on a variety of subjects in his systematic and exegetical theology, and also on dialectics, are left in complete order, so that his posthumous works are expected to appear in eight volumes. The celebrated translation of Plato remains, alas! incomplete.'

Thousands flocked to the house to see his corpse; which, as usual in Germany, was placed between flowers. His death took place on the 12th of February, and his funeral was attended on the 15th. Almost the whole city of Berlin, with its immense population, was in motion on this occasion, and thousands joined the funeral procession. Dr. Strauss, the cathedral preacher and rector of the University, delivered an address on the occasion; and about fifty clergymen were present, among whom were two Roman Catholics. A summary of Dr. Strauss' sermon is thus given by Stobwasser.

---

* Our Saviour's words, Matt. 26: 26, etc. 1 Cor. 11: 23—29.

† Late Professor in the London University.

"The preacher touched upon Schleiermacher's youth and remarked, that the whole tendency in the religious character of the deceased was to be ascribed to the fact, that his first theological education was received in the Brethren's church; 'in that little circle whose light is silently and beneficially diffused through the church of Jesus Christ.' He then adverted to his life and actions, his letters on religion, which arose in their time to shed their beams upon a very dark night. *He* it was, said the speaker, that first again confessed the name of Jesus Christ as the Son of the living God. *His* hearers were chiefly of the cultivated class, and he expounded the gospel to them in a scientific method, suited to their intellectual character. *Thousands were awakened by him and brought to a knowledge of themselves.* He was blamed for not going farther, because many of those, who were originally the fruits of his ministry, turned away from him to other preachers of the gospel; but he seemed to know that the part which the Lord had assigned to him, was to proclaim the gospel to the educated portion of the community. To lead inquirers further, he thought, must be left to the Spirit of God, by the reading of the holy Scriptures and the hearing of the gospel. Finally, the preacher related how the deceased had finished the circuit of his life with the profession, that the blood of Jesus Christ was the ground of his faith and his salvation."

Fifty students of the University were employed as marshalls to preserve the requisite order at his funeral. The catechumens of Dr. S. obtained liberty to walk next to his corpse, as orphans bereaved of their spiritual father. These were followed by his relatives; then the clergy; then other friends; and finally by 130 coaches in mourning, among which were several State coaches of the royal princes.

At the grave, Pischon delivered a brilliant eulogy upon the deceased, as a professor, teacher of religion, and preacher.

The whole account shews both the state of Dr. S's mind in his later and latest hours, and the state of public feeling towards him, which was so universally expressed. Can it be, that a man who lived thus and died thus, was not a disciple of Jesus? The answer to this question we must leave to the great day that will reveal the secrets of all hearts. Whatever Dr. S's speculative errors were, (and I cannot help believing that he did cherish some that in themselves would be dangerous to most minds), yet can we feel that a man who died thus was no believer in the Saviour of sinners? I feel constrained to say, that I mourn his loss to the world as an efficient and powerful writer; but I cannot mourn as one without hope for him. May his errors, whatever they were, be fully developed and shunned ; and may all the truths which he has helped to illustrate and confirm, be universally admitted and felt !

COMPARISON, ETC. BY DR. SCHLEIERMACHER.[*]

§ 1. *Introduction.*

To the following pages I might have given a more indefinite title, inasmuch as they are not designed fully to treat of the subject announced, but only to compare the relations of certain particulars to each other, that stand connected with what is said in my *Doctrines of the Creed,* or *Doctrines worthy of Belief,* (Glaubenslehre, § 190), and near the close of it, respecting the subject of the Trinity. If what is unsatisfactory and obscure in our creeds, with regard to the doctrine of the Trinity, was occasioned by going too far in opposition to Sabellianism, the points of difference and opposition between the two systems must be distinctly understood and duly appreciated, before our Symbols can be safely corrected. It matters not in what way the opposition to Sabellianism originated ; whether it came from apprehending that something in it was false and dangerous which was not so; or whether, for the expression of what was in itself really contradictory, phrases were laid hold of which signified more than was intended; still the nature of the whole thing must be rightly understood, before any mistakes can be properly corrected that may have been committed.

My present design is to exhibit only such points as may serve to communicate, if possible, some new impetus to the spirit of investigation. That it is desirable to animate with new life the spirit of historical investigation and of doctrinal reasoning, the entire literature of this department of religious knowledge bears ample testimony.

The Arian creed, in its various ramifications, forms another and different antithesis to the Trinitarian doctrine of our commonly received Symbols. But the mutual relations of these two latter systems have, with great diligence and in a great va-

---

[*] Published in the *Theologische Zeitschrift,* 1822, dritt. Heft, p. 295 seq.

riety of ways, been discussed. On the other hand, the relations between Sabellianism and our common Creed have hitherto been but slightly touched, or handled as it were in the gross, without going into any particulars of a nicer kind and more subtile nature. So far as developments of a historical nature merely are concerned, this is indeed to be justified; inasmuch as the Arian doctrines have occasioned much longer and more vehement contests in the church, than the Sabellian. But so far as the simple interests of *doctrinal* truth are concerned, this fact is merely an accidental circumstance; and the things which we ought to believe as the ultimate result of all our inquiries, can be fully developed, only when the Sabellian disagreement with our Symbols shall be as fully disclosed as the Arian has been.

The peculiar character of Christian piety began early to trace back that which appeared to be extraordinary and superhuman in the Saviour, to the divine Being himself, and to express its reverence toward it in poetic effusions of a Christian stamp, and in public addresses to the churches, as well as in apologetic writings. Nor did it confine itself to these; it gave utterance to the same feelings in the language of doctrinal instruction. In this way did Christianity take a middle place between Judaism and Paganism; inasmuch as the multiplication of gods is appropriately Pagan; while the denial of all distinction or difference in the Godhead, and especially of that by which it exists in a peculiar manner in Christ, is of Jewish origin, and is appropriately a Jewish rejection of the Son.

Such a view of the Saviour as divine is developed so frequently in the writings of the fathers since the Council of Nice, that it would be altogether superfluous to prove it here by the citation of particular passages. It is indeed so natural that the Christian church should take such a view, so long as it had Paganism on the one hand and Judaism on the other to contend with, that sentiments of this nature surely must have been much older than the time when the Council of Nice was held. Inasmuch, however, as this belief would appear polytheistic to the Jews, while the Gentiles at the same time would accuse Christians of being impious because they did not admit of manifold divisions or individualities in the divine nature, so was the church exposed to two shoals in the difficult voyage undertaken for the further formation and exhibition of this doctrine, between which it must take its course. On the one hand, it must give such a direction to that distinction of the Godhead which was appropriately Christian, as that it would by no means dash upon polytheism, but preserve the true characteristics of μοναρχία (sole supremacy); while on the other, it must not veer towards Judaism so as to become implicated in it. That which distinctly marked its removal from Judaism, was the Christian οἰκονομία. There was, indeed, a considerable width left for sailing between the two shoals; yet the signals on both for keeping aloof brought with them this disadvantage, that when one, directed by his reckoning or by the wind, took his course between them, he seemed to some to be too near one of these signals, while he himself believed that he was only holding a middle course; and yet, after all, he was actually sailing too near the other signal.

Judaism maintained the unity of the supreme Being; but according to this, God in his unity remained in a state of separation from man. He did indeed exhibit himself at times; he made his voice to be heard; and so the giving of the law and prophecy ensued. But his thoughts and his will could thus be made known to men only *from without*, by means of words and laws. The inspiration of the seer was, in earlier times, conversant only with external visions and voices and influences from without. Even had it proceeded purely from an *internal* source, it could not *then* have been looked upon in any other light, than in that of a kind of ephemeral and as it were magical operation. But this imperfection was to be done away. The Most High at length transferred his abode to man, and dwelt *in* him. This was the special object of the Christian dispensation. Real *Christian* faith was fully persuaded that this had been accomplished.

The Greeks had indeed spoken much and often of the divinity, as preparing particular men to become his temple, and of his dwelling in them. But by reason of the diversity of these habitations, the Godhead itself had as it were become divided, and was lowered down to a state of mutability like that of men; and thus the glory which would result from a real and internal union of the divine and human natures, was tarnished by all the abominations of idolatry. The pagan *indwelling* of the divinity was demoniacal, and its season of continuance soon passed away. The Most High, one and undivided, at last took up his abode in man; and the Sole Supreme (μοναρχία), by such a union with man, must needs destroy all idolatry.

If now a particular account of such a union of the Jewish, and simplification of the heathen, systems were to be made out, this might be done in different ways by different persons. One would be more affected with disgust of the Jewish stiffness and the literal interpretation of their sacred books ; another with the extravagant and deleterious nature of polytheism : one of course would be more concerned lest he should dash upon the Jewish shoal ; and another lest he should run aground upon the Gentile one. By this simple principle, now, may we account for all the various views which stand related to the Trinitarian doctrine of our Symbols, and which have given more or less occasion to its gradual development.

§ 2. *Opinions of Artemon.*

[PRELIMINARY NOTICE. Of Artemon, whose opinions are canvassed in the following section, we know little or nothing that is definite and certain. The ancient ecclesiastical writers differ so much about him, that even his name is not certainly known, some calling him Artemon, and some Artemas ; Theod. Haeret. Fab. II. 4. Of his country, his parentage, his place of development, or the circumstances of his life, we are, and it would seem that we must remain, ignorant. The scanty, imperfect, and contradictory opinions which are thrown out in relation to these subjects, may be found, if the reader is prompted by motives of curiosity or of interest to seek for them, in Euseb. Hist. Ecc. V. 28. Thedoreti Haeret. Fab. Lib. II. 4. Epiphan. Haeres. LXV. §§ 1, 4. Pamphili Apol. pro Origine, Lib. I. p. 235 in Vol. V. of Hieronym. Opp., edit. Martianay. See also Niceph. Hist. Ecc. Lib. IV. 20. Photii Biblioth. cod. 48. Such are the principal ancient sources. The modern ones worthy of particular consultation, are (most of all) C. W. F. Walch, Historie der Ketzereien I. p. 558 seq. ; Lardner's History of Heretics, p. 360 seq. Fabricii Biblioth. Graec. Vol. V. p. 276. P. Schaffhausen, Historia Artemonis et Artemonitarum. Bulli Judic. Ecc. Cathol. p. 27. Scanty and unsatisfactory notices are contained in most of the usual ecclesiastical histories, biographical dictionaries, etc.

In order to supply the reader, however, with adequate means of understanding the various allusions of Dr. S. in the present section, it will be necessary to state in particular some of the things which have been said by the ancient writers respecting

Artemon. Eusebius says (ut supra), that he had in his own possession an anonymous book, the author of which aimed to refute the heresy of Artemon; which heresy maintained that Christ was a mere man. The anonymous author avers, that the adherents to the doctrines of Artemon declare, that all the ancients, and even the apostles themselves, received and taught what they (the disciples of Artemon) received and taught; and that his state of things continued until the time of Victor, the thirteenth bishop of Rome after Peter; but that his successor Zephyrinus first introduced spurious doctrine.

To refute this, Eusebius appeals to the writings of distinguished men in the church, who lived before the time of Victor, and defended the divinity of Christ; and to the fact, that Victor himself expelled Theodotus of Byzantium from the church at Rome, for maintaining that Christ was a mere man. Victor was bishop of Rome ten years, i. e. from A. D. 192 to A. D. 202.

Eusebius also says, that Theodotus was the *first* who asserted that Christ was a mere man; and thus he tacitly intimates, that he preceded Artemon in the heretical opinion ascribed to him. He then cites the anonymous author as declaring, that some disciples of Theodotus had made Natalis a bishop among them; that this bishop subsequently abjured his errors; and that the party to which he had belonged, cultivated science very much, gave themselves to the logical examination of the Scriptures, and were very bold in their emendations and alterations of the sacred books. But whether this is meant of the followers of Artemon, or merely of Theodotus; or whether the anonymous author and Eusebius also both confound the two sects together, cannot well be made out from the obscure narration of Eusebius.

Theodoret (Haeret. Fab. Lib. II. 4.) says of Artemon, that he believed in God the creator of the universe, in the same way as the Christians; but that he asserted the Lord Jesus Christ to be a mere man; born, however, of a virgin, and of a power (ἀρετῇ) superior to that of the prophets. Like the anonymous author in Eusebius, he testifies of Artemon, that he maintained the apostolic antiquity of the doctrine which he held. Artemon moreover declared, that 'those who succeeded the apostles first began θεολογῆσαι τὸν Χριστόν, who is not God.' The reader will have occasion in the sequel to advert to the peculiar phraseology which is here quoted.

On the whole it appears probable, that Artemon lived near the close of the second, or at the beginning of the third century. Caius, a presbyter under Zephyrinus (about A. D. 210), is said by Photius (Biblioth. Cod. 48) to have written a book or books against the heresy of Artemon; which most have taken for the anonymous book quoted by Eusebius, as related above. But as this matter cannot be satisfactorily established, we can only speak of *probabilities.* Eusebius says, that Paul of Samosata, who lived in the latter half of the third century, only *renewed* the heresy of Artemon. It would seem by this, that the opinions of Artemon had been as it were forgotten, before Paul renewed them; and therefore the former must have lived as early as the first part of the third century.

Finally, as to the theological opinions of Artemon, all agree that he denied Christ to be God, i. e. he denied this in the sense in which the orthodox Christians of his day asserted it. But there are many different ways of denying such views as were then held. Accordingly, Pamphilus, Eusebius, and Epiphanius represent Artemon as holding the same sentiments in respect to the divinity of Christ, that Paul of Samosata held; Alexander of Alexandria makes him an Arian; and Theodoret, a Theodotian, Photinian, or Ebionite. Gennadius of Marseilles attaches him to the Praxean or Sabellian party. It will be seen, in the sequel, that Dr. S. agrees with Gennadius; and he has stated reasons for believing, that Artemon has been unjustly associated with Theodotus, either as to opinions or party. It is on the ground which Gennadius takes, that Dr. S. has extended to the opinions of Artemon the comparison which he makes between the Sabellian and Athanasian Creeds.

It does not seem probable, that the party of Artemon was ever considerable, or that it was of long continuance. Philastrius, Epiphanius, and Augustine, give him no express place in their list of heretics. Epiphanius adverts to him merely *en passant.*

As to Theodotus of Byzantium, who is frequently mentioned in the pages that follow, and in connection with Artemon, more that is definite is known of him. Although a σκυτεύς (*shoemaker*, but usually translated *tanner*), he is said by Epiphanius to have had a good acquaintance with learning. It is the general testimony, moreover, of the ancients, that in a time of persecution he abjured the Christian religion; and that, falling into disrepute at Byzantium on account of this, he went to Rome.

There he broached his opinions that Christ was a mere man, or
at least that he had not a divine nature, (for it is not certain
that he denied his miraculous conception) ; for which he was expelled from the church by Victor bishop of Rome, (fl. 192—
202).   Dr. S. seems to regard Theodotus as a man of very
little weight or stability ; and he is altogether unwilling to asso-
ciate Artemon with him.   He supposes that Theodotus appealed to the opinions of Artemon, in order to procure credit for
his own.   If this be well founded, it would seem probable that
Artemon had lived at Rome, or at least that his party were, or
had been, in some consideration and influence there.

The reader who wishes for more minute information respecting Theodotus, is referred to Euseb. Hist. Ecc. V. 28. Theo-
doreti Haeret. Fab. Lib. II. 5. Philastrius de Haeres. cap. 50.
August. de Haeres. cap. 33. Epiphanius, Haeres. L. IV. Also
the Appendix to Tertull. de Praescrip. Haeret.   Among the
modern writers, Walch, Historie der Ketz. I. 548 seq. Lardner, Hist. of Heret. p. 364 seq., particularly the former, may
be consulted with satisfaction.

It may not be uninteresting to remark, at the close of this
notice, that Samuel Crellius (ob. 1632), the celebrated Unitarian, who wrote a book to explain away the testimony of John
respecting the Logos, assumed the fictitious name of *Artemoni-
us* (an Artemonite), in order to avoid the prejudices which the
name of *Socinian* would have to encounter.   In so doing, Crellius took it for granted that Artemon was of the same sentiment
that Theodotus maintained ; a position that Dr. S. by no means
admits.   TR.]

Soon after the Godhead of Christ began in the Christian
churches to be presented in a more strictly *doctrinal* shape,
Artemon declared himself against it as an *innovation*, out of
fear, as it would seem, that it was an approach to polytheistic
Paganism.   The passage concerning this which Eusebius has
quoted from an unknown writer (Hist. Ecc. v. 28), cannot be
understood otherwise than as referring to the commencement
of a more definite *doctrinal* development.*   It would betray
such a degree of ignorance and prejudice in Artemon, as the tes-

* That the writer quoted here was the Roman presbyter Caius
[see on p. 334 above], I would not positively assert ; nor does it appear to me to be satisfactorly determined, that Artemon is to be sought
for in Italy rather than elsewhere.

timony of even his adversaries will not allow us to ascribe to
him, had he intended to deny that in hymns and hortatory dis-
courses the divinity of Christ had been often and long asserted.
But in a strictly *didactic* form, the doctrine of the divinity of
Christ was probably beginning to appear in apologetic writings
and others of a similar nature, at a time near to that in which
Artemon lived.

Inasmuch now as this man inclined to the side of cool and
deliberate consideration, so it may be naturally supposed, that
the views and phraseology in question with respect to the divine
nature of Christ, were regarded by him as harmless assertions,
so long as they were limited merely to the expression and communication of internal feeling; but when they came to be employed in strictly *didactic* discourse, where exact definitions
were to be made out, then he objected to these and the like
declarations. In case such didactic assertions had in this way
but recently begun to come into use, Artemon could notwithstanding those older expressions in hymns and hortatory dis-
courses, still say, that the practice of declaring Christ to be
God had commenced in his time.* Certainly the word θεολο-
γῆσαι† which is employed, has reference to a strictly *didactic*
use; and it is testified, moreover, in respect to Artemon, that
he laid great stress upon *logical* definitions of religious expressions, and on this account he subjected the meaning of passages
in the Scriptures to a logical investigation, when a strictly *doctrinal* use was to be made of them.‡

It appears moreover, that as he did not in his School, neglect
the knowledge of scientific matters on the one hand, so on the

---

* Theodoret (Haeret. Fab. II. 4) represents him as merely saying,
that this practice had commenced *since apostolic times.*

[† See the manner in which this word is employed by Theodoret,
in reference to Artemon, on p. 333 above. Θεολογέω properly means,
to act as a θεόλογος, i. e. to speak of God and divine things; and so
Dr. S. would seem to understand it here. But Theodoret affirms
that Artemon said, that "after the Apostles' time some began θεολογῆσαι χριστὸν, οὐκ ὄντα θεόν," which I cannot well interpret except
by translating it, *Some began to call Christ God, who is not God;* and
in this way the word θεολογέω is often employed in the fathers. TR.]

[‡ It will be seen by this remark, that Dr. S. applies to Artemon
and his School, what Eusebius says in a doubtful way, as mentioned
on p. 333 above. TR.]

other he examined in a critical way the text of the Scriptures;
and this, without feeling obliged to follow any particular dogmatic views, i. e. he did this in such a way as to act the part of
a mere philologist.   We see therefore in his case, that a historical and critical taste, which is so indispensable in theologizing,
inclined him to doctrinal doubts of a kind like those which afterwards frequently, and sometimes predominantly, developed
themselves.   There was this difference, however, between his
case and the one last mentioned, viz., that the fear of Jewish
superstition was in after times the more common feeling; while
in the case before us, when return to Paganism was yet quite a
possible thing, the fear which developes itself is that of exchang-
ing Christianity for heathen polytheism.

Thus constructed and fitted out, the vessel of Artemon sailed,
to be sure, sufficiently near to the Jewish coast.   Theodoret
testifies of him, that he preserved pure and unadulterated the
doctrine of μοναρχία; but still in such a way, according to his
view, as would infringe upon the Christian economy, οἰκονομίαν,
[i. e. the doctrines respecting the Godhead which are peculiar
to the Gospel.]

I would not venture, however, to assert that Artemon suffered shipwreck as to this part of Christian belief; for it is only
the Nazaraean view of this subject which appropriately constitutes that species of Christianity which returns back to Judaism.
Artemon appears to have developed his views respecting the
Godhead of the Redeemer, only in such a way as was adapted
to express his aversion to every thing, which could in the most
distant manner seem to be like polytheism.   We may suppose
his case to have been such, from the fact that the opinions of
Paul of Samosata are sometimes traced back to him;* and also from the fact that he did, in the most explicit manner, hold
to the birth of Christ from a virgin, and that Jesus was not to
be placed on a level with the prophets, but above them.   Here
we have, in the perfect freedom of Jesus' human nature from
sin, and in the more elevated measure of influence from the divine Logos, or from the exhibitions of the Spirit in Jesus,† some-

---

* E. g. in Theodoret, Haeret. Fab. II. 8. Augustin, de Haeres.
XLIV.

† Even the sect of *Melchisedeciani* were no more than a shoot from
the School of Artemon.   What they taught of the relation of Christ
to Melchisedek, was only the result of their mode of interpreting the

thing on which true faith in the absolute sufficiency of redemption may at least take hold, although it cannot here find a basis for support which is entirely satisfactory.

But inasmuch as Theodotus of Byzantium is mentioned as sympathizing in belief with Artemon; and by some, moreover, he is regarded as the teacher of Artemon, while others do not admit that there was any connection between them in the same school or sect; so, (because this is not the proper place for the investigation of such a point), I must content myself by saying, in order to justify what I have already suggested, that I agree to the latter opinion.* Moreover I do not think that unworthy of credit which is said of Theodotus, viz., that he came to his peculiar views in consequence of making little of denying Christ, which was so characteristic of the Gnostics; or at least, that he was forced to a public declaration and propagation of his views in regard to Christ, by the infamy which ensued upon his thoughtless step [of renouncing Christianity in the time of persecution].† With this agrees very well the story, that Theodotus, in order to gain credit again as a true confessor, endeavoured to make himself the visible head or leader of a party. The basis of this may be true, although that part of the story which has reference to the chastisement by angels may be false and visionary.‡ Nay, I would even go still further; I must believe, that through the paucity of historic materials, that has happened which often takes place, viz., a confounding of things together which are diverse; so that many of the arguments which Epiphanius ascribes to Theodotus, belong rather to Artemon and his School. To the latter only can I ascribe arguments

epistle to the Hebrews, which of course was accommodated to the ground-work of their own system. Their design no doubt was to shew, that their stand-point was purely Christian, and was at a great remove from Judaism.

* Theodoret (ut supra) definitely designates him as the Head of another φρατρία (brotherhood).

[† See the account usually given of this, on p. 334 above. TR.]

[‡ The anonymous author whom Eusebius quotes (see p. 333 above), mentions that Natalis, the chosen bishop of the Theodotians, was chastised by angels for his presumption in accepting office conferred by such a party; and that he was thus brought to repentance; and moreover, that he shewed the marks of the blows to the bishop of Rome, in order to move him to forgiveness. Eusebius does not say whether he himself gives any credit to this or not. TR.]

of a critical and logical character; and to him should I assign
the learned scholars whose names are worth preserving, rather
than to the frivolous σχυτεύς (*cobler* or *shoemaker*) of Byzantium.

If now we make proper distinctions among the dissimilar elements which are so variously treated by ancient historians, we
may find, in those early times, a phenomenon which has often
been repeated in the church. Artemon is a leader of those, in
whom a deeply-rooted earnestness produces efforts to check all
harsh and easily perverted expressions respecting what is of a
wonderful nature in our creed, and to keep such expressions
away from the region of *scientific* theology ; and of course of
those whose favourite object it is, to introduce and render
current the more moderate kind of expressions respecting such
subjects.

To such views of the importance of moderate and limited expressions, does the unreflecting spirit of skepticism in many
easily attach itself ; for they are ready to admit nothing but
what is the merest and most common matter of fact, and no
where do they manifest any desire for what belongs to the wonderful, nor appear to possess any capacity to relish it. It is a
favourite contrivance of this class of persons, to lean on such or
such a prop, and to represent themselves as belonging to this or
that party. Such people, in my opinion, have in Theodotus a
leader ; and it usually happens to them, as it did to him ; for he
came by such pretences to be so confounded with Artemon,
that to the latter was ascribed the blame which belonged to the
former ; while on the other hand, Theodotus took on himself a
part of the merit which could properly be ascribed only to Artemon.

§ 3. *Creed of Praxeas.*

[INTRODUCTION. Of Praxeas we find little that is of a personal nature in the ancient ecclesiastical writers. Tertullian
says that he was of Asia : Ex Asia hoc genus perversitatis intulit homo ; cont. Prax. cap. 1. The story among the ancients
concerning him was, that he had been thrown into prison on account of his stedfast adherence to the Christian faith ; and that
this circumstance greatly added to the credit which he had
among the churches.

The time in which he made his appearance at Rome, was
probably when Victor was bishop there (A. D. 192—202).

Praxeas persuaded this bishop to renounce his partiality for the
Montanists ; which circumstance seems to have given much
sharpness to the edge of Tertullian's opposition against him.
Philaster and Augustine say, that Praxeas lived in Africa ; and the
probability is, that he went from Rome to Africa, and most likely to Carthage, where Tertullian became acquainted with him.

A report also prevailed among the ancient Christians, that
Praxeas was there induced by some one, probably by Tertullian,
to recant all of his errors.   To this recantation (if he made it)
he does not seem to have adhered ; for he afterwards maintained his opinions with great zeal, and made many converts in
Africa.

Of his subsequent history we know nothing certain.   Later
report says, that he was excommunicated for heresy by a council of African bishops ; but this needs confirmation.

The amount of his sentiment respecting the Trinity appears to
be, that he was a *modalist* in his views; i. e. he regarded Father, Son, and Holy Ghost, as only designations of the different *modes* in which the same God disclosed or revealed himself
to men.   But as his sentiments are so amply discussed by Dr.
S. in the sequel, more need not be here said.

The reader who wishes to trace out all of importance that has
been said concerning Praxeas, may consult for ancient views,
Tertullian, Contra Prax. ; Philastrius, de Haeres. cap. 41.
Optatus of Milan, Lib. I. p. 10. IV. p. 128. Praedest. cap.
41.   Neither Irenaeus, nor Clement, nor Cyril, nor Epiphanius,
nor Theodoret, nor Eusebius, mention him ; and Philaster and
Augustine only *obiter*.

For modern views, he may consult Walch, B. I. Lardner, p.
407 seq. Tillemont, Memoirs, etc. Tom. III. p. 74, 618. Ittig.,
de Haeresiarch. § 2. c. 16.   Tr.]

If now the opinions of Artemon are not to be regarded as altogether inconsistent with Christianity, yet it is certain, that if
true Christian belief may consist with those forms of expression
used by him, they are still not to be regarded as the proper sup-
porters and guides of it.   Hence it was natural for Christians,
who wished indeed (like him) to shun every approach to polytheism on the one hand, still, on the other, to be desirous of
choosing expressions even for strictly didactic purposes, which
were stronger than mere negatives could be for designating the

higher nature of the Redeemer, and which would exhibit a more firmly grounded justification of the honours paid to him by the church.

This did Praxeas and Noetus; who, more independent probably of each other than Artemon and Theodotus, did still harmonize more exactly in sentiment and purpose. In order to avoid all semblance of approach to polytheism, (which it is difficult to do while the formula $\theta\epsilon\grave{o}\varsigma$ $\grave{\epsilon}\varkappa$ $\theta\epsilon o\tilde{v}$ is employed), they chose rather to acknowledge no difference between the divine Being in the Redeemer and in the Father.

We can trace indeed, in history, no connection of Artemon and Theodotus with Noetus; nor even with Praxeas, except in the way of inference. But although no historical clue is *apparent*, it is still not the less certain, that the latter were opposed to the former, and that the modes of expression employed by Noetus and Praxeas must have been designedly *antithetic* to those of Theodotus and Artemon, although we are now unable to shew that the sects of the latter existed in the countries to which Noetus and Praxeas belonged. In respect to Praxeas we know, that without any accusation of heresy, or rather with the unspotted reputation of a confessor, he came to Rome at the time when Victor was bishop, who had expelled Theodotus from the communion of the church. Since now the assertions which Tertullian accuses Praxeas of making are adapted to shun all appearance of polytheism, without abridging any thing of the divinity of the Redeemer; so is it altogether probable, that they are to be regarded as antithetic to those of Theodotus. If they had not some such object in view as that of making out a substantial contradiction of opinions already condemned, but had been employed simply and without any special cause to call them forth, they would almost inevitably have excited unfavourable notice at Rome, on account of the dissimilarity between them and the customary modes of expression. That Praxeas did receive the favourable attention already mentioned, we have good ground for believing; because we should certainly have found some notices of the fact, if he had been condemned in Rome, or a Synod had been convoked in Africa, in order to condemn him.* That this tol-

---

* When Philastrius (de Haeres.) says concerning the followers of Praxeas, (and without any good reason respecting the followers of Hermogenes): *Qui et ita* (i. e. in the same manner as the Sabellians)

eration towards him was still exercised, even after Tertullian had poured forth his invectives, must not be ascribed to the Montanism of Tertullian, which was afterward so much disliked at Rome. For at that time Montanism was so little disliked in that city, that, at least as Tertullian believed, nothing but the influence of Praxeas hindered its being approved and formally acknowledged.

Thus much may we admit respecting the historical connection of Praxeas with Theodotus. His doctrinal opinions, however, we can learn only from the attacks made upon him by Tertullian. In representing these we may suppose that Tertullian takes as many liberties, as advocates for one side are wont to take in respect to their antagonist. Yet no one ought to conclude, that all is perverted which Tertullian alleges in order to put to shame the enemy of Montanism. Essentially the opinion of Praxeas appears to have been, that, in case one did not allow himself to detract from the divine nature of the Redeemer, nor deny nor abridge it, he could consistently maintain the unity of the Godhead, only by not separating the divine in the Redeemer from that of the Father, and by not representing it as *subordinate*, but by explaining it as one and the same. According to this view, we may regard the expression, *duos unum volunt esse,** as an appropriate phrase of Praxeas and of his party. Yet one must be well on his guard, so as not to confound the expressions which Tertullian employs in describing the opinions of his antagonist, with the expressions of Praxeas himself. This applies to the first leading passage which is quoted as the sentiment of Praxeas;† for, as is elsewhere abundantly manifest, Praxeas did, in conformity no doubt with the usage of the New Testament, employ the term *Son*, not to designate the *divine* nature which dwelt in the Re-

---

sentientes, abjecti sunt ab ecclesia catholica, this must be understood as only an expression of the later opinion that prevailed respecting the Praxeans.

* Tertull. adv. Praxeam, 5.

† Perversitas ... quae se existimat meram veritatem possidere, deum unicum non alias putat credendum, quam si ipsum eundemque et Patrem et Filium et Spiritum Sanctum dicat; adv. Prax. c. 2. ['Perverseness ... which thinks itself to be in possession of simple truth, and supposes that God cannot be believed in as one God only, otherwise than by asserting Father, Son, and Holy Spirit to be one and the same.']

deemer, but for *the human nature as united with the divine.* ✱ ∨
In accordance with this sentiment, therefore, he could not well
affirm that the Father and the Son are one and the same.

Whether, moreover, Praxeas ever affirmed that in the composite name *Jesus Christ*, Jesus designated the *human*, and
Christ the *divine* nature, so that Tertullian could correctly say
that he made Christ and the Father one and the same, I would
not venture to assert.† But if he did make such a distinction
in the person of the Redeemer,‡ it is much more likely that
he gave the name *Jesus* to the human nature, than that he
gave the name *Christ* to the divine nature united with the human. This latter is quite improbable; inasmuch as Christ is too
plainly declared in the Scriptures to have been crucified.
Since now the whole argumentation respecting the use of the
expression *Son of God*, rests upon the fact that only the human nature could be born; so the appellation *Christ* could
not possibly have been applied by Praxeas to designate the divine nature in the Son, because it is so plainly said that Christ
was crucified.

Still more certain is it, on the same grounds, and from the
manner in which Praxeas separates between the Father and
Son, that he never could have used the expression, 'The Father was born, and suffered, and was crucified.' He may
have said: 'The Father descended into the Virgin ;§ but he

---

* Cont. Prax. c. 27, Ut aeque in una persona utrumque distinguant
[i. e. they, the party of Praxeas] Patrem et Filium, dicentes Filium
carnem esse, i. e. hominem, i. e. Jesum; Patrem autem Spiritum, i. e.
Deum, i. e. Christum. And in the same section: Qui Filium Dei
carnem interpretaris; with reference to a preceding passage. Again,
in the preceding part of the same section: Ecce, inquiunt, ab angelo
praedicatum est, propterea quod nascetur Sanctum vocabitur Filius
Dei. Caro itaque (it should be *utique)* nata est; caro itaque erit Filius
Dei. ['In like manner they distinguish, as really as we, Father and
Son in one person : saying, that the Son is flesh, i. e. man, i. e.
Jesus; but that the Father is Spirit, i. e. God, i. e. Christ. . . . You
who interpret Son of God as meaning *flesh.* . . . Behold, say they, it
was declared by the angel, Therefore that Holy [Child] which will
be born, shall be called the *Son of God.* Flesh surely it was, which
was born; consequently the Son of God must be flesh.']

† Itaque Christum facis Patrem; cap. 28.

‡ Si enim alius est Jesus, alius Christus; cap. 27.

§ Ipsum dicit Patrem descendisse in virginem; cap. 1.

could never have proceeded to say : ' The Father was born of
her, and suffered.' I the more believe this, because Tertullian
makes the accusation only in the way of a sally of wit,* and it
must be a mere erroneous deduction from the declarations of
Praxeas. For according to Praxeas, the Father never became, as God, properly *united with* the human nature of Jesus ;
although his *dwelling in* the man Jesus made him the *Christ.*
Consequently he could never, according to Praxeas, have suffered in Jesus.

In like manner I doubt, although Tertullian charges him
with it, whether Praxeas asserts the identity of the Spirit with
the Father and Son. In the whole book of Tertullian against
Praxeas, very little occurs in regard to any declarations of
Praxeas respecting the Spirit.† Yet Tertullian, as a Montanist,
had a special interest to make objections of this nature, if matter for them had been found ;‡ and considering his rhetorical

---

* Ita duo negotia diaboli Praxeas Romae procuravit . . . Paracletam
fugavit, et Patrem crucifixit ; cap. 1. [' So Praxeas accomplished the
devil's business in two respects, at Rome. . . . He drove away the
Comforter, and crucified the Father.'—In saying that he drove away
the *Paraclete,* Tertullian refers to the fact, that Praxeas persuaded the
bishop of Rome to abandon the cause of the Montanists, of which
Tertullian was a warm supporter, and which the bishop, before the
visit of Praxeas was made to Rome, had regarded with a favourable
eye. As Montanism consisted principally in extravagant positions
concerning the extraordinary operations of the Spirit, Tertullian accuses Praxeas of *driving away the Spirit,* and so of accomplishing the
business of Satan. TR.]

† The passage near the close of cap. 27 : *Sed spiritum Patrem ipsum vis haberi, quia Deus spiritus,* can be interpreted as having respect to the Holy Ghost only through an erroneous view of its proper
meaning. [*Spiritum* in this case means *a spiritual nature*]. The view
of Praxeas, [on which Tertullian comments in so severe a manner],
was merely, that there was a *twofold* nature in the Redeemer, one
part of which might be designated by κατὰ σάρκα, the other by κατὰ
πνεῦμα. That in other places Tertullian has assigned more signifi-
cance to πνεῦμα than Praxeas did, appears evident to me from the
manner of his expression, after he [Tertullian] had been endeavouring to shew that the way in which he himself supposed the Son to exist, was not at all at variance with the μοναρχία of the Godhead ; for
he merely adds : *Hoc mihi et in tertium Gradum dictum sit.*

[‡ The reason of this is, that the peculiar views of the Montanists
had respect almost entirely to the extraordinary operations and devel-

turn of mind, and his method of handling passages of Scripture, we cannot well suppose that he would have omitted to notice, in his own peculiar way, any assertions of this kind in the works of Praxeas.   Yea, I might venture to say, that the sally of wit, which I have quoted above, and which stands in the introductory part of Tertullian's remarks, would have been otherwise modelled and expressed, in case Praxeas had taught any thing very peculiar respecting the Spirit.

If there be any good foundation for these remarks, then do they constitute another reason for believing, that the doctrine of Praxeas was not something formed independently and by itself, but that it was formed in the way of opposition to the views of the Ebionites.   Or, if one chooses, he may state the subject thus, viz., that in the country where Praxeas lived, much question had not yet been made concerning the doctrine of the Spirit ; and the considering of the same as *person* (hypostasis), had not yet seemed to threaten the doctrine of μοναρχία (sole supremacy).   In this way we may come substantially to the same conclusion as before.   In fact, we may well imagine the possibility, that, so long as the doctrine of the Trinity was not yet fully unfolded in a didactic way, one might teach as Praxeas did, in order fully to vindicate divine honours to the Redeemer; and yet if the Spirit, as the source of all Christian graces and gifts, had been represented as a hypostasis, a kind of *subordination-theory* respecting him would have been more easily admitted than respecting the Redeemer.

If Praxeas, moreover, had no urgent call fully and definitely to declare himself respecting the Spirit, then he had no occasion to advance beyond the duality of Father and Son ; and it was therefore the more natural for him to view the Father and Αὐτόθεος [God in and of himself, God self-existent], as altogether one and the same.   He may then have used as equivalent the two phrases : ' The divine nature in Christ is αὐτό-θεος,'* and ' The Father went out of himself;' as Tertullian makes him paraphrase John 13: 1.† Yet it cannot be very

---

opments of the Holy Spirit ; so that Tertullian, being a friend of the Montanists, had a particular sensibility on this subject.   TR.]

* Ipse-Deus, Deus omnipotens, Jesus Christus praedicatus ; cap. 1. [' Jesus Christ is called αὐτόθεος, the omnipotent God.']

† Praxeas vult ipsum Patrem de semetipso exiisse, et ad semet ipsum abiisse ; cap. 23.   [' Praxeas would have it, that the Father came out of himself, and then departed to himself.']

probable that he used the expression, 'the Father went out of himself,' since he urges so often and strenuously, that the Father is in the Redeemer.* Rather may we suppose him to have said: 'The Father came *into* the flesh,' than that 'he went *out* of himself.'

Praxeas, as it would seem, found no occasion of distinguishing between God as he is in himself ($a\dot{v}\tau\dot{o}\vartheta\epsilon o\varsigma$), the simple divine Unity, and the Father who is one of the Trinity of persons. This state of things might have given occasion to one of the errors respecting the doctrine of the Trinity, which I have found fault with as exhibited in our ecclesiastical Symbols;† only one may say, with a good degree of probability, that if an insight into the nature of the divine Spirit had been further developed in the School of Praxeas, and had the necessity become apparent of placing him in the same rank with the Saviour, then two different ways of doing this would have disclosed themselves. The one was, to regard the Father and the $a\dot{v}\tau\dot{o}\vartheta\epsilon o\varsigma$ as ever being and remaining one and the same, and to speak of them as such ; and then there would be but one divine Being, strictly considered, with two *Phases* of himself, but no real Trinity. In the other way, the various relations of man to God might be compared with the like ones to the Redeemer and Spirit, in order to establish the position of a similarity of nature between these three divine persons. Even then, the Old and New Testament dispensations must be more thoroughly distinguished and separated than they usually had been, (because to insist much on this distinction had been deemed to savour of Gnosticism), in order to come to the conclusion that the Spirit must be referred to a third $\varphi\dot{a}\sigma\iota\varsigma$. By making in this way the Father, Son,

---

* Nam sicut in veteribus, nihil aliud tenent quam *Ego Deus, et alius praeter me non est* ; ita in evangelio responsionem Domini ad Philippum tuentur, *Ego et Pater unum sumus ; et qui me videt, videt et Patrem* ; et, *Ego in Patre, et Pater in me*. His tribus capitulis totum instrumentum utriusque Testamenti volunt cedere; cap. 20. [' As in respect to the ancient dispensation, they hold to nothing else but *I am God, and there is none other besides me;* so in respect to the gospel, they defend the response of the Lord to Philip, *I and the Father are one; he who seeth me, seeth also the Father ;* and again, *I am in the Father, and the Father in me.* To these three summaries of doctrine, they would that the whole of both the Old and New Testament should give place.']

† Glaubenslehre, II. p. 704.

and Spirit coordinate, they might then be distinguished from the absolute Unity of the divine Being more definitely than they had been by Praxeas.

We are, unable in a definite way to gather any thing from Tertullian, which serves to cast more light upon the main positions of Praxeas. But this circumstance gives us no liberty to raise any serious objection against the latter; for the probability is, that Praxeas did no further unfold his views than as they appear in Tertullian, and that he contented himself with presenting merely the main points of his doctrine. And as to these, it would be natural for him to go only so far as might serve to satisfy the exigency of the occasion, as judged of by him. This exigency was, in his view, so to maintain the unity of the divine Being as not in any way to detract from the glory of the Redeemer. That Praxeas effected his purpose, or reached this point, even Tertullian himself testifies; although he makes the suggestion, that the same point might just as well have been reached in the way which he himself had chosen.* · In respect to his doing full honour to the Redeemer, Tertullian says nothing very explicit of Praxeas; but he accuses him of infringing upon the divine economy of the gospel, by excessive partiality for the doctrine of divine unity.† He even entirely over-

---

* Quasi non sic quoque unus sit omnia, *dum ex uno omnia*, per substantiae scilicet unitatem; et nihilominus custodiatur οἰκονομίας sacramentum; cap. 2. ['Just as if all were not one in this way, *whilst all proceed from one*, viz., [one] by unity of substance, and yet the mysterious peculiarity of the gospel-dispensation is not given up.'—This sentence of Tertullian developes the common, I believe I might almost say the universal, idea of the orthodox fathers, respecting the unity of Christ and the Spirit with the Godhead. It was unity, because the substance of the latter was derived from the Father, and was therefore homogeneous with his. A specific Unity, therefore, i. e. a nature common to each person, is intended to be marked out by such descriptions, and not a simple numerical unity; as we have already seen in p. 293 seq.—The οἰκονομίας *sacramentum* here means, the distinctions or personality in the Godhead peculiarly revealed by the οἰκονομία or new dispensation. Tertullian designs to assert, that the distinctions may, in his way of explanation, be regarded as perfectly well preserved. This is true enough; but whether a real *unity* was in this way preserved, is a question that admits of much more doubt than Tertullian seems to have entertained. Tr.]

† Eundem Patrem et Filium et Spiritum contendunt, adversus οἰκονομίαν Monarchiae adulantes. ['They (the party of Praxeas) con-

looks the principal object of Praxeas, viz., that of maintaining the *divine* honour due to the Redeemer, and accuses him of *Judaizing ;** and nothing worse than this could well be said of even Artemon or Theodotus.

In this way of dealing, the person who demands the strongest expressions to designate that which is divine in the Redeemer, is likened to him who will allow of only the weakest ones. In this way the very important difference between these two classes of men is abridged as much as possible ; and thus Theodotus, who expressed himself so doubtfully respecting the pre-eminence of the Redeemer, is elevated as it were to a place with Tertullian and Praxeas, who both strenuously contend for the divine pre-eminence of the Saviour, although the first admits a two fold nature in the divine Being, while the other does not.† Of Praxeas it may be said, that he made near approaches to Sabellianism ; of Tertullian, that he came near to our ecclesiastical Symbols.

If now one will diligently compare the outlines of Praxeas' views, as they are presented in the pages of Tertullian, he will not be able to deny that the doctrine of Praxeas contains a simple and definitive assertion or declaration respecting the union of the divine Being with Jesus' human nature ; while, at the same time, Praxeas does not undertake in any way to

---

tend that Father and Son and Spirit are the same ; thus shewing their partiality for sole Supremacy in opposition to the economy of the gospel.']

* Ceterum Judaicae fidei ista res est, sic unum Deum credere, ut Filium adnumerare ei nolis; et post Filium, Spiritum ; cap. 31. ['But this is a Jewish faith, so to believe in one God, that you are unwilling to comprise the Son with him, and after the Son, also the Spirit.']

† Further can no one carry this matter, than does Tertullian at the close of his Tract against Praxeas : Viderint igitur antichristi, qui negant Patrem et Filium. Negant enim ... dando illis quae non sunt, auferendo quae sunt. ... Qui Filium non habet, nec vitam habet. Non habet autem Filium, qui eam alium quam Filium credit. ['Let the anti-christs look well to it, then, who deny the Father and the Son. For they do deny ... by attributing to them those things which do not belong to them, and by taking away those things which do belong to them.... He who has not the Son, has not life. But he has not the Son, who believes him to be something different from the Son.']

modify his views respecting the divine Being, so as to regard
him in one way when united with Jesus, and in another way
when he is not. Praxeas seems to view him simply as he is
in himself considered. We may indeed say, that he expressly
declines making any distinctions. To maintain the union of
the divine nature with Jesus and its existence in him, was undertaken by Praxeas in order to oppose the Ebionitish heresy,
and every thing which approximated towards it ; while the omission to make any distinction in the divine Nature, was designedly opposed to all those, who, although they entirely renounc-
ed the opinions of Ebion, yet would be inclined by their views,
as he supposed, toward a species of Gentile polytheism.

The next thing which Praxeas would have had to do, had
he proceeded to the further formation of his creed, would have
been more exactly to distinguish how we are to conceive of
the divine Being, as existing in union with a particular Being
[Jesus], and as universally present and existing every where.
Such a distinction the wants of Christians as to doctrinal
instruction seem to have called for ; and to the making of it
Praxeas would no doubt have been called, if the partizans of
Artemon and Theodotus had entered into and carried on a contest with him. It would have been very natural to object
against them, that they knew not how to make any such distinction. But it would seem that Praxeas had no special call
to develope his views, on this point ; and therefore his opinions, and those of his disciples (if he had any), seem, in regard
to this particular, never to have been made out, or at least not
to have been exhibited.

On the other hand, the views of Tertullian were more fully
disclosed. He every where brings in the *Spirit* as a subject of
his consideration ; respecting which, so far as Praxeas is concerned, we must remain in doubt. Nor can one boast that
even Tertullian would have expressed himself so definitely, unless he had been called out as it were to make use of *negative*
expressions, in order to clear himself from all suspicion of
leaning toward polytheism, so long as he admitted that there
are distinctions in the Godhead. To maintain the *unity* of the
Godhead, was the more a work of urgency in his case, inasmuch as he had always been a vehement opposer of the Gnostics ; who, in the sense above represented, went over to a kind
of Hellenism, [i. e. polytheism]. Where however it is not
Tertullian's main business to ward off suspicion, but only to

make direct and positive representations, there it of course becomes a matter of more difficulty to designate the distinctions in the Godhead ; for this must be done with the most careful foresight in the weighing of expressions.   Hence it comes, that on such occasions Tertullian expresses himself in a dubious and indefinite manner.*   Moreover in representations of this kind, it is very natural that tropical expressions should be frequently resorted to ; but in order to do this with any success, one must have a tact for rightly comprehending the force of them ;† and even then, for the most part, peculiar cautions are needed in order to avoid their being exposed to misinterpretation.‡ Hence it is no wonder, that in different passages the defining and lim-

---

* For example : *Οἰκονομία* ... quae Unitatem in Trinitatem disponit, tres dirigens ; cap. 2.—Unitas ex semet ipsa derivans 'Trinitatem ; cap. 3.—Ut invisibilem Patrem intelligamus pro plenitudine majestatis, visibilem vero Filium agnoscamus pro modulo derivationis ; cap. 14.—Qua Pater et Filius duo, et hoc non ex separatione substantiae sed ex dispositione ; cum individuum et inseparatum Filium a Patre pronunciamus ; cap. 19. [' The economy ... which arranges a Unity in Trinity, marking out or designating three.—The Unity deriving a Trinity from itself.—That we may conceive of the invisible Father, according to the plenitude of his majesty ; but of the visible Son, according to the limitations prescribed by his derivation.—On account of which the Father and Son are two ; and this, not by separation of substance, but by arrangement of it, inasmuch as we assert that the Son is not divided or separated from the Father.']

† As an example of tropical expressions the following passage may be cited : Protulit enim Deus Sermonem, sicut radix fruticem, et fons fluvium, et sol radium.   Nam et istae species *probolae* sunt earum substantiarum ex quibus prodeunt; cap. 8.   [' For God produced the Word, as the root does the fruit, and the fountain the stream, and the sun the rays of light.   For the specimens now mentioned are the offspring of those substances from which they proceed.'—The reader should take notice that every where the idea of *derivation* as to the *divine* nature of the Logos, is held fast by Tertullian, as well as by most of the later fathers. TR.]

‡ For an example [how things may be said on this subject, which may easily be misinterpreted], take the following: Omne quod prodit ex aliquo, secundum sit ejus necesse est de quo prodit; non ideo tamen est separatum.   ['Every thing which is derived from another, must necessarily be *second* to that from which it is derived ; however, it is not on account of this to be regarded as a separate thing.']

86

iting expressions of Tertullian, are subversive of one another.*
Besides this, the relation of the Trinity to Unity cannot be
maintained, if at one time [as in Tertullian] all three persons
are derived from the one God, and at another the second and
third persons are derived from the Father.† Nor can the relation of the Father to the Son be maintained, if at one time
entire similitude is insisted on, and at another dissimilitude is
conceded or taken for granted.‡

This last idea, indeed, lies so deep in the whole views and
representations of Tertullian, that it every where, unconsciously as it were, but still in a very marked manner, developes it-

---

* For example : Numerum sine divisione patiuntur ; cap. 2.—Pater enim tota substantia est ; Filius, vero, derivatio totius et portio ;
cap. 9. ['They (the persons of the Trinity) are the subjects of number, but not of division.—For the Father is the whole substance; the
Son, the derivation and apportionment of the whole.']

† Unus Deus, *ex quo* et gradus isti et formae et species, in nomine
Patris et Filii et Spiritus Sancti deputantur ; cap. 2. Compare this
now with the following: Ita Trinitas per consertos et connexos gradus *a Patre decurrens*, et monarchiae nihil obstrepit, et οἰκονομίας sta-
tum protegit ; cap. 8. In this passage, the Father corresponds to the
sun, and light and heat to the Son and Spirit. ['One God, from
whom all those gradations and forms and species are reckoned, by the
name of Father and Son and Spirit.—Thus the Trinity, by implicated
and connected gradations proceeding *from the Father*, casts no reproach upon the μοναρχία, and at the same time defends the consti-
tution of the οἰκονομία.'—In the first passage the three persons are
represented as coming from the *one God*; in the second, the Trinty
is presented as *a Patre decurrens*.]

‡ Unius substantiae, unius status, et unius potestatis ; cap. 2. Compare with this the following: Sic et Pater *alius a Filio*, dum Filio
major; cap. 9. Also with this : Tamen alium dicam oportet, ex ne-
cessitate sensus, eum qui jubet et eum qui facit, cap. 12 ; and moreover with this : Unum dicit quod pertinet ad unitatem, ad similitudinem, ad conjunctionem, ad dilectionem Patris, et ad obsequium Filii
. . . et ita per opera intelligimus unum esse Patrem et Filium, cap. 22.
['Of one substance, one state, and one power.—So the Father is another or *different* from the Son, since he is *greater* than the Son.—Yet
from the necessity of the sense, he who gives orders must be *different*
from him who executes them.—Oneness means that which pertains
to unity, to similitude, to conjunction, to the love of the Father and
obedience of the Son . . . and thus by their works we understand that
the Father and Son are one.']

self. For if the Father was originally sole and by himself, and had the Logos only *in* him;* and the Logos himself first attained to full and complete existence when he came forth out of the Father;† how could he then be *altogether like* to him from whom he came forth? Or how could the Son say: 'ALL which the Father hath is mine,' when *eternity* was not his? How I say could one be consistent in believing these latter assertions, and still persevering to maintain, that while the Logos was in God, he had not yet his appropriate existence? Or how can one maintain the *immutability* of the Logos, if he holds to his passing out of that state in which he was ἐνδιάθε-τος in God, and his coming into a state of separate and hypostatic existence? Or if we are to make distinctions so nice respecting the Godhead of the Son, that in and by himself considered we may give the name *God* to him, but when we compare the Son with the Father we must then call the former nothing more than *Lord* ;‡ how then is a *perfect similitude* between the two to be made out?

[* Ante omnia enim Deus erat solus. . . . Caeterum ne quidem solus ; habebat enim secum, quam habebat in semetipso, rationem suam scilicet . . . Hanc Graeci λόγον dicunt. 'Before creation, God was alone . . . Yet not alone, indeed, for he had with him that which he had in him, viz., his reason . . . which the Greeks name Logos.' Dr. S. has omitted to cite this. Tr.]

† Tunc . . . Sermo ₃speciem et ornatum suum sumit . . . cum dicit Deus: *Fiat lux.* Haec est nativitas perfecta Sermonis, dum ex Deo procedit. In the sequel he appeals to the following passage of Scripture in order to prove such a derivation of the Logos from the Father, viz., *Eructavit cor meum Sermonem optimum,* (Ps. 45: 1). ['Then the Word assumes his form and beauty . . . when God says: *Let there be light.* This is the perfect nativity of the Word, when he proceeds from God.—My heart eructates the Word who is most excellent.' These almost grossly offensive views harmonize very exactly with those of Justin Martyr, Tatian, Theophilus of Antioch, Athenagoras, and Hippolytus. Tr.]

[‡ The whole strain of Tertullian's reasoning, in cap. 13, is to establish the propriety of making such a distinction as to appellations. He says that we are justified in so doing by the fact, that we may call the light of the sun by the name of *sun,* when the light is considered in and by itself; but when the sun itself is also mentioned, it would not be proper to give to his light the same name. Tr.]

We may readily say then, in respect to Tertullian, that in developing his positive views of the doctrine of the Trinity, notwithstanding all his zeal against Gnosticism, his *probolae* [emanations] *Gnosticize;* and in his representations of the Logos, as existing indeed before all things, but (in order to create all things) as first coming forth substantially out of God, he *Arianizes.* Moreover his *ante omnia enim Deus erat solus* (cap. 5), agrees very exactly with the ἦν ποτε ὅτε οὐκ ἦν of Arius, respecting the Logos.

Finally, that these are not matters of mere oversight in debate, nor such departures from consistency merely the result of other errors of Tertullian, but that they are almost necessarily connected with the undertaking of Tertullian to make out some definite distinctions in the divine Being, in opposition to the simple phraseology of Praxeas—all this will be made apparent in the sequel, when we come to consider the relative opposition between the views of Noetus and Hippolytus.

THE

BIBLICAL REPOSITORY

AND

𝕼𝖚𝖆𝖗𝖙𝖊𝖗𝖑𝖞 𝕺𝖇𝖘𝖊𝖗𝖛𝖊𝖗.

No. XIX.

JULY, 1835.

ARTICLE I.

ON THE DISCREPANCY BETWEEN THE SABELLIAN AND ATHA-
NASIAN METHOD OF REPRESENTING THE DOCTRINE OF THE
TRINITY.

By Dr. Frederick Schleiermacher, late professor in the University of Berlin. Translated
with Notes and Illustrations by M. Stuart, Prof. of Sacred Lit. Theol. Sem. Andover.

§ 4. *Creed of Noetus.*

[THE circumstances of Noetus' history are very imperfectly
known. For what little knowledge we have, we are indebted
principally to the work of Hippolytus, contra Haeresim Noeti,
II. p. 5, seq. Epiphanius has repeated the principal things
there said concerning Noetus, in his Haeres. LVII., and Ana-
cephal. § XI. Tom. II. p. 145. Philastrius repeats the common report, in Haeres. LIII. Augustine, Haer. XXXVI. Tom.
VIII. p. 9, merely translates the Anacephalaiosis of Epiphanius.
Theodoret, Haeret. Fab. 117. 3, also gives the usual report,
but adds a few unimportant circumstances.

We have then in fact, as it would seem, but one source of
Noetus' history; and this is that of his professed antagonist,
Hippolytus.

According to the usual report, Noetus belonged to Smyrna;
whether as a *native* or merely as a resident, is not certain.
Epiphanius only says, that he was of Ephesus, τῆς Ἐφέσου πόλεως ὑπάρχων, p. 479; which seems to be a lapse of memory
here, for in his Anacephalaiosis he follows the usual report.

Nothing that is said by the ancient writers, determines whether Noetus held an office in the church or not. The report is,

91

that after he had begun to broach his opinions against the notion of separate hypostases in the divine Being, he was called to an account by the elders of the church at Smyrna, before whom he denied the truth of the information that had been given them against him. Upon the renewal, however, of his efforts to propagate his peculiar opinions, he and those who adhered to him were excommunicated from the church. Soon after this event took place he died. The time in which Noetus lived and acted at Ephesus is variously given by chronologers, viz., from A. D. 220 to A. D. 245. It is not certain that he was a writer. No treatise of his is definitely mentioned.

As to his creed, it neither appears that he called in question the divine origin and authority of any of the sacred books, nor that he entertained peculiar notions on any point of doctrine save that of personality in the Godhead. But inasmuch as the following pages are devoted to the exposition and discussion of his views, it is unnecessary here to enlarge on this point.

The modern sources worthy of particular consultation, are Walch, II. 1 seq. Martini Geschich. des Logos, pp. 142 seq. Lardner, Cred. of Gosp. Hist. Part II. Beausobre Hist. du Manich. I. p. 534. Tillemont, Memoires, etc. IV. p. 238. Worm, Hist. Sabell. II. p. 5.

As to HIPPOLYTUS, the opponent of Noetus, there seems to have been as little known with certainty about him as concerning his antagonist, among the ancient writers. Jerome (de illustr. Viris) speaks of Hippolytus as bishop of some place unknown to him (cap. LXI). Later writers say, that he was bishop of Portus Romanus in Italy. So Leontius Byzant., Johan. Zonaras; and this is found in the Greek Chronicon of Eusebius (p. 84), although the authority of the reading must be doubtful, after what Jerome says is well weighed. Nicephorus merely says, that he was ὁ Ῥωμαῖος συγγραφεύς. Several modern writers simply assert the fact, that he belonged to Portus Romanus, e. g. Miraeus and others; while they are divided among themselves whether this was Portus Romanus in Italy or in Arabia. Eusebius and Jerome speak of him as the writer of numerous commentaries on the Scriptures, and of many other books; in particular, one against Marcion, and another against all heresies. That he lived in the time of the Roman emperor Alexander, (regn. A. D. 222—235) appears from the fact, that in a work of his on the Paschal canons of computing time, he brings his computation down to the first year of this emperor's reign. Of course he was a cotemporary of Origen.

Neither Eusebius nor Jerome tells us, that the Hippolytus in question wrote against Noetus; but they speak, as we have seen, of a book which he wrote against Marcion, and another against *all heresies*. But Photius (Cod. 121) tells us that the last book of his work against all heresies, was in opposition to Noetus. The fact that he was a very voluminous writer, and that he had a particular zeal against those who were regarded as heretics, united with the fact that he was a cotemporary of Noetus, renders it quite probable that he wrote the book against the latter, which now bears his name. But the evidence, on the whole, is rather of a *conjectural* nature; and we must regard it as a somewhat doubtful question, who is the author of the work against Noetus which is ascribed to Hippolytus. There is no doubt, however, that the work is an ancient one; and so far as our present object is concerned, it is a matter of no great consequence, whether it belongs to the bishop Hippolytus, or to some other person.

The work itself is run in almost the same mold as that of Tertullian against Praxeas. One can hardly doubt that Tertullian's work was before the author. ' In one respect only,' says Münscher, ' does he distinguish himself from Tertullian. The latter asserts the specific generation of the Son, and says that it took place when God said : " Let there be light." Hippolytus abstains from presenting any definite views in relation to this particular subject; and shews himself in this respect to be not unlike the more cautious Irenaeus.' But Münscher is certainly mistaken here; as the following passage from Hippolytus (cont. Noet. § 10) will plainly shew : ἐγέννα Λόγον, ὃν λόγον ἔχων ἐν ἑαυτῷ ἀόρατόν τε ὄντα τῷ κτιζομένῳ κόσμῳ, ὁρατὸν ποιεῖ· προτέραν φωνὴν φθεγγόμενος, καὶ φῶς ἐκ φωτὸς γεννῶν, προῆκεν τῇ κτίσει κύριον, τὸν ἴδιον νοῦν· αὐτῷ μόνῳ πρότερον ὁρατὸν ὑπάρχοντα, τῷ δὲ γινομένῳ κόσμῳ ἀόρατον ὄντα, ὁρατὸν ποιεῖ, ὅπως διὰ τοῦ φανῆναι ἰδὼν ὁ κόσμος σωθῆναι δυνηθῇ : i. e. " He begat the Word, which Word, being in himself and yet invisible to the created world, he made visible ; when he uttered the first sound, and produced light from light, he sent forth to the creation a Lord, even his own *Νοῦς* ; him who before was visible only to himself, but invisible to the created world, he now made visible, that by his manifestation the world when beholding him might be saved." Here then is Tertullian, and

Justin, and Athenagoras, and Tatian, with their λόγος ἐνδιάθετος and προφορικός in full measure.—TR.]

A historical connection between Praxeas and Noetus we are
unable to establish. At most we can only make out, that both
were Asiatics. Of Praxeas Tertullian says this expressly;[*]
and in regard to Noetus, the historical accounts differ only concerning this, viz., whether he belonged to Smyrna or to Ephesus.[†] According to Epiphanius, Noetus was himself the author
of a fearful and pestilential heresy; but Theodoret considers
him only as renewing errors that had before been broached by
Epigones and Cleomenes, who are so entirely unknown to us,
that a reference to them casts no light on any connection which
they may have had with Praxeas. We may therefore well
make the supposition, that reasons such as operated on Praxeas
elsewhere produced the like effects and brought others to like
views. That there was a general agreement of opinion between
Praxeas and Noetus, there is no good reason to doubt.

That the principal design of Noetus, moreover, was to shun
every appearance of polytheism in the representation of the divine nature in the Redeemer, one may see from the very first
arguments which Hippolytus and Epiphanius cite from him.
The latter indeed, appears to have had some different views
from the former;[‡] although, as it would seem, their narrative
respecting Noetus was derived from one common source.

Noetus, in order to shew that the Godhead of Christ and the
Father is the same, appealed to the same texts that had been
cited by Praxeas for this purpose. Yet he seems to have laid
particular stress on those, in which the very same work is attributed both to the Father and to the Son.[§] I can easily be-

---

[*] Nam iste primus, ex Asia, hoc genus perversitatis intulit Romae;
cap. 1. ['For he, coming from Asia, first introduced this kind of per-
versity at Rome.']

[†] Νοητὸς ... Ἀσιανός, τῆς Ἐφέσου πόλεως ὑπάρχων; Epiphan. ad-
vers. Haeres. p. 479. Ὁ δὲ Νοητὸς, Σμυρναῖος μὲν ἦν τὸ γένος; Theod.
Haeret. Fab. III. 3. In the same manner also Hippolytus speaks.
['Noetus, an Asiatic, being of the city of Ephesus.—Noetus was of
Smyrna in respect to his descent.']

[‡] Martini is of a different opinion; see his Pragmat. Geschichte
des Logos, p. 142.

[§] Hippolytus (adv. Noetum), and Epiphanius after him, both seem
to dispose of the following matter without any embarrassment, and

lieve, that Noetus introduced the Spirit into his formula respecting the Godhead as little as Praxeas did. I know indeed that Hippolytus, and still more Theodoret, makes heavy charges against him; but much of this is only deduction in the spirit of controversy, and amounts to what Noetus himself never affirmed. I can easily believe that Noetus may have said, that there is no difference between the invisible God and him who made his appearance.* Tertullian, on the contrary, undertakes to shew a distinction in the divine Being, from the fact that there must be a difference between him who dwells in light inaccessible and him who makes himself visible to men.† In like manner, and in direct opposition to such views, Noetus may have undertaken to deny such a discrepancy between Father and Son, on the ground that God himself had never in reality become visible, but only his miraculous operations had been exercised upon finite and created things. And besides this, it is very natural to suggest, that the idea of *theophany* for the most part easily passes over, through the kindred one of the מֹפֵת־לָל [so familiar among the Rabbins as the name of a mediate theophany], into that of σημεῖον or τέρας. Noetus, moreover, had sufficient occasion to turn his attention to the idea of distinction between the invisible and the visible Deity, because all the Old

---

mention it as though it made nothing for the side of Noetus, viz., that on the one hand Christ says, he would again *himself* build up the temple [in case the Jews should destroy it], and on the other his resurrection from the dead [which was the building up of the temple that he meant to speak of], is ascribed to the *Father*. But a more accurate comparison of passages, e. g. Origen, IV. p. 199. c. D, shews, (what indeed belongs to the very nature of the case), that Noetus did not in fact pass by this passage without notice. Even his opponents felt themselves obliged to concede, that the raising from the dead is a thing that must be accomplished by peculiar power, and that such power has special claims to unity of subject. E. g. Hippol. VIII.: μία δύναμις τούτου, καὶ ὅσον μὲν κατὰ τὴν δύναμιν εἰς ἐστι θεός. ['One is the power of this being; and so far as it respects power, there is one God.']

* Ἀφανὴς μὲν ὅταν ἐθέλη, φαινόμενον δὲ ἡνίκα ἂν βούληται; Theod. Haeret. Fab. III. 3. ['Invisible indeed, whenever he pleases to be; but visible also, whenever he chooses to be so.']

[† This Tertullian attempts to do at great length, in his Treatise against Praxeas, cap. 14; to which the reader must be referred, as it is too long to be quoted here. Tr.]

Testament theophanies had already begun to be attributed to Christ.

If now we may suppose him to have affirmed, that there was no difference between the seen and unseen God ; yet we can hardly believe him to have said, that there was no distinction between the begotten and unbegotten God.* This last is a mere deduction of those, who held that the divine nature in Christ was that which was begotten before all worlds. These ought to have said, that Noetus made no distinction between the *unbegotten* God, and him *whom they called begotten.* But Noetus himself could never have affirmed any thing more, than that the *divine* nature in begotten man, was the unbegotten God himself ; and so he that was incapable of suffering, dwelt in man who could suffer. Surely he could not have said, as Theodoret charges him with saying, that the very same being was impassible and immortal, and yet was passible and mortal. Such an assertion could not be traced to any design of shunning polytheism ; because he that is capable of suffering, cannot be conceived of as one simple being, to say nothing of his mortality.

With such considerations in view, it would seem that the expressions, ὅταν ἐθέλῃ, ὅτε ἐβούλετο, and the like, in reference to the theophanies related in the Old or New Testament, are peculiar to Noetus. What a pity, that we have no means of developing with certainty what he intended to designate by them. It may be, that be intended only to designate the idea of the unceasing activity of the Godhead, (somewhat after the manner of our own voluntary exercises of the mind in continual succession), now withdrawing and concealing himself as it were within himself, and then revealing himself by connection with a finite being. If this were the case, and he expressed himself so indefinitely as the formula ὅταν ἐθέλῃ would seem to imply, there might be in this the meaning, that other and future revelations of the Godhead might still be looked for, besides those already made in the person of Christ ; and this would have been an anti-christian notion. But inasmuch as the principal object of Noetus was to vindicate the *divine* nature of Christ, it would not be proper to assume that he had any design of making such an assertion ; although one may concede, that the expression itself (ὅταν ἐθέλῃ) would not exclude such a meaning.

Indeed we cannot well say that our common Symbols are

---

* See Theodoret, ut supra.

not exposed to such a construction. If, in addition to eternal
generation, there is still another indescribable difference in the
Godhead, viz. that of the procession of the Spirit ; then (so far
as this representation in and by itself is concerned) there appears to be no good reason why there may not be many such
processions. Besides this, if the divine νοῦς or λόγος, i. e. intelligence or understanding, could come forth out of the Godhead, and coming forth become a hypostatic and separate being,
why may not every other divine attribute exhibit itself in like
manner ? In fact we cannot properly demand of a purely doctrinal representation of the Trinity, that all exclusion of any
greater number than *three*, should be absolutely incorporated
with it. We must seek the ground of such limitation as to
number, in the appropriateness of a revelation through Christ
and the Spirit in order to reclaim our sinful race. Only a *specu-*
lative view of the doctrine of the Trinity can attempt the making out of such an exclusive construction ; but on this very
ground, viz., that such a construction is not an indispensable one,
it cannot be regarded as truly belonging to the essence of theology.

If now Noetus represented to himself the manifestations of
the Redeemer, as disclosed in revelation, under the form of a
divine activity, as mentioned above ; then there must always
be attached to this mode of representation a high and scarcely
allowable measure of *anthropopathy,* in case the ὅτε and ἡνίκα
be referred equally to the divine counsel and to the accomplishment of that counsel ; for in a case such as he presents, an action of the Godhead is represented as one altogether of a transitory nature. This was certainly an embarrassing circumstance in his theory and a disadvantage to it ; for in the other
theory, the generation of the Son and the procession of the
Spirit may be represented as unlimited by time. On the other
hand, the theory of Noetus has this which is peculiar to itself,
and which constitutes a kind of off-set against the advantage of
the other theory just mentioned, viz., that divine activity or
energy in making special revelations, is definitely to be con-
trasted with that which is exhibited in the government of the
world ; a thing contended for by many who admit the usual
Symbols, but one which can hardly be made out with consistency by them. While nothing hinders our conceiving of each
particular event as determined on and necessarily accomplished
in such a way, that every particular occurrence seems to de-

pend on some antecedent one; yet the particular times of making a revelation appear to intervene between those occurrences, as something depending merely on divine pleasure, and each one of these times is determined for itself by a free and independent ὅτε ἠθέλησε.

It is unnecessary however to insist on this doubtful ground of preference. One may suppose that Noetus himself, in the further development of his system, would have separated the divine counsel as *eternal*, from its actual execution which was a *temporal* phenomenon; and then he might have stood on as good ground as those, who separate the eternal generation of the Son from his "becoming flesh and dwelling among us." He would then even have this ground of preference, viz., that his theory was very simple, while the other was compounded in a way that involves difficulty. For difficult indeed it is, when we assume an original plurality of persons in the Godhead, to determine whether the coming forth of the Son out of the Father is *merely voluntary*, or *necessarily grounded* in the nature of the divine Being. According to this last mode of representation, the persons of the Godhead seem to be subjected to a kind of law superior to themselves; somewhat in the manner in which the Grecian divinities are subject to eternal destiny. By the former mode, the Son is so definitively dependent for his existence on the will of the Father, that, if he pleased, he might have refrained from begetting him; and thus his dependence is made altogether like to that of other beings who are created.

Noetus, however, avoided this difficulty; and not only so, but the still greater one, viz., whether the incarnation which took place in time and space, depended solely on the will of the Father, or also on that of the Son. According to the first of these two suppositions, there must have been in the Godhead, command on one part and obedience on the other; a *dissimilarity* which involves an entire separation.* According to the second, it would hardly have been possible to make out the distinction between Father and Son, in case the exhibition of it had not been made by the incarnation; against which position the most zealous defenders of the common Symbols have

---

* So that one could not properly say, in such a case, μὴ δύο ἐξ ἑνὸς μερισθέντα νόει; Basil, Hom. XXIV. ['You must not suppose two divided out of one.']

warmly protested.*   All these difficulties Noetus avoided, inasmuch as he may be supposed to have acknowledged only one
divine Will, whose eternal counsel was carried into execution
in a definite way, and only at a definite period.

   That Noetus regarded the one and undivided Deity as taking
the place of a human soul in Christ, and dwelling directly in his
human body ; and that he thus was a predecessor of Apollinaris
(as Martini supposes) ;†—all this appears to me not to follow
from the passage of Hippolytus there quoted.   Nor do I think
it probable in itself ; for such an opinion would approximate too
near to the metamorphoses of the heathen gods, to leave any
room for supposing that it would have been adopted by a strenuous opposer of polytheism.   Besides all this, it would have
involved some consequences savouring of the tenets of the Docetae, which the opposers of Noetus would by no means admit ;
and the context therefore would have taken a different turn,
and occupied a more extensive ground.   The view of Apollinaris, moreover, could be held by those only who made a special
distinction in the divine Being, in reference to the incarnation,
and limited the latter only to a particular person of the Godhead.   And such appears to me to be the state of the case in
regard to the passage in question of Hippolytus ;‡ viz., that he

---

* E. g. Athanasius cont. Sabell. Greg. 10. 11. 15.

† Martini, Geschichte des Logos, pp. 143, 144. [Apollinaris, bishop
of Laodicea in Syria (A. D. 366—382) held that the Logos took the
place of a *rational* soul in Christ ; and, consequently, that God in him
was united with a human body and a *sensitive* soul.   As a man and
a scholar he was highly esteemed in his time.   A party was formed
at Antioch in his favour.   After his death they divided into two sects ;
one holding his peculiar opinions, and the other maintaining that God
became so united with the body of Christ as to make one substance
with it, and consequently paying divine honours to the *human* nature
of Christ.   On account of this, they received the name of *Sarcolatrae*,
i. e. worshippers of flesh.   The whole party was of short continuance ; and they were suppressed, in part, by imperial edicts.   Tr.]

‡ Hippol. cont. Noetum, § 17.   [The passage here alluded to runs
thus : "We believe . . . according to the tradition of the apostles, that
God the Logos came down from heaven into the virgin Mary ; so that
he, having become incarnate of her, taking to himself a human soul, I
mean a *rational* one, and thus having become truly human in all respects, sin excepted, might save him who had lapsed, etc."   Martini
contends that this is said in direct opposition to an opinion of Noetus ;

does not declare himself in it against Noetus, for then he would not have concluded the matter so briefly; but he intends merely to defend himself against those consequences, which some might be prone to deduce from the expression σαρχωθείς that he had employed, viz. that the λόγος had obtained merely a body by his birth of the virgin, and not a soul also.

Consequently one cannot well conclude, that Noetus had no knowledge of two natures in Christ; and the more so, in case he says (as Hippolytus acknowledges)* that Christ means the Son of God as to his *human* nature, while the Logos is not named *Son* by John, who says only that *he was with God*. Thus it would seem, that he acknowledged both the human and the divine in Christ; and therefore he, as well as his opponents, could speak of *two* natures in him: unless indeed one should assert, that the distinction into *persons* first occasioned the expression *nature* [in a like sense] to be applied to the divine Being; for in this particular sense Noetus would no doubt have denied to Christ a divine nature.

In the mean time, in case many an unfounded accusation or supposition can be laid aside, and several points be more definitely cleared up, still it would seem, that Noetus had explained himself no more definitely than Praxeas did, upon the point, how God united himself with the man Jesus, and wherein the distinction of his being in Christ definitely consisted. Theodoret, indeed, and the authorities to which he makes his immediate appeal, appear to have had knowledge of further developments which the doctrine of Noetus experienced by means of Callistus; but of these no relic has reached our times.

Let us now turn to Hippolytus, and inquire how he defended a *plurality* of persons against Noetus. In him we see the same strong leaning to the Arian schism, and anon the same approaches to Tritheism, as in Tertullian. The same difficulty exists, moreover, in respect to the separation of the Father as a *person* from the αὐτόθεος as the Unity, so as to constitute a Trinity; which separation, however, is imperiously demanded by the doctrine of a personal Trinity in the unity of the divine Being.

---

while Dr. S. maintains, that he says this to avoid a misconception which might be attached to his use of the word σαρχωθείς. Tr.]

* The Greek text is disturbed here, and needs to be corrected by the translation.

Hippolytus avers, that the Son, as well as other things, can bear no comparison with the Father.* He represents him as first coming forth out of the Father when he first uttered his voice [at the creation of the world].† Sometimes he speaks of one God and two persons ; and then again, of one Father and two persons ;‡ not ranking the Spirit with them in either of these passages, although in one of them he mentions him, but still, almost with a direct intention, declines to call him a *πρόσωπον.* In fact the unity of the Godhead is with him so indefinite, (so strenuously does he contend for *plurality* of persons), that he reduces it to harmony of sentiment and cooperation ; and strictly understood, he even denies that the Father, Son, and Spirit are *substantially* one.§

---

* *Πρὸς γὰρ τὸν πατέρα τίς λογισθήσεται ;* Cont. Noetum, V. ['Who can be brought into comparison with the Father ?']

† *Ὃν (λόγον) ἔχων ἐν ἑαυτῷ ἀόρατον, ὁρατὸν ποιεῖ προτέραν φωνὴν φθεγγόμενος ;* ibid. X. ['Who, having the invisible (Logos) in himself, makes it visible when he utters the first sound.'] If any one should construe *ὁρατὸν ποιεῖ* and *προῆκε* as not designed to assert eternal generation, but only incarnation, he must explain in the manner of Sabellius or of Beryll ; but this would be directly against the design of Hippolytus.

‡ *Δύο μὲν οὐκ ἐρῶ θεούς, ἀλλ' ἕνα · πρόσωπα δὲ δύο, οἰκονομίαν δὲ τρίτην, τὴν χάριν τοῦ ἁγίου πνεύματος.* ['I do not speak of two Gods, but one ; of two persons, however, and of a third *οἰκονομία,* the grace of the Holy Spirit.'] Here plainly the Spirit is not comprised among the two *πρόσωπα;* and the Father is not the *one God,* but *one person.* Immediately after he adds : *Πατὴρ μὲν γὰρ εἷς, πρόσωπα δὲ δύο, ὅτι καὶ ὁ υἱός · τὸ δὲ τρίτον, τὸ ἅγιον πνεῦμα.* ['The Father indeed is one, but there are two persons, for there is also the Son ; the third is the Holy Spirit.'] This I can explain in no other way than as follows; viz., that there are two persons, because there is a Son besides the Father ; and the Holy Spirit is moreover added as a third ; for the *δὲ* admits of no other explanation. Hippolytus appears to have arranged his expressions so as designedly to convey the idea, that the Father is not *derived* from the *one God,* the *αὐτόθεος,* the *Μονάς,* and to distinguish the Son and the Spirit by the fact, that they are derived from the source of the Father.

§ *Μὴ πάντες ἓν σῶμά ἐσμεν* [not *ἐστι,* as the text wrongly is] *κατὰ τὴν οὐσίαν ; Ἢ τῇ δυνάμει καὶ τῇ διαθέσει τῆς ὁμοφρονίας ἓν γινόμεθα ; Τὸν αὐτὸν δὴ τρόπον ὁ παῖς, ὁ πεμφθεὶς ὡμολόγησεν εἶναι ἐν* ['ἓν ?'] *τῷ πατρὶ δυνάμει, διαθέσει,* cap. VII. ['Are we all one body as to substance ? Or are we one in respect to power and unanimity ? In like

101

It is particularly worthy of note, when we compare the manner in which Hippolytus contradicts the argument drawn by Noetus from John 10: 30,* with that by which Tertullian endeavours to overthrow the argument of Praxeas deduced from the same passage, how each contradicts his antagonist by appealing to different considerations or views of this text. Tertullian refutes Praxeas by an appeal to the ἕν [one substance] in John 10: 30, which he considers as meaning something very different from what would have been designated by εἷς, [which might mean *one person* or *one individual hypostasis*] ; but he says nothing against Praxeas which is drawn from the use of the plural ἐσμέν there employed. Hippolytus, on the other hand, leaves the ἕν untouched, because he apprehends that Noetus might take shelter behind it, and he employs only ἐσμέν to make out his argument. Hippolytus then must fairly concede to Tertullian, his coadjutor in the contest, that the plural ἐσμέν does not stand in the way of Noetus ; and Tertullian must in like manner concede to Hippolytus, that the neuter ἕν may be easily reconciled with the views of Noetus. The interpretation of Scripture, however, is not that in respect to which the developments of these contests appear to most advantage. Least of all can we expect any thing of particular excellence here, in those who are wedded to particular creeds ; for then the *extraneous* influence of these creeds would act upon them, as we may naturally suppose ; and so the interpretation of Scripture would

---

manner the Son who was sent, confesses himself to be *one* [according to the emendation ἕν] with the Father, in respect to power and condition.' [The last clause, according to the text as it now stands, would run thus: ' In like manner the Son, who was sent, professes himself to be *in* the Father, with respect to power and condition ;' which scarcely makes any sense.] Still, I would deduce nothing more from this, than that the mode of representation, so destitute of simplicity and so intricate, has so confused the idiom, that in this case οὐσία is used in the same sense in which ὕπαρξις and ὑπόστασις are elsewhere employed.

Not less remarkable is the expression: οἰκονομίας συμφωνία συνάγεται εἰς ἕνα θεόν ; cap. XIV. ['The harmony of the economy (i. e. of the three persons in the Godhead) brings about a union in respect to the one God']. Here the Unity would seem to be represented as arising from the harmonious combination of the Trinity ; much in the same way as the personal unity of Christ is represented as consisting in the entire coincidence of his two wills.

* Ἐγὼ καὶ ὁ πατὴρ ἕν ἐσμέν.

become wavering through the influence of polemics, which are
so apt to occasion partiality and prevent the exercise of candour.
The consequence of all this usually is, the introduction of an
arbitrary and artificial method of interpretation ; and this once
introduced by party zeal, usually proceeds so far in the sequel,
that one is at length compelled to seek for some established
principles of exegesis.   •

§ 5. *Sentiments of Beryll, bishop of Bostria.*

[Of Beryll, bishop of Bostria a well known town in Arabia,
(flor. 230—244), very little is known with certainty, excepting
his conference with Origen.   That he was a man of learning,
the author of letters and other writings, is sufficiently vouched
for by the testimony of antiquity.   Eusebius says he had in-
spected many of his writings in the library at Jerusalem ; Ecc.
Hist. VI. 20.   But all his writings are lost ; and we know him
only by the history which his opponents have given of his sentiments.

Eusebius (Ecc. Hist. VI. 33) charges Beryll with having
held, ' that our Lord and Saviour did not exist as a distinct person, before the incarnation ; and that the divinity of the Father
(not his own) dwelt in him.'   The bishops in his neighbourhood,
it seems by his account, had many conferences with Beryll, but
were unable to convince him.   At length a Synod was conven-
ed, at which Origen was invited to be present.   He succeeded,
as the statement is, by his learning and eloquence, in winning
Beryll over to his favourite *hypostatical* views.   Eusebius says
that the acts of this Synod were extant in his time.   Jerome
(de Vir. Illus. c. 60) says, that the *Letters* of Beryll were extant in his time ; and among them a letter of thanks to Origen
for his efforts in correcting his errors.   The genuineness of this
is not generally admitted, at the present time.

What the real sentiments of Beryll were, has been greatly
contested ; inasmuch as the accounts of him are very imperfect,
and Eusebius and Jerome do not seem to agree in their statement concerning him.   They are, however, most amply and
ably developed in the following remarks of Dr. Schleiermacher.

The sources to be consulted, besides those already named,
are Socrates, Hist. Ecc. III. 7.   Gennadius, de Dogmat. Ecc.
c. 3.   Modern sources ; Walch, II. p. 126 seq.   Ceiller, Hist.

des Auteurs Ecc. III. p. 280. Bull. Judic. Ecc. Cathol. p. 28. Lardner, Credibil. of Gosp. Hist. III. p. 199 seq. Tr.]

If now Noetus so managed as to escape the difficulties and dangers that are naturally consequent upon the admission of a plurality of persons in the Godhead, (one may call this personality either ὑπόστασις, or ὕπαρξις, or πρόσωπον); and yet, after all, expressed himself as *indefinitely* as Theodoret supposes, respecting the difference of the two states or modes of the existence of the divine Being, viz., that of concealment within himself and that of disclosure to the world; granting, in the meantime, that he disclaimed ever so strenuously all expressions which would assign to this state of disclosure some definite relation to space and time; yet still, the method of Noetus' representation would easily give occasion to the supposition, that Christ made only a *transitory* development of himself, which, being dependent on and arising from the will of God, might again change and cease. Such a view, now, of the Redeemer's person would by no means satisfy the demands of Christian faith; for his regal dignity and governing power as Son, must endure at least until that undefined period, when all enemies shall be put under his feet. Thus much cannot be dispensed with.

The adding of this important circumstance to the view of Noetus, and thus supplying a want that was previously felt by Christians, appears to have been particularly accomplished by Beryll of Bostria. That he afterwards abandoned his opinion, through the influence of Origen, whose credit and personal superiority gave him great weight, can be no good ground for neglecting to examine that opinion, nor even for undervaluing it.

Should we concede that no historical connection between Beryll and Noetus can be traced, because our information respecting the times of the latter and his school is so scanty and uncertain; still, a connection in regard to opinion remains certain. If Beryll did not draw from Noetus, or even if he knew nothing of him, still his opinion discloses the same views. I could not say, with Martini, that Beryll entertained an opinion like to that of Noetus, but yet somewhat discrepant;* for

---

* Pragmat. Geschich. p. 149.

in fact it is altogether the same opinion, with the exception, that in regard to the continued abode of the divine nature in the person of Christ, it is expressed in a more definite manner. We have, indeed, no information on this point which was communicated by Beryll himself; but the few notices that we have from others, are harmonious.

I am aware of Huet's opinion,* that Eusebius and Jerome do not agree in their statements respecting Beryll. This arises, however, from his not rightly understanding and translating Eusebius.† The words ἰδία οὐσίας περιγραφή do not mean *propria substantiae differentia*, as Huet translates them. This is contrary to the well-known use of περιγράφειν and περιγραφή. They must mean *propria substantiae circumscriptio*. Nor can we assume, in order to vindicate Eusebius, that Beryll used οὐσία in the room of ὑπόστασις, (as we have seen above to be the case with Hippolytus); but the whole expression is a periphrastic explanation of ὑπόστασις or ὕπαρξις, in the very sense of the church Symbols. For if we assume a plurality in the divine Being, yet so that the essence of all three persons is the *same*, and then go on to aver, that, separately from the modification of the second person by his union with the human nature, and of the third person by his union with the church, nothing but what is strictly appropriate to Godhead remains; how then can we explain *personality* in the Trinity otherwise than by saying, that the divine Being is circumscribed in such a way in each person, that in respect to the others he has certain limitations, and is at the same time more definitely designated as he is in himself? And this idea may be very well expressed by the use of the word περιγραφή.‡ That Eusebius, however, in

---

* Origeniana, I. 3. 8.

† ' Τὸν σωτῆρα καὶ κύριον ἡμῶν λέγειν τολμῶν, μὴ προυφεστάναι κατ᾽ ἰδίαν οὐσίας περιγραφήν, πρὸ τῆς εἰς ἀνθρώπους ἐπιδημίας · μηδὲ μὴν θεότητα ἰδίαν ἔχειν, ἀλλ᾽ ἐμπολιτευομένην αὐτῷ μονὴν τὴν πατρικήν· Hist. Ecc. VI. 33. ['Daring to affirm, that our Saviour and Lord had no existence as to the peculiar circumscription of his substance, before the incarnation; neither a proper Godhead of his own; but that the Father's only took up its abode in him.' The reader will note, that this is what Eusebius says respecting the opinions of Beryll. Tr.]

‡ See passages cited and compared, under περιγράφειν and περιγραφή, in Stephani Thesaurus. In particular the passage in Origen (Comm. in Johan. IV. p. 47), which has respect either to Noetus or Beryll, probably to the latter, should be compared here; where the expression κατὰ περιγραφήν occurs several times.

the passage quoted, does not employ language which is simply
his own, but in fact uses that of Beryll, or at least expressions
that appropriately describe the transactions of Bostria, is probable for two reasons; the first, that language like this was not
commonly employed in the like disputes in the time of Eusebius;
the second, that Eusebius probably had before him, in writing,
an account of the transactions at Bostria, as may be seen from
inspection of the passage in him which is now under examination. This probability is much increased by the fact, that Beryll could very appropriately have made use of the same phraseology, in making a representation of his own opinions. He
assumed with Noetus, that the Godhead took up its abode and
acted (ἐμπολιτευομένη) in the Redeemer; consequently he
must represent this dwelling and acting as of a different kind
from that which is common to all beings by virtue of God's omnipresence and universal agency; and therefore he might well
describe the specific difference between the two modes of indwelling and acting, as being (in respect to the Redeemer) an
ἰδία τῆς θείας οὐσίας περιγραφή. According to this view of the
subject, something might be said of the Redeemer in relation to
his divine nature, which could not properly be predicated of
any thing else. The sum or *tout ensemble* of these relations,
(which constitutes what we call the divine nature in Christ), was
in fact an *ἰδία τῆς θείας οὐσίας περιγραφή*, i. e. an appropriate
circumscription of the divine Being.

Beryll, then, might properly say, that the divine nature sub-
sists now not merely in and by itself, but also in its own circumscription or peculiar limits. *Person* he could not appropriately
call this peculiar *περιγραφή*, because he (in common with his
opponents) thought that the development of the three persons
in the Godhead could not be something merely temporary and
local; and therefore that the word *person* (*ὑπόστασις* or *πρόσωπον*) could not properly be applied to the divine Being, inasmuch as this word (in his view) designated only a unity that is
temporary and local. *Person*, therefore, as he defined it, could
be predicated only of the man Jesus; and still, at the same
time, he viewed the dwelling and acting of the Godhead in Jesus, as something appropriate only to the one and undivided
Being.

Huet, then, does injustice to Eusebius, when he blames him
for finding fault with Beryll because he maintained that Christ
has no *ἰδία θεότης;* because there can be but one *θεότης*, since

on other grounds we must adopt the principle of Tritheism.
The expression criticised upon does not belong to Eusebius,
but to Beryll. Eusebius might quote this in the sense of its
author; but he could not give it his approbation, because Beryll attached to it a meaning the correctness of which Eusebius
would not allow. It was the opinion of the former, that if we
maintain the existence of several persons in the Godhead, without reference to this or to that indwelling of the Son and of the
Spirit, then such persons would be not mere *circumscriptions*
(περιγραφαί) of the divine Being in such a sense as he admitted,
viz., circumscriptions in reference to the connection of the Godhead with humanity, (and no other περιγραφαί could he admit
in common with his opponents); but they would then be of
such a nature as would divide and dissever the Godhead, in regard to what is correlate and antithetic in it (e. g. Father and
Son); and therefore one Godhead would thus be one thing,
and another a different one.

Beryll would have always said, no doubt, that the *unbegotten* Godhead was somewhat different from the *begotten* one in
Christ. To him it would have seemed to be substantially of
the same import, to assert that the Son of God before his incarnation had subsisted as a peculiar περιγραφή of the Godhead,
and to assert that during the incarnation a peculiar Godhead
dwelt in the person of Jesus. The case, however, was different with his opponents; for inasmuch as they admitted the
former of these propositions, and denied the latter, so they
could not regard the two assertions as in any measure equivalent. In like manner Beryll regarded as substantially equivalent, the assertion that the Godhead simply which dwelt in the
Redeemer was not to be distinguished from that of the Father,
and the assertion that the Godhead dwelling in the Redeemer
did not subsist before the incarnation in a peculiar περιγραφή
of the divine Being, but previously to this was from eternity
simply Godhead; while his opponents could not agree to this,
inasmuch as they admitted the former and denied the latter.
We may therefore well conclude, that the phrase in question
out of Eusebius, was one taken by him from the doings of the
Synod at Bostria, and employed by them in settling the controversy between Beryll and his opponents.

If now it appears, that Beryll denied only the περιγραφή of
the person of the Logos at a period antecedent to the incarnation; but did not at all deny, nor was even accused by his op-

ponents of denying, that when this περιγραφή had once commenced, it would continue to exist; then we may confidently
believe, that he admitted its continued existence after the ascension of Christ: in like manner as the Romish creed admits
its continuance at least until the final judgment; and Christians
in general have in fact believed it will continue forever in future time, inasmuch as we do without doubt connect the happi-
ness of believers in the eternal world, with the continuance of
such a union in the person of the Redeemer.

What Jerome says moreover concerning Beryll,[*] agrees not
only in a general way with the explanation here given of the
passage in Eusebius, but affords us some particular testimony
for Beryll in regard to this point. In explaining what Jerome
says of Beryll's views, we are not to suppose his assertion, that
the bishop of Bostria denied the existence of Christ before the
incarnation, to have any respect to the pre-existence of Christ's
human soul; for there is no evidence that the question respecting this was then agitated. Indeed no essential difference between the human soul of Christ and other human souls can be
supposed, if we admit that he possessed a nature truly human.
What Beryll then is here said to have denied of Christ, cannot
have respect to his humanity, but only to his *Godhead;* nor has
it respect to this, when considered simply and in itself; for there
can be no doubt that he admitted the reality of this, as Eusebius
expressly testifies. The point of denial was, that the Godhead
of Christ existed *before* the incarnation as a *person* in and by
itself.

The manner of the expression in Jerome, on which we are
commenting, is easy to be explained. In the strictest sense,
Jerome himself did not believe that Christ existed before his
birth; and one is fully entitled to say of him, (as Huet says of
Eusebius), that if Beryll asserted this, and Jerome blamed him
for so doing, he himself must have been a heretic. Jerome,
however, here understands the word *Christ*, just as if the word
Logos had been employed, i. e. as designating the second person in the Godhead; and he ascribes to Beryll only the opinion,
that his *personality* (ἰδία οὐσίας περιγραφή) commenced with
his incarnation.

---

[*] Ad extremum lapsus in haeresim quae Christum ante incarnation-
em negat; De Viris Illust. cap. LX. ['At last lapsed into the heresy,
which denies that Christ had an existence before the incarnation.']

The very same thing Gennadius also asserts ;* in a manner indeed which is somewhat confused, yet so that we are not at a loss on the whole for his meaning, if other witnesses be consulted.

If now any thing had been known, which could establish the fact that Beryll believed the Godhead would ever withdraw from his connection with the human nature of Christ, then would Jerome unquestionably have said, not only that 'Beryll denies Christ before his birth,' but with still more reason : 'He denies him after his ascension, or after the final judgment,' according as Beryll might have decided.

I say this with the more confidence, inasmuch as the question, whether human souls have an individual existence before birth, is not of much interest to Christian faith ; but the endless being of souls has always been a position which has most earnestly been contended for. The human soul of Christ, then, might have existed forever, and yet Christ in his true character be denied. But if Beryll, by more definite declarations, had removed from the positions of Noetus all suspicions of such a nature, then every imaginable interest of Christian belief appears to remain unassailed by these opinions, and this advantage is gained, viz., that the unity of the divine Being is preserved altogether pure, and not only remains uninjured but is not even in appearance assailed.

---

* Neque sic est natus ex virgine, ut et divinitatis initium homo nascendo acceperit, quasi, antequam nasceretur ex virgine, Deus non fuerit ; sicut Artemon, et Beryllus, et Marcellus docuerunt ; de Dogm. Eccl. c. 4. ['Neither was he so born of a virgin, that the man by birth received the beginning of divinity, as if, before he was born of a virgin, he was not God ; as Artemon, Beryll, and Marcellus taught.'] We pass by Marcellus here, because he may be accused of approximating near to Sabellius; and on essential points must have agreed with Beryll. But as to Artemon ; it is only by the most arbitrary deductions and inferences, that we can rank him with Beryll ; viz., one must say, that by the Godhead of the Father he meant only the universal presence of God in every thing ; and that this only dwells in the Redeemer, and therefore he differs from other men in nothing that is important. This was a heresy from which Origen not only kept himself free, but in the most definite manner he distinguishes the opinion of Beryll from that of those, who hold that Christ is a mere man. But apart from this, it is clear that even Gennadius holds the opinion of Beryll to be merely, that the *peculiar* subsistence of the Godhead of Christ first began with the incarnation.

The idea of *redemption*, as it demands that both the human and the divine should exist in the Redeemer without detraction and without diminution, cannot be more purely preserved, than in a system where there is no special occasion on the one hand to introduce any thing peculiar to the Docetae, nor on the other to represent God simply considered, or the Father because he is God supreme, as greater and better than the divine nature which dwells in the Redeemer; while this at the same time is represented as inferior and dependent. It is in this latter way, that Tertullian, Hippolytus, and Origen, as the opposers of Beryll and others, have almost every where represented the Godhead of Christ.

It is certain, moreover, that the more full and complete the Godhead in the Redeemer is acknowledged to be, and the less any circumstances are added which diminish or degrade it, the more complete must we suppose his humanity to be. But if any person ascribes to him only a Godhead of an inferior kind, one merely approaching true divinity or elevated towards it,* so must the human nature of the Redeemer be more or less changed in its phenomena.

The kingdom also of the Redeemer, in which he gathers and governs his disciples by the power imparted to him, and renders them always happy—this remains stable, in case the Saviour ever retains his Godhead.

What more than this, then, can one demand for the interests of Christian belief, since the two points that have just now been subjected to view, have ever been the corner-stones of all Christian preaching?† And why should we rather lay stress, in respect to true Christian belief, upon an *eternal* plurality in the Godhead, which has no relation to any thing without, than content ourselves with such a distinction in it as is connected with Christian revelation? For this is the only difference that existed between Beryll and his opponents. One thing however may be said, (which is matter of common interest so far as the

---

* Ἀληθινὸς οὖν θεὸς ὁ θεός. Οἱ δὲ κατ᾿ ἐκεῖνον μορφούμενοι θεοί, ὡς εἰκόνες πρωτοτύπου. Ἀλλὰ πάλιν τῶν πλειόνων εἰκόνων ἡ ἀρχέτυπος εἰκὼν ὁ πρὸς τὸν θεόν ἐστι λόγος. Origen, in Johann. IV. p. 51. ['God [supreme] is then the true God. But the Gods made in conformity with him, are images of the Prototype. Then again, the archetypal Image, which is the Logos that is with God, [is the model] of many more images.']

† Acts XXVII.

analogy of the scriptural *usus loquendi* is concerned, and thereby a multitude of useless logomachies may be avoided), viz.,
that, according to the views of Beryll, one may find it difficult
to see a reason, why the Godhead in connection with Jesus
should be called *Son,* while in and by itself it is called *Father.*
It was by considerations of this nature, that Origen appears to
have designed to check the progress of Beryll's opinions.* Yet
even this argument does not seem to have produced much effect, after the defenders of personal discrepancy in the Godhead had begun to soften down, through the reasoning of Noetus.   Hippolytus himself grants, that before the incarnation of
the Logos, he was indeed perfectly *Logos,* but not perfectly
Son.† The latter he became, only after the incarnation. And
this, in fact, accords entirely with the Scripture method of
speaking, where λόγος and θεός are used together.

Allowing now that the word *Son* does not designate merely
the divine nature of Christ, but the *whole person* of Christ, why
does not this theory accord entirely with that of Beryll? If God
as he is in himself is the cause or ground of this connection
[between divinity and humanity], and the whole person of
Christ, as such and by virtue of the indwelling of the Godhead,
is the archetypal image of God, why cannot such a relation between the two be well expressed by the relative words *Father*
and *Son*?

It is not however merely that the interests of Christian faith
are promoted by such a creed as that of Beryll, as much as by
the one that was opposed to him, (inasmuch as the Christian
economy suffers nothing by this creed, and the doctrine of μοναρχία remains entirely uninjured) ; but even the deeper scien-
tifical views, which the handling of Christian doctrine demands
and which belong to the proper theologian, become by this

---

* Λεκτέον πρὸς αὐτοὺς πρῶτον μὲν τὰ προηγουμένως κατασκευαστικὰ
ῥητὰ τοῦ ἕτερον εἶναι τὸν υἱὸν παρὰ τὸν πατέρα, καὶ ὅτι ἀνάγκη τὸν υἱὸν
πατρὸς εἶναι υἱόν, καὶ τὸν πατέρα υἱοῦ πατέρα. Orig. in Johan. IV. p.
199. D. [' We must address them with words which have been previously furnished, viz., that the Son is different from the Father, and
that the Son of a Father must necessarily be a Son, and the Father of
a Son [must necessarily be] a Father.']

† Οὔτε γὰρ ἀόρατος καὶ καθ' ἑαυτὸν ὁ λόγος τέλειος ἦν υἱός· καίτοι
τέλειος ὢν λόγος μονογενής· Cont. Noet. XV. [' For the Logos, as invisible and in and by himself, was not a perfect Son ; although he was
perfect as only begotten Logos.']

111

opinion neither more abstruse nor more unfruitful. Not more abstruse ; for by this theory we are saved from making any ef- fort to account for it, how there can be diversity of relations and persons in the Godhead in and by itself, or in what these consist, inasmuch as all (on the ground now in question) is view- ed as having relation to the Godhead as *revealed* to men. Not more unfruitful ; for if we could even give an adequate and sat- isfactory account of all these distinctions and relations of the Godhead as it originally was in and of itself, this would have no important bearing on the operations of divine grace ; which, after all, are the appropriate objects of true evangelical doctrine and instruction.

On the unfolding of true Christian doctrine, then, the theory of Beryll would seem to have an influence equally advantageous at least with that of his antagonists. His scheme, as well as the other, would lead men to investigate the question, how far the relation of the divine to the human nature in Christ could be further unfolded. The attempt however fully to do this, was made in the church later than the times of Beryll. But had the church retained the opinion of this bishop, this would not at all have impeded its investigations relative to this subject. One may even say, that it does not become any easier to comprehend, in what way Christ differs from all other human beings in conse- quence of the union of the divine nature with the human, if, in order to do this, we assume that the divine Being which united with Christ did from all eternity exist in an *ἰδία οὐσίας περιγρα- φή* [separate circumscription of being]. I might rather say, that such an assumption is adapted to mislead us, inasmuch as we have to suppose to ourselves, that the divine Being, in its union with the human nature, is different from God as he is in himself, and is in a measure first lowered down and reduced to a subordinate rank.

On these rocks the theory of Beryll is not so much exposed to dash. This appears still more evident when we consider, that besides the formulas common to both creeds, by which they were constrained to make attempts to explain what in all the actions and developments of the Redeemer, was the result of human, and what of divine agency, and how both natures or beings, constituting a unity of person, stood related to each other ; besides this, I say, there was another idea to be unfold- ed, which, although not altogether peculiar to the theory of Be- ryll, is more easily understood and explained by it than by any other, viz., the determining how the existence of God in Christ stands related to that indwelling of his in all men, which is essentially connected with his omnipresence and universal agency. This is a view of the subject the right use of which must produce some very definite and accurate results. But this view cannot well be made use of, when one strenuously maintains *eternal* personality ; because then, as experience shews, in doctrinal deductions made by Christian teachers, there is ever a leaning more and more to distinguish the personality, rather than to maintain the unity, of the Godhead ; the consequence of which is, that omnipresence and universal agency are eventually ascribed only to the Father.

If now we take all these considerations into view, we shall be more disposed to think that Beryll, when he had a conference with Origen at Bostria, ought rather to have converted him, than he to have converted Beryll. More particularly shall we be inclined to such an opinion, when we call to mind how conscious the great Alexandrine teacher must have been, of strenuous effort to shun the dangers that attended the assumption of three eternal or ante-mundane persons in the Godhead. Not without good reason has it been objected against him, that in his strenuous efforts to establish *diversity* between Father and Son, he has infringed upon the *unity* of the Godhead. Adopting the declarations of Clement of Alexandria, who says at one time that " the nature of the Son is nearest to that of the Father ;"* and then again (using the like phraseology) says, that he who has true γνῶσις is most nearly related to God ;† Origen in a similar way assumes the existence of a multitude of beings or natures who have become divine by that which was communicated to them, and then sets the Godhead as incarnate in Christ at the head of them all, for the reason that Christ is the nearest to the αὐτόθεος.‡ Christ, thus constituted, he

---

* Τελειωτάτη δὴ ... ἡ υἱοῦ φύσις, ἡ τῷ μόνῳ παντοκράτορι προσεχεστάτη· Strom. VII. p. 831, edit. Potter. ['The nature of the Son is the most perfect, he being nearest of all to the only almighty [God'].

† Προσεχέστερον δὴ ὁ γνωστικὸς ᾠκείωται θεῷ· Ib. p. 652. ['The [true] Gnostic is most nearly like to God.']

‡ See the afore-cited note from Origen in Johann. p. 51, on p. 20 above. Compare also the following: ... πολλαχοῦ κεῖται λογικαὶ τινῶν θείων ζώων, δυνάμεων ὀνομαζομένων, ὧν ἡ ἀνωτέρω καὶ κρείττων Χριστὸς ἦν· οὐ μόνον σοφία θεοῦ, ἀλλὰ καὶ δύναμις προσαγορευόμενος·

maintains to be the first of all beings in consequence of his τὸ πρὸς τὸν θεὸν εἶναι, i. e. his intimate communion with God, by which he attracts as it were divinity to himself.* He further holds, that the Logos is God in this way and on this account, and continues to be such by virtue of the τὸ πρὸς τὸν θεὸν εἶναι, and by his uninterrupted and constant intuition of the βάθος of the Father.†

These views incline so evidently to maintaining, that the Godhead of the Son is one which is as it were in a state of becoming divine, in part commencing and in part already commenced, and not a complete and actually existing thing, that one may easily see the reason, why Origen strove not to confound the Son with the Father; and this, so long and so much that he came at last nearly to make an entire separation between Father and Son.‡

In this way also, Origen came so near, on the one hand, to

ὥσπερ οὖν δυνάμεις θεοῦ πλείονές εἰσιν, ὧν ἑκάστη κατὰ περιγραφήν, ὧν διαφέρει ὁ σωτήρ, οὕτως, κ. τ. λ. Comm. in Johann. p. 47. ['Every where are placed some rational living creatures of a godlike nature, who are called δυνάμεις, of whom the higher and more preeminent is Christ, who is named not only the Wisdom but the Power of God. Inasmuch then as there are many Powers of God, each one according to his own circumscription, from whom the Saviour differs; so etc.']

* ... ᾧ πάντας ὁ πρωτότοκος πάσης κτίσεως, ἅτε πρῶτος τῷ πρὸς τὸν θεὸν εἶναι, σπάσας τῆς θεότητος εἰς ἑαυτόν, τιμιώτερός ἐστι τοῖς λοιποῖς παρ' αὐτοῦ θεοῖς, κ. τ. λ. Ib. p. 51. ['... to whom he is altogether the first-born of all creation, since he is first by being with God; and thus attracting divinity to himself, he is more honourable than other gods who are with him, etc.']

† Τῷ εἶναι πρὸς τὸν θεὸν ἀεὶ μένων θεός, οὐκ ἂν δ' αὐτὸ ἐσχηκώς, εἰ μὴ πρὸς τὸν θεὸν ἦν, καὶ οὐκ ἂν μείνας θεός, εἰ μὴ παρέμενε τῇ ἀδιαλείπτῳ θέᾳ τοῦ πατρικοῦ βάθους. Ib. p. 51. ['By being with God he always continues to be God; for this he would not have obtained unless he had been with God; nor would he have continued to be God, unless he had continued to abide in the unceasing contemplation of the Father's depths.']

‡ Ἀλλ' ὅμως τῶν τοσούτων καὶ τηλικούτων ὑπερέχων οὐσίᾳ, καὶ πρεσβείᾳ, καὶ δυνάμει, καὶ θεότητι ... καὶ σοφίᾳ, κατ' οὐδὲν συγκρίνεται τῷ πατρί, κ. τ. λ. Ib. p. 255. ['But at the same time that he surpasses such and the like beings, in substance, and in dignity, and in power, and in Godhead ... and in wisdom, he is in no respect to be compared with the Father, etc.']

the doctrine of the Gnostic emanations, that he appears to have rejected their terminology principally because he supposed that it might involve something of a *corporeal* nature in it ;* while, on the other hand, he opens to us the prospect, by our own future τὸ πρὸς τὸν θεὸν εἶναι, i. e. intimate communion with God, of becoming divine and like to the Logos.† This hope he checks and moderates merely by insisting, that it is only by the unceasing contemplation of the deeps of God from all eternity, that the Logos became and continues to be God ; and that he is in the same way exalted beyond comparison above all else which becomes divine, yet still, without diminishing at all the distance between him and the Father, or the superiority of the latter.‡

After all, remarkable as these passages are which thus magnify the difference between the Father and the Son, there are not wanting passages in Origen, wherein he speaks almost entirely in the same manner as those do who deny such a discrepancy. Thus when he wishes to distinguish the generation of the Son from the production of the Gnostic προβολαί (emanations or offspring), he says that " the Father is the Father of the Son without division or separation."§ This might be explained as merely asserting, that the Father does not produce

---

* Εἰ γὰρ προβολή ἐστιν ὁ υἱὸς τοῦ πατρός, καὶ γεννᾷ μὲν ἐξ αὐτοῦ ὁποῖα τὰ τῶν ζώων γεννήματα, ἀνάγκη σῶμα εἶναι τὸν προβάλλοντα καὶ τὸν προβεβλημένον. De Princip. IV. Tom. I. p. 190. ['For if he is the offspring of the Father, and produces from himself all the various kinds of living creatures, that which produces, and that which is produced, must necessarily be corporeal.']

† Comp. 1 John 3: 2.

‡ On this account he calls him τὸν ἀγέννητον καὶ πάσης γεννητῆς φύσεως πρωτότοκον ['the unbegotten and first-born or head of all produced nature'] ; although he immediately afterwards names the Father, τὸν γεννήσαντα αὐτόν ['him who begat him.'] Cont. Cels. Tom. I. p. 643. In like manner, πάντων μὲν τῶν γεννητῶν ὑπερέχειν, οὐ συγκρίσει, ἀλλ' ὑπερβαλλούσῃ ὑπεροχῇ, φαμεν τὸν σωτῆρα. Comm. in Johann. p. 235. [' We affirm that the Saviour is preeminent over all created beings, not in the way of comparison, but by an exceeding preeminence.'] The addition here in the original of καὶ τὸ πνεῦμα τὸ ἅγιον shews, that the expression σωτήρ is to be referred to the Godhead of the Redeemer.

§ Περὶ πατρός, ὡς ἀδιαίρετος καὶ ἀμέριστος ὢν υἱοῦ γίνεται πατήρ. Vol. I. p. 190. [' Respecting the Father, that he is the Father of the Son without division or separation.']

the Son out of his own substance. But one must remember, that Origen holds the generation of the Son to be eternal, and always continued, and therefore never completed.* The Father is always begetting ; the Son is never completely begotten and fully produced from the Father.† Why then could not Beryll have used this view to his own advantage ? Or rather, why could he not shew that Origen was still more remote than himself from the real doctrine of the Trinity ; inasmuch as, according to Origen's view, the Son never yet since his incarnation has truly had his *ἰδία τῆς οὐσίας περιγραφή*, i. e. his own circumscription of being or personality ? For if *the being begotten* is the circumstance which is to explain the relation of the second person of the Trinity to the first, i. e. of the Son to the Father, then we may say, that the Father is not truly Father, so long as the generation is incomplete ; nor is the Son truly Son, so long as the being generated is not complete, but only after this is completed. So long then as the generation continues, the Father is named Father without actually being so ; and so the Son also is called Son without actually being so ; in accordance with what Origen says in a passage already cited : " The Father is the Father of the Son without division or separation." If therefore the generation is incomplete, and is from all eternity, then Father and Son have never yet been fully developed as such, and the Godhead after all is to be divided only in imagination into plurality of persons, while in reality it remains but one and the same.

According to Origen's principles, then, we might pass by Beryll, and go back even to Noetus, and say with him, that since the incarnation, the Godhead of the Redeemer does not

* Ἀλλ' ὁ συμπαρεκτείνων τῇ ἀγεννήτῳ καὶ ἀϊδίῳ αὐτοῦ ζωῇ, ἵνα οὕτως, εἴπω, χρόνος ἡμέρα ἐστὶν αὐτῷ σήμερον, ἐν ᾗ γεγέννηται ὁ υἰός. Comm. in Johann. p. 23. [' But he continues to extend it to his unbegotten and eternal life ; so that thus, as I may say, [all] time is *today* in which he is begotten']. Here, plainly, this day has as little a morning as an evening, and as little a morning as a yesterday. In other words, the generation is ever continued, but never completed.

† Ἐὰν οὖν ἐπιστήσω σοι ἐπὶ τοῦ σωτῆρος, ὅτι οὐχὶ ἐγέννησεν ὁ πατὴρ τὸν υἰόν, καὶ ἀπέλυσεν αὐτὸν ὁ πατὴρ ἀπὸ τῆς γενέσεως αὐτοῦ, ἀλλ' ἀεὶ γεννᾷ αὐτόν· κ. τ. λ. Homil. IX. in Jer. Tom. III. p. 181. [' If then I should reply to you concerning the Saviour, that the Father has not begotten the Son, and made him free from being born, but is always begetting him, etc.']

exist appropriately in a *κατ᾽ ἰδίαν οὐσίας περιγραφήν*, but (at the most) it is only in reference to the human nature in which it dwells and on account of which it is called *Son*, that we can speak of *person* in respect to it; for God, in himself considered, is a simple *unity*, without distinction and without plurality.

The passages already quoted from Origen do not stand alone, but are intimately connected with many other like formulas of the same author. Origen could not comprehend how God could exist without continually creating; inasmuch as he would then have been destitute of the glory of dominion, up to a certain point; and must also have passed over from a state of previous inaction, to a state of activity in creating; which would be to suppose him mutable.*   In like manner, he supposed, the Fa-

---

* Quemadmodum pater non potest esse quis si filius non sit, neque, dominus quis esse potest sine possessione, ita ne omnipotens quidem Deus dici potest, si non sint in quos exerceat potentatum: et ideo, ut omnipotens ostendatur Deus, omnia subsistere necesse est.   Nam si quis est, qui velit saecula aliqua transiisse, cum nondum essent quae facta sunt, per hoc videbitur Deus profectum quendam accepisse, et ex inferioribus ad potiora venisse, si quidem melius esse non dubitatur, esse eum omnipotentem quam non esse. De Princip. I. 2. 10.   [' As a father cannot be a father who has no son, nor any one be lord without some dominion ; so God cannot be called *omnipotent*, unless those are in existence over whom his power may be exercised : and consequently it is necessary that all things should have an existence, in order that God may be exhibited as omnipotent.   If now there be any one, who supposes that some ages passed away before things were called into existence ; his opinion will make out that God has made some advances, and come out of an inferior to a more perfect state ; since it cannot be doubted, that it is better he should be omnipotent, than not to be so.'—That is, if I rightly understand this last sentence, it is much better to suppose that things have always existed, and so have evidence that God has always been omnipotent, than it is to deny their perpetual existence, and thus disrobe the divine Being of his attribute of omnipotence, without which he would no longer be God.

On the sentiment of this whole passage it is difficult to say, whether the weakness of the reasoning, or the extravagance of the mode of thinking, is the predominant quality. If the reasoning is true ; then every event that happens, must have been happening from all eternity ; or else it involves the supposition, that God has advanced from one state of being and acting to a different one, and is therefore mutable. The death of Jesus, then, must have been happening from all eternity ; or else it never could happen.   And so of every event which we are accustomed to call *new* or *strange*.   Such is the *logic*.

The *extravagance* of the whole supposition ; the egregious over-

ther could not dispense with the glory of having a Son ; nor could he pass from a state of not begetting to a state of begetting ; which would imply change or mutability in him.* Nor did he

looking (what less can we name it ?) of even the first principles of intelligent, rational, and free agency, whose essence consists in *powers* and *attributes*, not in the mode of their development ; astonishes one who has been taught to look with veneration upon the profound learning of Origen. Just as if this or that particular direction given to the powers of a free agent, (be this God or any other free agent), would make a change in the nature of the Being, and this because a change is produced as to things which are *ad extra ?* But such statements do not need refutation. Certainly the intelligent reader does not need any effort to refute such weak and extravagant assertions.

Seldom indeed do we meet with a writer of such singular qualities as Origen. It may well be said of him : " Quod sentit, valde sentit." When he is contending with views like those of Sabellius, he becomes a downright Arian; I mean, that his language is incapable of being fairly construed so as to mean any thing short of absolute Arianism. Such clearly are the passages already cited above; and many more of a similar tenor might be easily produced. Then on the other hand, when he comes to contend with those who infringed upon the honour or worship due to the Redeemer, he expresses himself almost in the manner of a Patripassian. How little ought such vehement feelings to be trusted, without sober judgment and discretion to guide them ? Whither must the ship go, which has passion and vehemence to hoist her sails when the wind is blowing with violence, and has no sober and steady pilot at the helm ? What incalculable mischief has been done in theology, by vehement assertion made by reason of excited feeling, and made without any due regard to the symmetry or harmony of the whole system of religious truth ! As an illustration of this we may say, that Arians, Patripassians, Trinitarians, and even Unitarians, may all find what seem to be proof-passages for their respective systems in Origen. Such must be the fate of those who have more sail than ballast or steerage. Tr.]

* Οὐ γὰρ ὁ Θεὸς πατὴρ εἶναι ἤρξατο, κωλυόμενος, ὡς οἱ γινόμενοι πατέρες ἄνθρωποι ὑπὸ τοῦ δύνασθαι μήπω πατέρες εἶναι. Εἰ γὰρ ἀεὶ τέλειος ὁ Θεός, καὶ πάρεστιν αὐτῷ δύναμις τοῦ πατέρα αὐτὸν εἶναι, καὶ καλὸν αὐτὸν πατέρα εἶναι, καὶ καλὸν αὐτὸν πατέρα εἶναι τοῦ τοιούτου υἱοῦ, ἀναβάλλεται καὶ αὐτὸν τοῦ καλοῦ στηρίσκει ; Orig. apud Euseb. cont. Marc. I. 4. ['For God did not begin to be a Father, having before been prevented ; as men who are fathers cease from being so by reason of inability. For if God is always perfect ; and the power belongs to him of being a Father ; and it is good that he should be the Father of such a Son ; could he put off such a thing, and deprive himself of a good ?'—Here is the same extravagance and futility of

stop with this. Assuming the principles already mentioned, he proceeded to the position, that God cannot pass from a state of creating to one of not creating, i. e. to one of destroying, (for the continued preservation of things he regarded as equivalent to a continued creation); and in like manner, that he could not pass from a state of begetting to one of not begetting. In accordance with this principle, he represented the Son as continually and eternally begotten, because, if he once admitted that the hypostatical state of the Logos was complete and had fully its own separate state of existence, then it would follow that the Son would no more continue to be begotten; which would contradict his theory.

If now Origen, from one stand-point, came in this way as near as he could to that Arianism which assigns to the Son a separate existence, and yet he did not give up the eternity of the Logos; and from another stand-point, assuming the perpetual *identity* of the divine perfections, he identified the Logos almost numerically with God, even as nearly as it is possible to go, if in truth any mutual relation between Father and Son is to be preserved; how can it be explained, that the much more simple positions of Beryll did not commend themselves to his approbation; for these would have freed him from such a state of oscillation? Hardly any other answer can be given to this question, than that Origen, as well as all the earlier ecclesiastical fathers, who contributed to the formation of the Symbol in after times in respect to the doctrine of the Trinity, were especially influenced in their representations of the Logos, by their views of John 1: 1—3. One might doubt of this in respect to Origen, if he should consult merely his treatise περὶ ἀρχῶν; although what has just been said is quite clear in respect to Hippolytus and others. In the treatise περὶ ἀρχῶν,* Origen, in the Christological part, appears to have taken his ground-work, as to the divine hypostasis of the Logos, more immediately from those passages which represent him as the *power* and *wisdom* of God.† But this passage in the epistle to the

logic, as before. Any thing which is good, must on this ground have been always in existence from eternity. So then, because the Scriptures are a blessing, they were given us from eternity! And thus of all other blessings; for all are good in the sight of God, as really and truly as the having of a Son, although not in the same degree. Tr.]

* Lib. I. cap. 2.			† 1 Cor. 1: 24.

Corinthians would never have been interpreted by him as having relation to *hypostasis*, (certainly not had Rom. 1: 16 been compared with it), unless the custom had already existed, of interpreting the text in 1 Cor. 1: 24 as having reference to the Logos. To do this, one interchanged the σοφία of this text with the λόγος of John, inasmuch as the two words are very nearly related in some of their meanings. Moreover a distinction was not made, such as the Scripture requires (Hippolytus himself being judge), between λόγος and υἱός. Hence the passage 1 Cor. 1: 24, [Christ the wisdom of God and the power of God], seemed to Origen to afford the best New Testament ground for a comparison with the passages in Prov. VIII., and with several in the Apocryphal book of Wisdom, respecting the Son and Wisdom. These the Alexandrine teachers applied to the Logos.

If now we consider, that the *hypostatical* view of the passage in John I., (as Origen has beyond all doubt fully and plainly represented it in his Commentary on this evangelist), rests principally on the two following considerations, viz., first that θεός without the article has a sense different from ὁ θεός, and secondly that πρὸς τὸν θεόν conveys a meaning different from that which would be conveyed by ἐν τῷ θεῷ—all this I say being duly considered, it seems difficult to believe, that such an interpretation as that of Origen could come from a simple and impartial view of the passage. There must have been a strong *previous* inclination to such an interpretation, and to the belief of such a hypostatical condition of the Logos. What could be plainer, than that the want of the article before θεός in the phrase καὶ θεός ἦν ὁ λόγος, merely determined that θεός belonged (notwithstanding its position) to the predicate of the sentence, and that such an artificial distinction built on a grammatical circumstance of such minuteness, was not at all in the spirit of John. In like manner, one need only see how θεὸς ἦν ὁ λόγος is included between ἦν πρὸς τὸν θεόν on either hand (vs. 1, 2), and call to mind how πρός is used as corresponding to the Hebrew ב and אל, in order to satisfy himself that no more is to be attributed to the expression ἦν πρὸς τὸν θεόν, than that it is the counterpart or antithesis of v. 14, viz., λόγος σάρξ ἐγένετο.

Hence those who favoured the views of Noetus and Beryll, never felt themselves excited to any doubt about the genuineness of the passage in John 1:1, nor betook themselves to such a variety of artifices in respect to it, as later opposers of the divine

nature of Christ have done. To them the passage appeared to
have a meaning quite simple, and altogether accordant with
their views. They only warned against confounding λόγος and
υἱός, as the connection of their expressions shews, and as one
must conclude from the declarations of Hippolytus; and this
they did, because they considered υἱός not as the equivalent of
λόγος simply, but of λόγος σὰρξ γενόμενος. More than this they
were not necessitated to do, in order to harmonize all which the
Scripture says of the distinction between the Son and the Father, with the opinion that the divine nature in the Son is the
same with that of the Father.

How then shall we declare ourselves, in respect to circumstances of such a kind, which arose not from mere interpretation, but from a previous inclination to hypostatize the divine
nature of the Son which had already obtained predominance in
the-church creed? The undeniable oscillation of the theories,
between the *equality* of the so-called persons in the Godhead
and the *subordination* of the same, shews plainly that not only
a religious interest, but also one not purely of a religious nature,
bore sway in all this. A mere religious interest could never
have produced any oscillation, nor any contest between this party and that which did not admit an *original* personal distinction
in the Godhead. Noetus and Beryll were learned men, as
general report says, without any participation in such an oscillating state of opinion. What Beryll added to the creed of Noetus, was only a more complete development of his principles,
without being any departure from them. We are forced then
to the conclusion, that the oscillating party were under the influence of a cosmological or philosophical interest, namely, that
of finding a point of union for the order of spiritual beings—
something to fill the void between the simply infinite Being, the
αὐτόθεος, and finite intelligences.

Inasmuch now as this interest in process of time elevated itself above the purely religious one, Arianism arose, which placed
the Son at the head of finite beings, and gave him a beginning
before the beginning of things. Origen was kept back from
embracing this view, because in him the religious and philosophical interests had found a common point of union in his
sentiment respecting the absolute immutability of the Most High;
on which account he denied both the beginning of the Son, and
the beginning of all other things. Taking his stand here, he
was, on the one hand, brought very near to the opinion of Noe-

tus; he would not concede that the Logos in Christ could be exempted from the continued generation of the Father, lest he should thus detract from the "*exceeding pre-eminence*" which belonged to his mediatorial dignity; while, on the other, his philosophical views drew him to the *subordination-theory;* for only by the distance between Father and Son could he find a measure by which he could estimate the distances between other spiritual and living intelligences.*

If now we have good reason for believing that Beryll was not swayed by such views, because he in common with many other earlier and later fathers who were learned and intelligent, contented himself with the usual views of creation in time, on account of which such an interposition as Origen maintained seemed less necessary; so it must follow, that Beryll was not moved to give up his views by feeling that the demands of such a theory could not be satisfied by the views that he defended. What then induced him to give it up?

In answer to this question we must first inquire, how far he did give it up; and how far we may trust to the representations of Eusebius on this point? This historian appears to have had the records of the Synod of Bostria before him, and to have made his narration from them. But who can assure us, that Beryll's explanations are not, in one way or another, cut short; or that something of them was not overlooked by the dominant

---

* Ὥστε, κατὰ τοῦτο, μείζων ἡ δύναμις τοῦ πατρὸς παρὰ τὸν υἱὸν καὶ τὸ πνεῦμα τὸ ἅγιον, πλείων δὲ ἡ τοῦ υἱοῦ παρὰ τὸ πνεῦμα τὸ ἅγιον· καὶ πάλιν, διαφέρουσα μᾶλλον τοῦ ἁγίου πνεύματος ἡ δύναμις παρὰ τὰ ἄλλα ἅγια. De Princip. I. 3. 5. [' So that, according to this, the power of the Father is greater than what the Son or the Holy Spirit has; and the power of the Son is greater than that of the Holy Spirit: and again, the power of the Holy Spirit far exceeds that of all other holy beings.'—If this be not Arianism, it is something even below it, at least in respect to the divine Spirit. Tr.] This passage, the original Greek of which is found only in the well known letter of Justinian which is written in Greek, runs quite differently in the Latin version of Rufinus. Its authenticity, however, is sufficiently confirmed by the sentiment in passages already cited above, out of Origen's Comm. in Johannem. That a philosophical and speculative interest lay at the bottom of such sentiments, is plain from the arrangement itself of Origen's book; where he goes from treating of the Trinity, to the consideration of rational beings in their order, specially the higher ones. The same thing is shewn, by his ranking Christ with other beings that *become* gods; see Note * above, on p. 20.

party, or designedly passed by, either of which would not be a thing ungrateful to them?

The colloquy between the parties, and the letter of thanks to Origen written by Beryll, which Jerome quotes (Vir. Illust. art. Beryllus), cannot be regarded as additional testimony; inasmuch as we can hardly suppose such compositions to have been any thing more than factitious writings, by which those transactions were published, and placed in the light that was grateful to the dominant party.

The doubt, moreover, whether Beryll did go over entirely to the views of Origen, is the more natural, since, although we cannot assume it yet we cannot deem it improbable, that, in an assembly where all was managed with frankness and moderation and where there was no reason to expect spies, to which moreover Origen was invited on account of his distinguished learning and intelligence, he kept in the back-ground one part of his theory, viz., that of *subordination*, and was purposely silent respecting it, or artfully concealed it. As little can we feel assured, that Beryll was not only induced to admit the *eternal* personality of the Godhead of Christ, (a thing which appeared superfluous to him in the Christian economy), but at the same time was also persuaded to admit a diminution of his Godhead, which stood directly opposed to his own previous convictions. If we suppose the latter, we must then suppose that Origen undertook to shew, that the full and entire Godhead of the Redeemer was not an indispensable thing in the scheme of redemption. But in this way Origen never would have proceeded; at all events, we have no evidence in his writings that he did so. Even those passages of Scripture which he quotes, in order to prove that the Son is different from the Father,[*] are so handled, that Beryll would not have felt himself moved by them. Beryll himself, who used the word *Son* only to designate the *incarnate Logos*, in which he allowed the Divinity to exist κατ' ἰδίαν τῆς οὐσίας περιγραφήν, would of course allow the Son, in this respect, to be distinguished from the Father.

---

[*] See Note [*], from p. 199 of Origen's Comm. in Johann., on p. 21 above, and the texts in the original connected with it. Let any one compare now what Epiphanius cites for the like purpose againt Noetus, and he may easily satisfy himself how easily Beryll could have replied to such arguments.

The only point, then, where union seems to have been required between the two, was that which respects the interpretation of such Old Testament passages as might be thought to have a bearing on the doctrine of *eternal generation.* In respect to these, we may easily imagine that Beryll found some perplexity, in consequence of the usual mode of exegesis which was applied to them. But we can hardly suppose that he felt necessitated to go any farther than to concede, that on account of the tenor of such passages, one might be led so to express himself, as if, because of the divine decree respecting the incarnation which is of paramount importance and is the true basis of all the phenomena of the Christian religion, even from eternity there had been in the divine Being a special reference to this, and the Godhead as determining on this was the Father, and as determined, the Son. And with this, or something like it, might the friends of the doctrine of personality afterwards have contented themselves, as a *substantial* consent to their views.

That Origen himself was not conscious of any signal victory over Beryll, appears from the fact, that neither in his Commentaries, nor in his work against Celsus, which is generally reputed as later,* does he mention the theory of Beryll as a thing brought to an end, but as still in existence.

---

* Εἰ δέ τις ἐκ τούτων περισπασθήσεται, μή πη αὐτομολοῦμεν πρὸς τοὺς ἀναιροῦντας δύο εἶναι ὑποστάσεις πατέρα καὶ υἱόν. Cont. Cels. VIII. 12. ['But if any one shall be in perplexity by reason of these things, lest we should go over to the camp of those who deny that Father and Son can be two hypostases.'] One may believe, perhaps, that this might be more properly referred to Noetus than to Beryll; but that the latter is meant, seems sufficiently evident from the words that follow: ὡς οἴεσθαι ὅτι ἡ τῆς ἀληθείας οὐσία πρὸ τῶν χρόνων τῆς τοῦ Χριστοῦ ἐπιφανείας οὐκ ἦν · ['Like supposing, that the substance of truth did not exist before the times of the appearance of Christ.'] This looks very much like one of the arguments which Origen employed against Beryll. In like manner, I apprehend that the following passage applies rather to Beryll than to Noetus, viz., ἤτοι ἀρνουμένους ἰδιότητα υἱοῦ ἑτέραν παρὰ τὴν τοῦ πατρός, ὁμολογοῦντας θεὸν εἶναι · Comm. in Johann. p. 50. [' Or those who deny that the peculiar characteristics of the Son are different from those of the Father, declaring him to be God']. That this applies to Beryll is made probable by the following context: καὶ τὴν οὐσίαν κατὰ περιγραφὴν τυγχάνουσαν ἑτέραν τοῦ πατρός· ['And the substance which exists in a circumscription different from that of the Father.']

The theory of Sabellius, then, which we are yet to examine, is not to be regarded as any thing altogether new ; but it must be taken in connection with the formulas of Noetus and Beryll, and regarded as the more full development of them.

§ 6. *Views of Sabellius.*

[It is very remarkable, that we should have almost no definite information respecting the personal history of Sabellius ; considering the unusual interest which his opinions excited, in ancient times, both for and against him.   That he lived in Africa, at Ptolemais a town of Pentapolis or Cyrenaica, some distance on the Mediterranean shore west of Egypt, is generally conceded.   Later authors ascribe to him the office of bishop or elder ; but they are too late to be safe guides.   It is merely the influence which he seems to have had in the church, that would lead us to suppose that he was invested with some office.   The probable time of his publishing his sentiments, may be stated at 255—259.   Dionysius of Alexandria (Epist. in Euseb. Hist. Ecc. VII. 6) mentions the heresy of Sabellius as having recently sprung up.   Philastrius and Augustine say, that he was a pupil of Noetus.   This may have been the case ; but the distance between the two countries where they lived, renders this circumstance somewhat improbable, although not impossible.

That he was a writer, cannot well be questioned.   The younger Arnobius (de Deo uno, etc. p. 570 in Feuardent's edit. of Irenaeus) says, that in the fifth century some of his writings were still extant.   Of what nature these were, he has not told us.

That the opinions of Sabellius were urged with zeal and ability by him, seems altogether probable from the fact, that many bishops in the neighbouring countries, and in Egypt, received them.   Moreover the burning zeal which Dionysius bishop of Alexandria manifests against them, shews that he felt the danger from them to be great.   His excessive sensitiveness also betrays the conviction in his mind, that they would soon become predominant.   It is probable, that his strenuous efforts to suppress Sabellianism, joined with the successive ones of Athanasius, Basil, and others, may have checked very much the rapid progress which it was making.   Epiphanius however, (Haeres. 62) about A. D. 375, testifies that the adherents of Sabellius were still to be found in great numbers, both in Mesopotamia and at Rome. Facts like these account for the uncommon zeal which Dionysius, Athanasius, and Basil, as well as Hilary and others, shew against what they supposed to be Sabellianism. They shew us, also, that many in the churches were stumbled at the hypostatic theory of the Alexandrine School, and eagerly embraced an opportunity to throw it off; which always happens where such matters are carried to excess.

The second general council at Constantinople (A. D. 533), in their seventh canon, declared that baptism by Sabellius was not valid; which shews that at so late a period Sabellianism was still extant, and at or around the metropolis of the Roman empire. In fact, the frequent and vehement opposition made to this opinion by Augustine, Basil, Hilary, Euthymius, and others, shews beyond all question that Sabellianism had spread far and wide, and that it was considered as being fraught with danger in respect to the Nicene Creed.

Various names were given by the ancients, in the way of reproach, to the Sabellian party. They were called *Patripassians, Monarchians, Unionites, Praxeans*, and finally *Hermogenites*. The ground of the three first names is evident. The opponents of the Sabellians believed them to maintain, that there was only one person in the Godhead, and that this person was the same with that of the Father. Hence the three first names. *Praxeans* was an epithet of reproach, because they were accused of holding sentiments like those of Praxeas, whom Tertullian attacks with such uncommon vehemence. But as to the epithet *Hermogenites*, which was intended to shew that (like Hermogenes) they held to the eternal existence of matter and denied the proper creation of the world, there is no evidence that Sabellius, or his disciples in general, held such an opinion. It is probable, however, that some zealous and considerably distinguished Sabellian in the course of time broached this view; and party zeal took occasion from this to give the adherents of Sabellius a new and more reproachful name. The history of church or state will present us with abundance of the like examples.

It is remarkable that both in ancient and in modern times, the epithet *Sabellianism* should have been, and should continue to be, employed as a *generic* designation of almost all the different shades of opinion, which deny the hypostatic theory of the Trinity, and yet maintain the Godhead of Christ. This shews the great pre-eminence which the system of Sabellius obtained, over all the opinions which had some particular affinities with his.

The common apprehension of Sabellianism has been, that it removes all distinction of personality or hypostasis in the Godhead ; and that it considers Father, Son, and Holy Ghost to be mere names of the Godhead under different developments of one and the same person, who was both *Μονάς* and Father. This view of Sabellianism has been called in question by many distinguished writers; yet the current opinion seems hardly to have been arrested.   Morus, Souverain, Beausobre, and Lardner, have endeavoured to shew, that Sabellius taught only that a *δύναμις θεοῦ*, not a divine *ὑπόστασις*, dwelt in the man Christ Jesus.

Mosheim seems to have come much nearer to a true representation, in his Comm. de Rebus Christ. p. 690 seq.   He represents Sabellius as having denied that there was any plurality of persons in the *Μονάς* itself, and of course that there was any substantial and real individual personality in the Godhead as such and simply considered ; but still he avers, that Father and Son and Spirit were considered by him as altogether distinct ; and yet that they are parts or partitions of the divine *Μονάς*, called by the names Creator and Redeemer and Sanctifier, or Father and Son and Holy Ghost.

It will be seen in the exhibition of Dr. Schleiermacher, which the sequel presents, that Mosheim was quite mistaken in regard to the last part of this representation, viz., that the Godhead is divided.   Indeed it seems plain from the exhibition of this subject as made by Dr. S., that it was with Sabellius not a matter of doubt or hesitancy at all, whether Father, Son, and Holy Ghost were to be acknowledged as distinct *πρόσωπα* of the Godhead ; for he even excommunicated those who denied this. The true question, therefore, turns on this, viz., what is it which constitutes what we name *πρόσωπον* or person in the Godhead? Is it original, substantial, essential to divinity itself?   Or does it belong to and arise from the exhibitions and developments which the divine Being has made of himself to his creatures? The former Sabellius denied ; the latter he fully admitted ; and Dr. S. himself seems fully to sympathize with his views, in regard to this point.

Supposing this to be, and it really appears to be, a correct account of genuine Sabellianism, then that which has been called so in modern times ; that which makes out the Sabellians to be the same as Patripassians, and represents them as denying the distinctions in the Godhead ; is altogether a mistaken view of the subject. The mischiefs arising first from erroneous and inadequate conceptions respecting the true nature of an opinion, and then from zeal to proscribe it and proclaim it as heretical, are of a serious nature. It is time that in some way or other they should be curtailed. I trust the views of Dr. S. will help us better to know, at least, what Sabellianism truly is. It is only then, that we can be able to judge, whether it is indeed a fatal heresy.

The ancient sources for consultation are Euseb. Ecc. Hist. VII. 6. Theodoret, Haeret. Fab. II. 9. Philastrius, Haeres. LIV. Augustine, de Haeres. c. 41. Epiphanius Haeres. LXII. The modern ones which deserve most attention, are Mosheim, de Rebus Christ., p. 690 seq. Walch, II. p. 14 seq. Lardner, Credib. of Gosp. Hist. IV. p. 593 seq. Worm, Hist. Sabelliana. Beausobre Hist. du Manich. I. p. 533 seq. Many other writers, ancient and modern, have discussed and attacked the opinions of Sabellius. None have proved them so critically as Schleiermacher. TR.]

———————

BERYLL proceeded thus far in his system, viz., that while he fully recognized the divine nature of Christ, he still believed that the Logos by his incarnation received a peculiar περιγραφή (*circumscription, limitation*) ; in other words, that something was attached to him in these circumstances, which would not have been attached to him if they had not occurred. In this respect therefore he was ready to concede, that the Godhead in Christ might be distinguished from the Godhead as it is in and of itself. In order clearly to represent his views of the Christian economy, he felt constrained to admit a two-fold method of existence in the Godhead ; which still did not at all interfere with the divine unity or μοναρχία.

He was therefore on his way toward the doctrine of a Trinity, in a more strict sense than can be asserted of Noetus. The formulas of the latter seemed more to indicate something that was transitory in the Godhead, some lowering down of the Infinite One towards the finite, and then again some recontraction of itself back again. Consequently, there was something in all this of an oscillating nature; on account of which the divine economy in Christ would be presented to us only as a thing which in its operations was temporary and limited by place, and which in fine might at some future period be exchanged for another economy.

Beryll had attained to his views, without being swayed by any philosophical or cosmological speculations; or (as is often but not correctly said) without any *Platonizing;* which was indulged in only by those who strenuously defended the doctrine of personality, and this in a manner that opposed the sentiments of Beryll.   Too much therefore is asserted, when it is said, that 'without Platonizing, the Fathers would never have come to believe in the doctrine of a Trinity.'   At most it can only be said with truth, that perhaps we should not have obtained the Nicenian or Athanasian Creed.   The views expressed in this, are no doubt intended to be a correction of the earlier Arian tendencies in such Fathers as we have already quoted; but still these views do, after all, rest substantially on the same basis as Arianism, inasmuch as their object is to explain the revelation of God in Christ by a *divine plurality*, to which the divine Unity becomes quite subordinate.   In all probability, views like those of Sabellius, which might have been deduced from such theories as those of Beryll and Noetus, would have gained the predominance rather than these, unless an interest in a measure foreign to that of simple Christian piety had predominated.   This laid too much stress on *plurality;* so that the μοναρχία of the Godhead was infringed upon, or, in order to preserve the appearance of maintaining it, formulas were introduced which either were not tenable or were not intelligible. If the Sabellian views had peaceably obtained admission, in the sequel they would doubtless have received more accurate and definite limitations.   But they were overwhelmed in the stronger opposite current, before they had time to be fully unfolded.

Beryll was on the way to the Trinitarian doctrine, whether he actually attained to it, or stopped in his course; for, according to the best information we have, his assertion, that before the incarnation there was no personal distinction in the Godhead, has relation only to the *second* person, and not to the third. The same is also probable, as we have seen above, respecting Noetus and Praxeas; whereas in Origen, Hippolytus, and Tertullian, *three* persons are fully admitted.   The views of Noetus and Praxeas were not fully unfolded, nor really moulded into the shape of trinitarian doctrine, until the time of Sabellius. In the mean time, the difference between their views and those of Sabellius must not be passed over without some remarks.

To explain this, as Schmidt has done,* by the introduction *at that time* of the formula of baptism, and the consequent predominance of the *hypostatical* views over the earlier ones, does not appear to me satisfactory ; although in matters of historical criticism I should attribute much weight to his opinions. It is not only *not* proved, that Noetus and Beryll held the Son and Spirit to be one and the same, and that Sabellius first made a distinction between them ; but the very opposite of this is much more probable, viz., that from the first they did admit, although not both in the same way, a distinction between the Son and the Spirit.

The whole matter seems to me to stand thus. Admitting a distinction to exist between the Son and the Spirit, as a truth to build upon, one might then choose a different path to walk in, according as he assigned more or less of important meaning to these or to those passages of Scripture.

On the one hand, the Spirit might be considered as represented to be the Comforter, proceeding from the Father, and like to Christ ; so that both Christ and the Spirit participate, as it were, in the work of redemption and in reclaiming the human race. In this way the Spirit was conceived of by the Montanists ; which would appear abundantly in the work of Tertullian against Praxeas, were it not that he has introduced the mention of the Spirit but occasionally and as it were *obiter*.† But other fathers, who were not Montanists, shew a partiality for this mode of representing the Spirit ; as if the mission of Christ would have been inappropriate without it; yea, as if the apostles themselves would have continued to deny the Saviour, unless the Spirit had been given to them. And it is natural that all those should incline to this mode of representation, who *hypos-*

* J. E. C. Schmidt, Bibliothek für Krit. und Exegese II. St. 2. p. 207.

† Yet the passage is strong enough at the close of his work against Praxeas (cap. 30): Hic (Filius) interim acceptum a Patre munus effudit, Spiritum Sanctum, tertium nomen Divinitatis, unius praedicatorem monarchiae, et οἰκονομίας interpretatorem, et deductorem omnis veritatis. ['He [the Son] poured out the gift received from the Father, the Holy Spirit, the third name of the Godhead, the preacher of one sole supremacy, the interpreter of the [new] economy, and him who brings down from above all truth.']

tatized both the Word and the Wisdom of God, and consequently must have admitted the existence of several divine hypostases. Of course they would not object to the supposition, that besides the Son there was at least one more hypostasis.

On the other hand, the Spirit was represented by some as *dependent on Christ*, and as receiving every thing from him. They held it to be the office of the Spirit, to call to mind the words of Christ; and that, without any *original* productive power of his own, he becomes as it were the reflection and the echo of the original operations of the Godhead in the person of Christ. He now who laid special stress upon this view, could, without identifying Son and Spirit, still maintain that the Spirit was not a περιγραφή of the divine Being. So far as he is poured out from on high, such an one might aver that he was the *breath of life* which proceeded from Christ, who is himself necessarily the animating principle [" he has life in himself"]; and so far as the Spirit dwells in the disciples, he is the proper cause of spiritual life, which is excited by his breathing upon them. Thus, in neither of these respects would the Godhead of Christ be represented as the Spirit; nor would he necessarily constitute any other union of the divine Nature with the human, besides that of the Logos incarnate.

It appears then to be quite natural, that the one side should early personify the Spirit in their way; and that the other should make shift to manage their theory in their own way, without any personification.

If now we suppose, in the first place, that Noetus and Beryll referred every thing which is said respecting the Holy Spirit, to the operations of Christ, and in such a way as that just recited; and secondly, that their opponents made the inquiry : 'What then was the Holy Spirit in the times of the Old Testament dispensation ?' The most natural answer which Noetus and his followers could give, would be, that ' it was the occasional and transitory descent of the Godhead into the souls of men.' To this their opponents might reply and say, that 'in such a case the Holy Spirit, under the *ancient* covenant and under the *new*, was not one and the same.' To this the former might have again replied in an appropriate manner, and cleared themselves from such an accusation. But to draw out such a reply, would occupy more room than can now be spared.

In the meantime it should be noted, that Origen accounts the maintenance of such a sentiment respecting the Spirit as heretical, in a passage which seems to have often eluded the researches of some.* When now we take into consideration, that Noetus had disciples and followers, and that dispute (the records of which have not been preserved) must in all probability have been continued against them; also that the passage in Origen, which I have just quoted, immediately follows those passages which relate to Noetus and Beryll; we can hardly doubt that the relation and connection now assigned to the passage in question, are the true ones.

In fact, an objection of such a nature might be urged against Beryll himself, who must have held, that the Spirit under the Old Testament stood so related to the divine Nature simply, as the Holy Spirit under the New Covenant stood related to the peculiar περιγραφή of the Godhead in the person of Christ.

So long now as the Holy Spirit was thus explained by this party, those who belonged to it could not well form for themselves a doctrine of the Trinity. A kind of *Duality* was rather admitted, which was designated by the usual and scriptural expressions *Father* and *Son;* yet this same party did not (as the other party did) make use of the word *generation* or *begetting*, in order to designate the *divine* relation between the Father and Son.

In fine, it seems as if even Sabellius, by whom the idea of a Trinity was first made out on this side, did for a while content himself, like Noetus and Beryll, with a kind of *Duality*, without introducing the Spirit as essential to the completion of the Godhead; for otherwise one must assume (which is very improbable), that several things are expressly laid to his charge, by those who lived in his neighbourhood and within the circle of his influence, which still do not in reality belong to him, but to his predecessors. I refer now particularly to a writing of the Alexandrine clergy addressed to their bishop, Alexander, and

---

* Sed si qui sunt, qui Spiritum Sanctum alium quidem dicant esse in prophetis, alium autem qui fuit in apostolis Domini nostri, Jesu Christi, etc. Opp. Tom. IV. p. 695. [' If there are any who say, the Holy Spirit is one in the prophets, and another in the apostles of our Lord Jesus Christ.'] The supposition of Huet, viz., that Origen mentions this only as a *possible* heresy and without any actual knowledge of any such opinion, is too improbable for reception. Rather might one say, that the opinion is ascribed to those, who separate the God of the Old Testament from the God of the New; but I prefer the explanation given in the text.

cited by Athanasius; in which the expression υἱοπάτωρ is attributed to Sabellius.* Whether this properly belonged to Sabellius or to some earlier person, thus much is certain, viz., that on the one hand it must have been older than the Sabellian trinitarian creed, and on the other it must have designated a more accurate development of this mode of representation as usual among this party, than had been made by Beryll.

One must not overlook the fact, that the word υἱοπάτωρ, as appears in the passage cited, is designed to designate the divine Unity, which those who leaned to this way of thinking usually named *Μονάς*; while those who were strenuous defenders of original personal distinctions in the Godhead, more commonly used to employ the formulas, μία θεότης or μία οὐσία. If now an expression was needed in order to designate the relation between οἰκονομία and μοναρχία, and yet to preserve the idea that the Godhead remained one and the same and not at all different in itself during all its various revelations to men ; then υἱοπάτωρ could be used only at a time when the Spirit was not yet recognized as a part of these appropriate revelations of the Godhead ; for otherwise the expression would not have been *Son-Father*, but *Spirit-Son-Father* (πνευματο-υἱο-πάτωρ).

On the other hand however, Beryll, if his views have been correctly represented in the preceding pages, could hardly have employed such an expression as υἱοπάτωρ. For if he, as well as his opponent Origen, regarded the Father as αὐτόθεος, but the Son as a special and peculiar περιγραφή of the divine Being ; then υἱοπάτωρ could not be regarded by him as properly descriptive of the divine Being in his simple unity, (which differed in nothing from the Father) ; nor could he so connect Father and Son in one appellation, without any designation of the diverse relations which they sustained ; inasmuch as the Father was viewed by him as the Godhead itself, while the Son was considered only as a peculiar περιγραφή (circumscription) of the Godhead in connection with the man Jesus.

When one duly weighs these circumstances, he will find it to be quite probable, that the expression (υἱοπάτωρ) was intended to designate a distinction between the Godhead in itself considered (the true *Μονάς*), and the Father [considered merely

---

* Οὐδ' ὡς Σαβέλλιος, τὴν Μονάδα διαιρῶν, υἱοπάτορα εἶπεν. Athanas. de Synodis, 16. ['Not as Sabellius, who, destroying the Unity, said *Son-Father.*']

as a distinction or person]; also to designate an equality between the Father and the Son, in their relation to the Godhead as it is in and by itself. The *Father* must therefore, in the sense in which Sabellius employed this word, be conceived of as a πρόσωπον, or (to abide by the more favourite terminology of this School) as a περιγραφή or σχηματισμός of the divine ·Being,* separately from the *Μονάς*; so that the Godhead of the Father as such, and the Godhead of the Son, would be regarded as holding the like relation to the divine Being in himself considered or as *Μονάς*.

If now a form like that of the common Symbols in respect to the *Trinity*, was developed before Sabellianism had fully attained to the doctrine of the Trinity; yet it is also true, that Sabellianism distinguished between the personality of the Father and the divine *Μονάς*, before this distinction was made by the more common creed of the church. That such a distinction never was made in a complete manner, in the formation of the Nicenian or Athanasian Creed, is evident of itself; and on this point something more will be said in the sequel.

To the expression νιοπάτωρ, already remarked upon above, a passage in Hilary relates,† which does not seem to have been

---

* Ὃς καὶ αὐτὸς, πολλαχοῦ συγχέων τὴν ἔννοιαν, ἐπιχειρεῖ διαιρεῖν τὰ πρόσωπα, τὴν αὐτὴν ὑπόστασιν λέγων πρὸς τὴν ἑκάστην τότε παρεμπίπτουσαν χρείαν μετασχηματίζεσθαι. Basil. Ep. 236. 7. ['Who even himself, every where confounding ideas, undertakes to destroy personality; affirming that the same hypostasis takes different forms, as every occasion that happens may require.'] In what sense, however, Sabellius could make some distinction of persons, the same opponent of him tells us: ἕνα μὲν εἶναι τῇ ὑποστάσει τὸν θεόν, προσωποποιεῖσθαι δὲ ὑπὸ τῆς γραφῆς διαφόρως κατὰ τὸ ἰδίωμα τῆς ὑποκειμένης ἑκάστοτε χρείας· Epist. 214. 3. ['That God is one hypostasis; but that he is, by the Scripture, differently distinguished as to personality, according to the peculiarity of each exigency that takes place.'] We must recur to this passage again in the sequel, in order that one may not make less out of it than was actually meant.

† Neque unum esse ex geminatis nominibus unionis; De Trinit. X. 6. ['Neither that he is one from the coupled names of union.']— In like manner Athanasius has the same expression in mind, in his Ep. ad. Serap., Tom. I. p. 700: Διὰ τοῦτο Σαβέλλιος ἀλλότριος τῇ ἐκκλησίᾳ ἐκρίθη, τολμήσας εἰπεῖν ἐπὶ τοῦ πατρὸς τὸ υἱοῦ, καὶ ἐπὶ τοῦ υἱοῦ πατρὸς ὄνομα. ['On this account Sabellius was judged to be an outcast to the church, because he ventured to call the Father by the name of Son, and the Son by the name of Father.'] It is worthy of

well understood by his Benedictine editor ; for how could one
better express, in Latin like that of Hilary, the idea of *υἱοπάτωρ*, than by *geminata nomina unionis ?* [*the coupled names of
union*, i. e. two names joined in order to designate one united
being]. How Arius, because of the appellative *υἱοπάτωρ*, could
say in one of his epistles, that Sabellius *μονάδα διαιρεῖ*,* (when

---

remark, that the passage of Hilary leads to the supposition of *several*
double names [geminatis *nominibus*] ; and among these may have
been *υἱο-πνεῦμα* and *πνευματο-πάτωρ*.   This supposition is confirmed,
if (with some MSS.) we read in Athanasius, *τὸ τοῦ πνεύματος ὄνομα*
instead of *τὸ τοῦ πατρὸς ὄνομα*.   But this reading is not well support-
ed ; and moreover, the *plural* is often used in such cases, where only
a single instance is concerned.

* Hilary (de Trinit. VI. 11) comments in the following manner on
the rejection of Sabellianism by the Arians : Volentes enim nihil inter
Patrem et Filium esse unum, divisae a Sabellio unionis crimen ex-
probrant, cujus unionis divisio non nativitatem intulit, sed eundem di-
visit in virgine.   ['For although they plead for no unity at all between the Father and the Son, yet they reproach Sabellius with the
crime of dividing the unity ; the division of which unity did not introduce the nativity, but make a division of him (the Father?) in the
virgin.'—I understand this last clause to mean, that in Hilary's view,
the Sabellians did not admit of any division, i. e. personality, in the
Godhead antecedently to the incarnation, so that it was not a separate person of the Godhead which became incarnate, or (as he says)
introduced the nativity, but that the division, i. e. personality, first
commenced in the womb of the virgin, when the conception took
place.   That *eundem* means the *Father* I doubt not, because Hilary
every where confounds the Father with the *Μονάς*. Tr.]   So much
may be elicited from these obscure words, viz., that (in Hilary's view)
Sabellius believed the distinction between the Father and the Son first
commenced with the incarnation, and therefore was posterior to it ;
which was in fact the opinion of Beryll, [instead of Sabellius.]   On
this point we cannot accede to the views of Hilary ; who could not
put himself in the attitude of one who really believed in the distinction
between the *Μονάς* (as the source of every *περιγραφή* of the Godhead)
and the Father, [which was the real opinion of Sabellius].   The
same thing, as we shall see in the sequel, happened to many others.
    That such mistaken views were entertained by Hilary, is evident
from several other passages in him ; e. g. . . . Ut unius Dei, ut putant,
inviolabilem fidem series, ex solido in carnem deducta, conservet ;
dum usque ad virginem Pater protensus, ipse sibi natus sit in Filium ;
De Trinit. I. 16.   ['(They maintain) that, as they suppose, a continu-
ation, brought down from the entire whole into flesh, will preserve

Sabellius is commonly accused of the *haeresis unionis*);* and how Athanasian theologians, who were opposed both to Arius and Sabellius, could agree in their views respecting this point; one may best learn from a passage in Basil, in which however the immediate subject of discourse respects only the Father and Son, and the distinction which Sabellius makes between the Father and the *Μονάς*, though indeed not wholly overlooked, is not rightly comprehended.†

So much is true, viz., that Father and Son, according to Sabellius' views, proceeded from the *Μονάς*; but he would not have said that the *Μονάς* is therefore a *ὑπερκειμένη οὐσία*,‡ [substance or essence anterior or superior]; nor that it made a *partition* of itself when Father and Son were deduced from it; although this division of unity was charged upon him. If we should go back to Beryll, we might find a probability that some expressed themselves in this way, viz., that before the incarna-

---

the inviolable faith concerning the Godhead; while the Father, extended even to the virgin, himself becomes his own Son']. Here we see plainly enough, that Hilary, through ignorance of a distinction between the Father and the *Μονάς*, says that concerning the Father which he should say only of the *Μονάς*.

* Thus Athanasius (cont. Apoll.) expresses himself: *Σαβέλλιος δὲ ... δεδοικὼς τὴν ἐξ Ἀρείου διαίρησιν, τῇ ἀναιρετικῇ κατατάπτωκε πλάνῃ.* ['Sabellius ... through fear of the Arian *division*, fell into the error which abolishes all distinction.'] And so Hilary (de Synod. 26): Idcirco ne per hanc occasionem temporis abnegati, haeresis unionis irreperet. ['Therefore lest by reason of this denial that there was a time (when the Son was generated), this *heresy of the union* should creep in.']

† *"Ὅταν δὲ εἴπω μίαν οὐσίαν, μὴ δύο ἐξ ἑνὸς μερισθέντα νόει· ἀλλ' ἐκ τῆς ἀρχῆς τοῦ πατρὸς τὸν υἱὸν ὑποστάντα, οὐ πατέρα καὶ υἱὸν ἐκ μιᾶς οὐσίας ὑπερκειμένης.* Homil. XXIV. ['But when I speak of one *substance*, do not suppose that there are two divisions of this one; but (you must suppose) that the Son subsisted from the beginning of the Father, and not that Father and Son were from one substance which existed anterior to them.']

‡ Elsewhere Basil (Ep. IX) himself sets forth a formula which would be a sufficient antithesis to Sabellianism. This is, *ὅτι οἱ ταὐτὸν τῷ ὑποκειμένῳ, πατὴρ καὶ υἱός·* ['That they, the Father and the Son, are the same in substance']. He should then have said in the passage above quoted: *ἐκ μιᾶς οὐσίας ὑποκειμένης* [not *ὑπερκειμένης*].

tion there was no *ἰδία περιγραφή* of the Godhead.   But the originating of a *περιγραφή* could not be named a *partition* of the Godhead ; because, if the Son were abstracted, there would as it were be no other *part* remaining.   Nor could any one possibly so mis-interpret Beryll, as to suppose him to have held, that *after* the incarnation the Godhead no more existed in and of itself, or that it consisted merely of Son and the Godhead *minus* the Son, [i. e. what remained after subtracting the Son].

After Sabellius began to distinguish between the Father and the *Μονάς*, and to represent the first as an *ἰδία περιγραφή* of the divine Being, then his opponents thought that they had discovered that part of the Godhead which seemed to be lacking according to his views ; and they erroneously understood him now to maintain, that the Godhead, after personality became developed, was divided into half Father and half Son.   Or in case they did not go so far, but allowed him still to hold to the existence of the *Μονάς*, yet they considered his views to be such as would represent the *Μονάς* to have been purely and truly a *Μονάς* only *before* the incarnation, but since that time to have become a *υἱοπάτωρ*, i. e. a Godhead compounded of Father and Son.*   This erroneous opinion respecting Sabellius seems to have arisen from supposing him to have taught, that the Father himself became Son.†   Yet the phraseology, which is with much appearance of probability attributed to Sabellius in relation to this subject, viz. *πλατύνεσθαι*,‡ and also *ἐκτείνεσθαι* (which words not improbably were a part of his phraseology),§ seem to prohibit all correct supposition of actual partition or division.

That Sabellius did not derive the Godhead of the Son from that of the Father, Basil has recognized, by the fact that he attributes to him, in the way of objection, that according to him Father and Son were *ἀδελφά*, [i. e. pairs, twins].|| But strict-

---

* *Οὐχ ἓν ἐκ τριῶν πρᾶγμα συντιθείς ·* Athanas. cont. Sabell. Greg. 12. ['Not compounding one thing out of three.']

† Dum usque ad virginem Pater protensus, ipse sibi natus sit in Filium; Hilary, de Trinit. I. 16. ['While the Father, extended even to the virgin, himself becomes his own Son.']

‡ Vide Athanas. cont. Arian. Orat. IV.   § Ibid.

|| *Οὐ γὰρ ἀδελφὰ λέγομεν, ἀλλὰ πατέρα καὶ υἱὸν ὁμολογοῦμεν ·* Homil. XXXIV. ['We do not call them *pairs* or *twins*, but we confess Father and Son.'] This should be read with the passage from him that is cited above.

ly taken, this is not true respecting Sabellius. His view was, that only the ἰδία τῆς θείας οὐσίας (or τῆς Μονάδος) περιγραφή which belonged to the Son, was ἀδελφός [i. e. in all essential respects like] to the Father. Sabellius, accurately interpreted, maintained that the Son was θεάνθρωπος [i. e. the incarnate Logos] ; which one may plainly see from the fact, that according to his views the Logos first became Son by taking to himself the human nature.* It must therefore have been with him only an *accommodation* to the reigning modes of speech, when he used the phraseology υἱοπάτωρ ; if indeed this is not to be explained in another way, of which I shall speak in the sequel.

But even if it should be supposed that Father and Son are ἀδελφά [of the same grade and nature], according to this mode of representation, and that both sustain the same relation to the *Μονάς* ; also that the Son as God is not derived (as Sabellius' opponents affirmed) from the Father ; still Sabellius had good reason, even after he distinguished between the Father and God as he is in himself, to hold fast the expressions *Father and Son*, as having a sense mutually relative. This however we can fully understand and appreciate, only when the very diffi-

---

* Τὸν λόγον ἐν ἀρχῇ μὲν εἶναι λόγον ἁπλῶς· ὅτε δὲ ἐνηθρώπησε, τότε ὠνομάσθαι υἱόν· πρὸ γὰρ τῆς ἐπιφανείας μὴ εἶναι υἱόν, ἀλλὰ λόγον μόνον· Athanas. cont. Arian. Orat. IV. 22. ['That the Logos in the beginning was simply Logos ; but when he became incarnate, then he was called *Son ;* for before he made his appearance he was not *Son*, but was only *Logos.*'] With this agrees the assertion, that in the Old Testament, *Son* does not at all occur. So in the sequel : πόθεν δὲ ἄρα τὴν τοιαύτην ὑπόνοιαν ἐσχήκασιν, ἔρεσθαι καλόν· φασὶ δὴ διὰ τὸ μὴ εἰρῆσθαι ἐν τῇ παλαιᾷ περὶ υἱοῦ ἀλλὰ περὶ λόγου, καὶ διὰ τοῦτο νεώτερον ὑπονοεῖν τοῦ λόγου τὸν υἱὸν διαβεβαιοῦνται, ὅτι μὴ ἐν τῇ παλαιᾷ, ἀλλ' ἐν τῇ καινῇ μόνον, περὶ αὐτοῦ ἐλέχθη. ['Whence they have acquired such an opinion, it may be well to declare. They say, it is because in the Old Testament nothing is said of the *Son*, but of the *Logos ;* and on this account they affirm that we must consider the Son as more recent than the Logos, because the Son is not spoken of in the Old Testament, but only in the New.'] From this [if it be correct] it would follow, that Sabellius did not understand Ps. II. and other like passages, of Christ. But still it should be remarked, that in Sabellius' own theory, the expression Logos stands in the background, and that such assertions occur only in contest with the party of his opposers. It is uncertain, moreover, whether they belong to Sabellius, or to his followers ; indeed, the latter would seem the more probable. Still, they are certainly in accordance with the views of Sabellius.

cult question shall have been answered : ' In what way, and in what respect, has Sabellius represented Father and Son each to be a peculiar περιγραφή of the Godhead ?'

To infer from his expression υἱοπάτωρ that he held to this sentiment, would be going too far. But the fact itself, viz., what his opinion was, is not only clear from the passage out of Basil (Hom. 24), but in part also from Bas. Epist. 214. 236. In the latter, however, Father and Son are merely placed on the ground of equality ; and if this were all the evidence we had, it might remain doubtful, whether both were not intended as tropical expressions, which the Scripture employs in respect to various relations. One might indeed allege, that if either of the appellations, Father and Son, marks an ἰδία περιγραφή of the Godhead, then does also the other; and also that *Son*, used as a *tropical* expression, cannot possibly be employed in the same sense as *Father*, and consequently that *Father* in such a case must be something different from a tropical expression. If moreover such expressions now as προσωποιεῖσθαι ὑπὸ τῆς γραφῆς διαφόρως [to be represented as different persons by the Scriptures],* and the like,† may be referred to the mere *modus* of representation in Scripture, and nothing that is distinctive or definitive respecting the Godhead lies at the basis of them ; still this method of explanation is not applicable to those passages which belong not to the Scripture, but which Sabellius employed in order to explain his views respecting the evolution of the Trinity from the Unity.‡ Athanasius, indeed, argues respecting the passage in question, on the ground that the Μονάς and the Father are one and the same ; and elsewhere he substitutes one for the other.§ That the assertions which he employs,

---

* Basil. Epist. 214.

† Τὸν αὐτὸν θεὸν ἕνα τῷ ὑποκειμένῳ ὄντα, πρὸς τὰς ἑκάστοτε παραπιπτούσας χρείας μεταμορφούμενον· νῦν μὲν ὡς πατέρα, νῦν δὲ ὡς υἱόν, νῦν δὲ ὡς πνεῦμα ἅγιον διαλέγεσθαι· Basil. Ep. 210. 5. ['To affirm that the same God, who is one in substance, according to the various exigencies of the case assumed different forms ; now as Father, then as Son, and again as Holy Spirit.']

‡ Ἡ Μονὰς πλατυνθεῖσα γέγονε Τριάς· Athanas. cont. Arian. Orat. IV. 12. Or, ἐπλατύνθη ἡ Μονὰς εἰς Τριάδα. Ibid. 14. ['The Unity extended became a Trinity.—The Unity was extended into a Trinity.']

§ Οὕτω καὶ ὁ πατὴρ ὁ αὐτὸς μέν ἐστι, πλατύνεται δὲ εἰς υἱὸν καὶ πνεῦμα· Ib. 25. And in the sequel : ἔσται ὁ πατὴρ λόγος καὶ πνεῦμα

however, are not such as Sabellius himself employed, is clear from the fact, that if Sabellius had so interchanged πατήρ and μονάς and made them altogether equivalent, it cannot be explained how Athanasius himself could have lighted upon the suspicion as he plainly did, that after all it might*be, that the *Μονάς* of Sabellius was something different from the Father.[*] To have suggested such a thought, so strange to him and to those of the like belief, and to the Arian divines, there must have been some very strong and forcible declarations of Sabellius respecting this subject. On the same ground too, [viz. the *strangeness* of such views to Athanasius], we may explain the fact, that although Sabellius may have very explicitly declared himself respecting the point in question, yet Athanasius was too little accustomed to considering the subject in this light, to be able to hold fast in mind such views. Ever and anon, therefore, he relapses into his usual mode of representation, viz., as if *Father* and *Μονάς* were one and the same. And on this ground it is, that he undertakes to contradict Sabellius.

Allowing now the truth of what has been said, two suppositions may then be made respecting the phrase υἱοωάτωρ as above mentioned. Sabellius, in the first place, may have regarded the Son as a peculiar περιγραφή of the Godhead, and placed him on an equality with the περιγραφή of the Father; as Beryll did. And this I apprehend to have been his view. Or, in the second place, like Noetus, he may have looked upon the development of the Godhead in the Son, as something in its nature *transitory ;* and so of the development in the Father. The latter opinion seems to have been ascribed to him by all those, who, passing Beryll by, ascribe to Sabellius the same opinion as that of Noetus, and accuse him of renewing the Noetian heresy. The opinion, however, that Sabellius leaned upon the more correct sentiments of Beryll, and proceeded to

---

ἅγιον, ᾧ μὲν γινόμενος πατήρ, ᾧ δὲ λόγος, ᾧ δὲ πνεῦμα, πρὸς τὴν χρείαν ἑκάστου ἁρμοζόμενος· καὶ ὀνόματι μὲν υἱὸς καὶ πνεῦμα, τῷ δὲ ὄντι πατὴρ μόνον. ['Thus the Father is the same, and is merely extended into a Son and Spirit.—The Father will be both Logos and Holy Spirit; at one time becoming Father, then Son, and again Holy Spirit, accommodating himself to the exigencies of each occasion; so that in *name* there is a Son and a Spirit, but in *truth* only a Father.]

[*] Ἐκτὸς εἰ μὴ ἡ λεγομένη παρ᾿ αὐτῷ Μονάς ἄλλο τί ἐστι παρὰ τὸν πατέρα· Cont. Arian. Orat. IV. 13. ['Unless indeed the Unity spoken of by him, is something different from the Father.']

still further development of these, appears to have more weighty
reasons on its side ; as may be seen from the following considerations.

In the disputation of Athanasius, now commonly ascribed to
Vigilius, but which exhibits some good knowledge of definitions
and the means of defence employed by the various parties
among ancient theologians ; which, moreover, is far from being
partial to Sabellius ; it is merely objected to him, (which Eusebius also objects to Beryll), that he denied the pre-existence of
the Son.* That the incarnation, however, was nothing more
than a *temporary* descent of the Divinity into humanity, which
was followed by an ascent or withdrawal, (like the mutable
condition of the Son, which Theodoret charges Noetus with
maintaining) ; and all in such a way, that the Trinity may be
supposed to consist of nothing more than *theophanies* which are
transitory in their nature ; this, or the like to this, I say, is not
at all charged by Vigilius upon Sabellius. Athanasius does indeed accuse him of having learned from the Stoics, that God
alternately expands and contracts himself.† But to this declaration we may oppose that of Vigilius again, who represents Sabellius himself as accusing the strenuous advocates of personality in the Godhead, because they ascribed to the Deity expan-
sion and contraction ; and to such an ascription he objects, on
the ground that it is contrary to his simple nature.‡ Consequently we cannot suppose that Sabellius himself employed such
modes of representation.

When we accurately examine the expression of Athanasius
quoted above, we shall find that it relates to an assertion of Sa-

---

* Sabellius, unam confitendo personam, Filium ante cunctorum
originem saeculorum subsistere denegavit ; Opp. Athanas. II. p. 645.
['Sabellius, in confessing one person only, denied that the Son subsisted before the commencement of all ages.']

† Τοῦτο δὲ ἴσως ἀπὸ τῶν Στοικῶν ὑπέλαβε διαβεβαιουμένων συστέλ-
λεσθαι καὶ πάλιν ἐκτείνεσθαι τὸν θεόν· Cont. Arian. Orat. IV. 13.
['This perhaps he took from the Stoics, who affirm that God contracts and again expands himself.']

‡ Necesse est, enim, ut se ipsa minuendo contrahat, aut dilatando
diffundat. . . . Quae, quoniam simpliciilli et ineffabili naturae congru-
ere minime possunt, etc. Opp. Athanas. II. p. 624. [' For it (the
Godhead) must necessarily contract itself by diminution, or expand
itself by dilation. . . . Which things, as they are by no means congruous with that simple and ineffable nature, etc.']

bellius respecting the Son, which is of such a nature as to convey the idea, that he could return back to the Unity and cease to exist any longer in an *ἰδία περιγραφή.** But such an assertion is only one of those hypothetical declarations, which are often made in order to place a sentiment in as strong a light as possible. To Sabellius and his friends, no doubt, it seemed very important to maintain, that *Trinity was not essential to Godhead as in itself considered, but only in reference to created beings and on their account.* Indeed their opponents themselves recognized this; inasmuch as they named the whole doctrine respecting the Trinity *the secret of the οἰκονομία,* i. e. of the gospel-dispensation. Still they did not hold this position fast; inasmuch as they further asserted, that if the Logos were not *οὐσιώδης* and *ὑφεστώς* [essential and substantial], then must God be a Being compounded of essence and attribute.†

Now according to this mode of representation, hypostasis in the divine Being must be something necessarily existent and independent of all *οἰκονομία.* ˙ Such a view of the subject Sabellius felt himself bound very strongly to oppose, in order to preserve a proper balance between *μοναρχία* on the one hand, i. e. the doctrine concerning the essential unity of the Godhead, and the *οἰκονομία* on the other, i. e. the doctrine respecting those distinctions in the Godhead which have relation to the method of salvation as published to men. This opposition he could not express in a stronger manner, than by the declaration, that the appropriate *περιγραφή* of the Godhead which took place through the incarnation, had such an exclusive relation to men, that if men were to cease, this also would do the same. This opinion did not bind him however to hold to the idea, that the Son ever returns to, and is absorbed by, the Godhead; unless indeed he maintained, that all created beings were absorbed by it in a similar way; of which some intimations given by Athanasius would seem to accuse him.

From the opinion expressed above arose, no doubt, as Epiphanius informs us, the belief that Sabellius had compared the Son to a ray of light, which goes out from the sun and is reflected

---

* It seems to be pretty certain, that Athanasius gives us the assertion of Sabellius, in nearly his own words, in the following formula, viz., *δι᾽ ἡμᾶς γεγέννηται, καὶ μεθ᾽ ἡμᾶς ἀνατρέχει, ἵνα ᾖ ὥσπερ ἦν·* Cont. Arian. Orat. IV. 12. ['For our sake he was born, and with us was he brought up, that he might be what he was.']

† Ibid. 2.

back again.*   Appropriately, however, he could regard the
reception of Christ into heaven, only as a change of his *human*
condition; not as if the relation of the divine in him toward
the Godhead in itself considered, was thereby changed.   And
the difference between Son and Spirit could in his view, in respect to this point, consist only in this, that the Son lived and
acted in our world only a short time, but now exerts his active
power in heaven; while the Spirit continues still to act upon and
in the church on earth.   Confounding these together, Epiphanius might attribute to Sabellius, what in a strictly doctrinal sense
he never avowed.

   That Sabellius did not hold the Trinity to be only a *transitory* development, is plain from the imagery which he employed
in relation to this subject.   I make no particular account here
of that similitude, which Epiphanius charges him with employing, viz., that 'the Father is the body, the Son the soul, and
the Spirit the spirit.   Although Athanasius himself alludes to
this;'† yet I cannot suppose it to be a genuine sentiment of Sabellius.   For if Sabellius had placed the third person of the
Trinity as much higher than the first, as the spirit of man stands
in rank above his body, stronger objection would have been
made to this representation among the orthodox, and more suspicion would have attached to him on account of this, than on
all other grounds.

   There is another comparison, however, which he seems to
have designedly placed in opposition to the usual one; which
is, that the Father is like the natural sun; the Son is like the
radiance of the light from it; and the Spirit may be compared
to the points of the same.   Sabellius, however, compares the
circular form of the Sun as connected with its motion, its power
of giving light and of sending forth heat, with the distinctions in
the Godhead;‡ for these are not mere transitory phenomena,

---

* Haeres. LXII. 1.   † Athanas. cont. Sabell. Greg. 13.

‡ Ἤ ὡς ἐὰν ᾖ ἐν ἡλίῳ, ὄντι μὲν ἐν μιᾷ ὑποστάσει, τρεῖς δὲ ἔχοντι τὰς
ἐνεργείας· φημὶ δὲ τὸ φωτιστικόν, καὶ τὸ θάλπον, καὶ αὐτὸ τῆς περιφε-
ρείας σχῆμα· Epiph. Haeres. LXII. 1.   ['Or as in the sun, there being but one hypostasis, there are still three powers: I mean the light-
giving, the nourishing, and the circular form itself.']   In this case,
however, the αὐτό [as employed by Epiphanius] means something
quite contrary to the opinion of Sabellius, who would have regarded
the σχῆμα as nothing more than one of its powers; and thus Sabellius

but active powers which continue as long as there are living beings on whom the sun can act and by whom it may be noticed. Hence this similitude represents very well the views of Sabellius respecting the relation of Trinity to Unity in the Godhead, save that one must not undertake to illustrate the *appropriate* functions of each of the persons in the Godhead, by those three powers of the sun.

It cannot be ascertained in a satisfactory manner, whether Sabellius regarded the three persons of the Trinity as *ἐνέργειαι* of the Unity or *Μονάς*, and employed the word *ἐνέργεια* in the room of the *περιγραφή* which was employed by Beryll. But still, this opinion seems to be rendered probable, by another similitude which Sabellius is said to have made use of, viz., that the Trinity stands related to Unity, as the gifts of the Spirit in the church stand related to the Giver. The gifts are bestowed where and when the Spirit will, and wherever he is; yet each is as it were a peculiar *περιγραφή* of the same Spirit. His power is but one and the same; but yet its metes and bounds, and manner of being put forth, are different in each particular instance*—a mode of illustration which plainly shews, to say the least, that Sabellius did *not* regard the personality of the Godhead as a *transitory* phenomenon.

Considering this point now as made out, let us advance nearer to the question: 'In what sense was the *Father*, separately from the divine Unity in itself considered, regarded by Sabellius as a peculiar *περιγραφή* of the Godhead?'

is traduced by the reporter of his opinions, who supposes this *σχῆμα* to be the same as the *αὐτοήλιος* itself; for in his view, the Father was the same as the *αὐτόθεος*.

* *Μαίνεται δὲ καὶ παραδείγματι χρώμενος τῇ τοῦ πνεύματος χάριτι· φησὶ γὰρ ὥσπερ διαιρέσεις χαρισμάτων εἰσί, τὸ δὲ αὐτὸ πνεῦμα, οὕτω καὶ ὁ πατὴρ ὁ αὐτὸς μέν ἐστι, πλατύνεται δὲ εἰς υἱὸν καὶ πνεῦμα·* Athanas. cont. Arian. Orat. IV. 25. ['He raves, and appeals to the example of the grace of the Spirit; for he says, that as there are diversities of gifts, but the same Spirit, so also the Father is the same, but extends himself into Son and Spirit.'] Here one must put *θεός* or *μονάς*, where Athanasius employs *πατήρ*; and on the other hand he must arrange *πατήρ* along with Son and Spirit; and then must not suffer himself to be misled by the comment of Athanasius, who, either from misunderstanding or artifice, treats the comparison employed, just as if the three divine persons were supposed to exist in the same way in relation to particular men, as the gifts of the Spirit exist in relation to particular individuals.

A passage in Theodoret relative to the opinion of Sabellius, and particularly to his opinion on this point, first occurs to us here.* This assigns the business of legislation or law-giving to the Father. But it is plain that we cannot interpret this passage according to the letter. The ἀνθρωπῆσαι [becoming incarnate] which is predicated of the Son, and the ἐπιφοιτῆσαι [being conversant with—indwelling] which is predicated of the Spirit, will not compare well with the office of legislation assigned to the Father; for the one is *state* or *condition*, while the other is *action*. If now we seek for the *action* which is predicated of the Son and Spirit, so as to complete the comparison; and should trust to the representations of Epiphanius respecting Sabellius,† so far as this point is concerned; still legislation is not the whole, or only official business of the father. It would not be so, even in case one should boldly and without any solid support assume the position, that according to Sabellius, the Trinity are concerned only with operations upon men of a *spiritual* nature. Sabellius, with other ancient fathers, would not have disdained to regard even heathen wisdom as something preparatory to Christianity; and this, as well as legislating for the Jews, he must have ascribed to the Father.

Another passage in Hilary‡ gives us only some obscure intimation; because one does not well know how to interpret *na-*

---

* Τὸν αὐτὸν ὡς πατέρα νομοθετῆσαι, ὡς υἱὸν ἐνανθρωπῆσαι, ἐπιφοιτῆσαι δὲ ὡς πνεῦμα. Fab. Haeret. III. ['That the same Being, as Father, gives laws; as Son, becomes incarnate; as Spirit, is conversant with us.']

† Πεμφθέντα δὲ τὸν υἱὸν καὶ ἐργασάμενον πάντα ἐν τῷ κόσμῳ, τὰ τῆς οἰκονομίας τῆς εὐαγγελικῆς καὶ σωτηρίας τῶν ἀνθρώπων ... τὸ δὲ ἅγιον πνεῦμα πέμπεσθαι εἰς τὸν κόσμον, καὶ καθεξῆς καὶ καθ' ἕκαστα εἰς ἕκαστον τῶν καταξιουμένων, ἀναζωογονεῖν δὲ τὸν τοιοῦτον καὶ ἀναζέειν, κ. τ. λ. ['The Son having been sent, and having done all things in the world which had respect to the gospel-economy and the salvation of men ... and the Holy Spirit to be sent into the world, both in due order and in all respects to each one of those who are deemed worthy, to regenerate such an one and to quicken him, etc.']

‡ ... Ut in assumpto homine se Filium Dei nuncupet, in natura vero Deum Patrem; et unus ac solus, personali demutatione se nunc in alio mentiatur; de Trinit. VII. 39. ['That he might name him *Son of God* in his incarnate condition; in nature, however, he would name God the Father; and although he is one and sole, yet by a change of person he feigns himself to exist in different ways.']

145

tura, i. e. whether it is to be taken as the Greek φύσις, or in the sense of οὐσία. One cannot therefore decide whether he is to construe the passage *in naturâ vero Deum patrem,* as meaning that he is called Father considered in reference to his own nature ; or whether (putting the words *in natura* in contrast with *assumpto homine)* we are to interpret the phrase as meaning, that he is called Father as considered in reference to the creation. The first supposition seems to be the more probable ; inasmuch as Hilary does not appear to have apprehended the distinction made by Sabellius between the Father and the Godhead in and of itself. Yet still, that the latter mode of interpretation harmonizes well with the opinion of Sabellius, may be made out from two different considerations.

In the first place, Sabellius must have ascribed the creation and government of the world, so far as these were not directly involved in the administration of the kingdom of grace, to the Godhead as it is in itself, and not to the Trinity as such ; or else he must have ascribed it solely to the Father. For the Son *as such,* did not exist before the incarnation ; [i. e. the *human* nature as well as the divine, was necessary in his view to constitute *Son* in the appropriate sense of this word]. In like manner the Spirit did not exist as such [i. e. in his ἰδία περιγραφή], before the creation of man. Even in case Sabellius held the Old and New Testament dispensation to be substantially the same, he might have entertained such a view. But if now in fact Sabellius held that the Trinity as such is concerned merely with the *spiritual* affairs of men, and that all other providential control is to be assigned simply to the Godhead [and not to the Father as such] ; then the similitude employed by him, in respect to the Spirit and his gifts, would have been inept ; for the Spirit operates only by his gifts ; and after the analogy of this, the Godhead must then operate only by some person of the Trinity, and not in and of itself. It would follow from this, that only the Father was regarded by Sabellius as creating and preserving.

In the second place ; if Sabellius had ascribed the creation and government of the world only to the Godhead as it is in itself ; while he ascribed to the Father as a peculiar περιγραφή of the Godhead only legislation and what was immediately connected with it ; this would have given to his doctrine such a distinct and remarkable cast, that no one would then have failed to perceive (for this failure often happened) the great difference that he made between the Father and the Μονάς. This would happen, only in case Sabellius was wont to ascribe to the Father nearly all those operations *ad extra*, which others commonly did; and so they were easily led by this to imagine, that he employed the word Father in the same sense as they did, [i. e. as equivalent to the Μονάς.]

Assuming this as probable, we may now see how Sabellius could retain the expressions *Father* and *Son*, in order to communicate his views respecting the Trinity, in such a sense that the first member of the Trinity was named *Father*, not merely as the Creator of all things, but also in relation to the second person of the Godhead; although Sabellius did not in reality derive the second person from the first. If the second person was a peculiar περιγραφή, or (if I may be allowed the expression) *phasis* of the Godhead, only in relation to the incarnation, yet *this depended on that arrangement of the world in which the first person or Father had developed himself;* and *this relation of dependence, or this causal and consequential connection of things, might very well be expressed by the terms* FATHER *and* SON. Yea, even if it were established as a general truth, that *Son of God* meant appropriately the *God-Man*, yet Sabellius could employ the expression *Son* tropically and in the way of accommodation respecting the divine nature in the Redeemer, although this was the same as that in the Father, because a peculiar ὄνομα (if we may so speak on the present occasion) was appropriate to that nature, insomuch as it dwelt in a particular person which was connected with, or in a sense dependent on, an arrangement of the world made by the Father.

How long Sabellius satisfied himself with such views respecting Father and Son only, as two denominations (ὀνομάσιαι) in the Godhead peculiarly related to each other, without adding to them the Spirit, we do not certainly know. This however should be remarked, viz., we are not to consider that Sabellius, for the greater length of time, and in most of his conversation and writings, made mention only of Father and Son, merely because Basil and Athanasius, in making opposition to his views, hardly ever speak of any Being but Father and Son. We do not feel necessitated here to inquire after a special reason why Sabellius admitted the Spirit to like claims with those of the Father and Son; because we are satisfied that this reason lay in the gradual unfolding of Christian sentiment. In like manner we find it altogether natural to suppose, that each of the two parties did, for a long time, take more interest in the questions respecting Father and Son, because these questions presented more points for discussion, and more that was interesting, than those which related merely to the Spirit. Moreover, in later times, Sabellius was controverted principally in connection with the Arian disputes ; and consequently his views respecting Father and Son were much more frequently drawn into question, than those in regard to the Holy Spirit.

In respect to the Spirit, his views are disclosed principally by the two passages already cited above from Epiphanius, where the Spirit is compared with the warming influence of the sun ; and by that in Athanasius, where the Spirit with his gifts is made the similitude of the divine Unity and Trinity. In the former passage, the Spirit is represented in immediate relation to individual men ; but this view is corrected by an accurate consideration of the latter passage. For if the Spirit as he is in himself, is as such in particular men, how shall we distinguish him, on the one hand, from his own gifts, which constitute what comes from him and belongs to particular men ? And on the other hand, how shall he be taken as an appropriate image of the *Μονάς*, in case we consider him as personally so divided and multiplied?

Hence we come to the conclusion, that Sabellius' view must have been for substance as follows, and that it may be thus represented. That the Holy Spirit operated only in believers, his opponents held. But that the Holy Spirit as such dwelt *personally* in particular individuals, could not have been held by Sabellius ; for then he would have represented him as *manifold.* And since the Godhead, as viewed by him, was the same in all the persons of the Trinity, therefore every particular individual thus dwelt in, would have been a *Christ*, [because God would be in him]. Consequently Sabellius could have supposed only that the Spirit dwelt in the *community* of Christians, i. e. the church, as one in one. But every spiritual *δύναμις* of believers, with whom the Spirit that animated the whole connected himself, was a *χάρισμα*, i. e. a peculiar exertion of the active power of the Spirit, whose being or presence therein was circumscribed in a peculiar manner.

This, rightly made use of, may afford us now some of the needed explanation in respect to Sabellius' mode of representation. The Spirit developed himself as *χάρισμα*, only as he united himself with the psychological powers or functions of

men, and manifested himself in this way.   In like manner the
simple Unity of the Godhead becomes σχῆμα or πρόσωπον (in
the sense which Sabellius attached to these words),* only by union with something else, but still in such a way as to suffer no
change in itself; even as the Spirit remains one and the same,
in all the diversity of χαρίσματα which it bestows.

The self same one Godhead, then, when developed in the
person of the Redeemer, is according to him the second πρόσωπον in the Trinity; but still without undergoing any change of
its own proper nature by this union.   This seems to be equivalent to saying, that before union with the Redeemer, this second person as such (κατ᾽ ἰδίαν τῆς θείας οὐσίας περιγραφήν)
had no proper existence.   Once united, however, the state or
condition that ensues is *abiding;* and the one and the same
Godhead developed himself therein in a peculiar way, so long
as the person of the Redeemer exists, or (as we have seen
above) so long as his office continues; and all the virtues and
active powers of the Redeemer, while this second πρόσωπον thus
develops itself in him, stand in the relation to him as the gifts
of the Spirit do to the Spirit himself.

In like manner, when the one and the same God unites himself with the church, he becomes the third person, the Spirit,
who develops himself by the abundance of gifts, which have a
kind of organized symmetry or relation.   In and by himself,
however, the one God remains in this case unchanged and undivided.   Here also it may be said, that the Spirit did not become
a peculiar πρόσωπον, before that community existed wherein he
operates and dwells in his peculiar manner, viz. the church.

From this view of the subject it is plain, that whether Sabellius held the Spirit of the Old Testament to be the same as τὸ
πνεῦμα τὸ ἅγιον, depended on the fact, whether he acknowledged a true church under the Old Testament.

The question still remains, *how the personality of the Father
was constituted.*   If this sustained a relation to the Unity, such
as that sustained by the other persons, in what way was the
Godhead affected, or how did it develope itself, in order to be
called *Father?*

---

* ᾽Επεὶ τόγγε ἀνυπόστατον τῶν προσώπων ἀναπλασμὸν οὐδὲ ὁ Σαβέλλιος παρῃτήσατο, εἰπὼν τὸν αὐτὸν θεὸν ἕνα τῷ ὑποκειμένῳ ὄντα, κ. τ.
λ. Basil. Ep. 210. [Since Sabellius himself did not reject the formation of persons that did not convey the idea of hypostasis, saying that
the same God, being one in substance, etc."]

To these questions we have no *data* which will furnish us with an *explicit* answer. We must therefore resort to analogy. If the second person as such developes himself in the person and office of the Redeemer ; and the Spirit, as third person, developes himself in giving to men spiritual life and sanctification, and for this purpose dwells in believers ; then, if the appropriate office of the Father as such is creation and preservation and legislation, (which comprises every thing that may be only for spiritual purposes and yet not include redemption itself but only what is preparatory to it), it follows that we must come to this conclusion respecting the Father, viz. that one and the same God so unites with the world, [i. e. developes himself by action in and upon it], that he becomes the first person or the Father, manifested by all the powers of life and animation which form the organic structures of the universe ; and these stand related to him as their Father, in such a manner as the χαρίσματα of the Spirit stand related to him. Before the creation of the world, then, according to his view, he was not Father, strictly speaking, but the pure divine Unity, not yet developed, but existing in and by himself.

No one however must here admit the idea, that Sabellius regarded the world as pre-existing in its chaotic elements, (as Anaxagoras supposed it did, before the νοῦς acted upon it), and that afterwards the Godhead arranged and adapted it for use. This would be altogether against analogy. Sabellius did not hold, that the person of the Redeemer first existed, and then the Godhead united with it ; but that the person itself sprung from the union. In like manner, he did not view the church as first having existence, and then the Spirit as uniting with it ; but the church itself took its rise, and the peculiar περιγραφή of the Spirit was developed, by his union to it. In this way, every development of personality in the Godhead, even the second and third, must be regarded as in its nature *creative;* how much more then may we contemplate the first person in this light, and regard the rise of the creation and the becoming a Father, as coexisting, or as resulting from the same act.

If now Sabellius believed that the world took its rise in time, (although we know nothing certain respecting his opinion on this point, nor even whether he made it a question), then the first member of the Trinity would, in this respect, have been altogether like the others, inasmuch as that before the creation it had no peculiar περιγραφή. Even if he believed that the world was eternal, still the only point of difference, in his view, between the Father and the other persons of the Godhead, would have been, that the two latter had a definite point of time at which they began to develope themselves, but the former not so. Yet even in such a case, (which however is by no means a probable one), the dissimilarity between the persons would have been almost wholly made to vanish, by reason of the exactly similar relation of the three persons to the Unity.

This relation itself, as viewed by Sabellius, cannot be better described than by saying, that the Most High, in and of himself and considered apart from the idea of Trinity, the true *Μονάς*, would be altogether in and by himself and altogether unknown to other beings. But this could take place only on condition, that no other beings besides himself had an existence. *The Trinity, therefore, is* GOD REVEALED ; and each member of the same, is a peculiar mode of this revelation. The Godhead, however, in each of these, is one and the same and not a different one ; but still, it is never revealed to us as it is in itself, but as it is developed in the persons of the Trinity.

Hence, even when Sabellius so explains a particular passage of Scripture as if he took away the distinction between the persons of the Godhead, he does this because he appropriates the sense of it, (although the words are those of Christ),* to the Godhead as remaining in itself one and the same ; so that one can truly say, that the antithesis between *God unrevealed* and *God revealed* was never more completely and strictly carried out, in connection with the idea of a Trinity, than by Sabellius. According to him, *the whole Trinity is God revealed ; but the divine Being as he is in and of himself and in his simple unity, is God concealed or unrevealed.*

It needs only to be mentioned in order to be plain to every one, that such views must have had a very important influence on the further formation of doctrines respecting the divine *attributes*, if it had only been considered as settled, that the Godhead in itself is an indescribable and simple nature, of which we

---

* Id sine dubio restat intelligi, ut unus idemque in se ipso manens, de se ipso singulariter dicere videatur : Ego in Patre, et Pater in me ; et, Qui me vidit, vidit et Patrem ; Opp. Athanas. II. p. 644. ['That undoubtedly yet remains to be understood, that he who continues to be one and the same in himself, should appear to speak in the singular number concerning himself : I am in the Father, and the Father in me ; and, He who hath seen me hath seen the Father.']

cannot affirm that it is compounded of substance and attributes ; and that all *attributes* belong only to one of the three persons, or to all three in common. All this, moreover, must plainly have remained in a perpetual state of oscillation, so long as the Godhead as it is in itself, and the Father who is only one of the three persons, were confounded together.

It appears also, in case one holds fast to analogy, that all living creatures in the world must hold such a relation to the Father, as the gifts and graces in the church do to the Spirit ; and then it would seem, as if the doctrine respecting sin and grace in their antithetic relation, would, under the influence of such views, have obtained a more simple and definite development, than it could possibly do under the influence of the Athanasian creed. Yea one might say, perhaps, that then a more certain and immoveable station had been found, which was intermediate between the Manichaean γνῶσις on the one hand, (which held the Father of Jesus and the δημιουργός to be different beings), and the ἀφέλεια [uniformity, voidness of all distinction] of the Ebionites on the other, which regarded Christianity only as a kind of purified Judaism. But these views might both need some further development ; which, however, cannot here be made for want of room.

That Sabellius should strenuously insist on it, that God unrevealed or the *Μονάς*, and God revealed or the *Τριάς*, were not different but one and the same, was of course to be expected. The more pure his theology was from foreign philosophy, (that it could be traced to the Stoic or Heraclitan School was a mere phantasy of his opponents), the more would he be desirous of fully satisfying the demands of Christian belief ; which, without some such limitation as that just mentioned, was in danger of falling into, or rather of remaining in a state of division which could not be healed. With such views as he entertained, he was fully entitled to employ the expression ὁμοούσιοι respecting the persons of the Trinity ; and in fact it would seem that he did at first employ it in a sense not remote from that in which it was employed in the Schools.* But that

---

* From what Hilary says of Paul of Samosata, one may conclude that the latter made use of the expression ὁμοούσιος, in respect to the Father and the Son. Hilary (de Synod. 86) says : Male *homousion* Samosatenus confessus est.... octoginta episcopi olim respuerunt. ['He of Samosata fraudulently professed his belief in ὁμοούσια ... eighty bishops in former times rejected it.'] Many places in Hilary

he employed the formula μονοουσία, some have assumed only through mistake.* When Basil, however, disputes his right to make use of ὁμοούσιοι, and claims this word exclusively for his own party,† this claim rests on an explanation of the word which

---

appear to confirm this view; e. g. de Synod. 81, 82.—Still I apprehend that Hilary entertained erroneous views respecting the opinion of Paul of Samosata; and that the latter leaned much more to the views of Artemon and Theodotus. I should think it safer to hold to what Athanasius (de Synod. 43) has suggested: οἱ τὸν Σαμοσατέα κατακρίναντες ἐπίσκοποι γράφοντες εἰρήκασι, μὴ εἶναι ὁμοούσιον τὸν υἱόν τῷ πατρί. ['The bishops who condemned him of Samosata, in their writing with regard to this have said, that the Son is not *homoousian* with the Father.'] This must be compared with de Synodis 45. 47, τοῦ Παύλου σοφίζεσθαί τε θέλοντος καὶ λέγοντος, εἰ μὴ ἐξ ἀνθρώπου γέγονεν ὁ χριστὸς θεός, οὐκοῦν ὁμοούσιός ἐστι τῷ πατρί, κ. τ. λ. ['Paul wishing to play the sophist, and saying, Unless Christ had become God through the incarnation, then he would not have been *homoousian* with the Father']. It seems to result from this comparison, that Paul said to his opposers: 'If you reject my views, then you must maintain that the Son is homoousian with the Father;' which they were not prepared to assert, [and so condemned the use of ὁμοούσιος, in such a sense as Paul had employed it].

That Paul did not himself invent the word ὁμοούσιος, may be shewn from Hilary, who tells us that Dionysius of Alexandria rejected it; and this a long time before the eighty bishops condemned Paul. [Dionysius died about 241; Paul flourished about 270]. Who then brought ὁμοούσιος into use, and employed it in contest with Dionysius? Plainly it must have been Sabellius; who is the only man that can be thought of as referred to by Basil in the following passage: νῦν μὲν ἀναιρῶν τὸ ὁμοούσιον διὰ τὸν ἐπ' ἀθετήσει τῶν ὑποστάσεων κακῶς αὐτῷ κεχρημένον, Ep. IX. 2. ['Now indeed condemning ὁμοούσιος, because wickedly perverted by him in respect to the rejecting of the hypostases.']

Farther back than this dispute, we are unable to trace the doctrinal use of ὁμοούσιος.

* Οὔτε γὰρ υἱοπάτορα φρονοῦμεν, ὡς οἱ Σαβελλίου, λέγοντες μονοούσιον καὶ οὐκ ὁμοούσιον, καὶ ἐν τούτῳ ἀναιροῦντες τὸ εἶναι υἱόν· Athanas. Expos. Fid. 2. ['Neither do we consider him as Son-Father (like the Sabellians), nor affirm that he is μονοούσιος and not ὁμοούσιος, and by this destroy his Sonship']. Here λέγοντες must be connected with [ἡμεῖς] φρονοῦμεν, and not with Σαβέλλιοι; as the whole connection clearly shews.

† Ὅταν γὰρ μίαν οὐσίαν, μὴ δύο ἐξ ἑνὸς μερισθέντα νόει... σὺ γὰρ ἀδελφὰ λέγομεν κ. τ. λ. Homil. 4. ['When I speak of one substance,

is neither grammatical nor favoured by the usus loquendi of the fathers. According to this explanation, the Son was called ὁμοούσιος with the Father, because he had his origin from the Father; in accordance with the Nicene Creed. The Holy Ghost, then, could not, according to this view, be ὁμοούσιος with the Son; because he originated not from him, but from the Father. The Son and Spirit, therefore, were more properly ἀδελφοί than ὁμοούσιοι; and consequently ὁμοούσιοι could not be applied in the same sense to all the members of the Trinity; which, however, was asserted by the opponents of Sabellius in general.

With this peculiar mode of explaining ὁμοούσιος no passage of any writing harmonizes, which stands unconnected with the

do not suppose two divisions of one thing . . . for we do not speak of ἀδελφά, *twin things*']. But this appears to be particularly in opposition to the objections made by Paul of Samosata against his opponents' views, viz., that, if the Son is ὁμοούσιος with the Father, then a ὑπερκειμένη οὐσία, i. e. a substance antecedent to them, must be supposed, in which both participate.

One must compare here Athanasius (de Synod. 45), where he says: οὐκοῦν ὁμοούσιός ἐστι τῷ πατρί, καὶ ἀνάγκη τρεῖς οὐσίας εἶναι, μίαν προηγουμένην, τὰς δὲ δύο ἐξ ἐκείνης. ['Therefore he is not homoousian with the Father, and as if there must necessarily be three substances, one precedent, and the other two derived from it.'] Just as if he objected Sabellianism against them,—as Basil represents it, i. e. the Μονάς as being the antecedent substance, and Father and Son as divided out of the same.

But Basil says the same thing still more definitely, in respect to Sabellius; Ep. 52. For first he limits the meaning of the word as follows: οὐ γὰρ τὰ ἀδελφὰ ἀλλήλοις ὁμοούσια λέγεται, ὅπερ τινὲς ὑπειλήφασιν· ἀλλ' ὅταν καὶ τὸ αἴτιον καὶ τὸ ἐκ τοῦ αἰτίου τὴν ὕπαρξιν ἔχον τῆς αὐτῆς ὑπάρχῃ φύσεως, ὁμοούσια λέγεται. ['For not things that are twin to each other does ὁμοούσια mean, as some have supposed; but when both the cause, and that which has its subsistence from the cause, are substantially of the same nature, they are called ὁμοούσια.' —This is beyond all question a *forced* definition]. This goes directly against the supposition of Paul of Samosata. Basil then continues: αὕτη δὲ ἡ φωνὴ (i. e. in the sense above given) καὶ τὸ τοῦ Σαβελλίου κακὸν ἐπανορθοῦται· ἀναιρεῖ γὰρ τῆς ταυτότητα τῆς ὑποστάσεως, καὶ εἰσάγει τελείαν τῶν προσώπων ἔννοιαν· οὐ γὰρ αὐτότι ἔστιν ἑαυτῷ ὁμοούσιον, ἀλλ' ἕτερον ἑτέρῳ. ['But this same word also corrects the error of Sabellius; for it denies a sameness of substance, and presents a perfect conception of personality; for the same thing is not homoousian with itself, but one thing with another.]

strange assertion of Basil.*   When, however, this father says,
that the expression ὁμοούσιος must lead to some definitive limitation of πρόσωπον, Sabellius would by no means be displeased
with this.   How could he have pronounced those to be heretics who *deny* Father, Son, and Spirit,† if he had himself made
no distinction between them?   For any omission to make this
distinction must have been altogether a denial of one or other
of the persons of the Trinity.

It appears, moreover, and I trust satisfactorily appears, from
what has already been said, how definitely Sabellius distinguished between the members of the Trinity ; and how exactly one
may define the peculiar province of each person, according to
the views of Sabellius, if he will diligently and carefully attend
to the respective characteristics of each.

Still we know, that his opponents sometimes accused him of
only denying a proper hypostasis in the Godhead while they admit that he allowed of πρόσωπα ; and yet at other times they
accuse him of admitting only one πρόσωπον, to which in different relations he gave different names.‡   [How can these seem-

---

* Ὁμοούσιον λέγεται τὸ ταυτὸν τῇ φύσει καὶ τῇ ἀϊδιότητι ἀπαραλλάκ-
τως · Greg. Thaumat. de Fide, 2.   [' *Homoousian* that is called, which
is without variation, the same in nature and in permanency'].—Ὁμο-
ούσιόν ἐστιν ὁ τὸν αὐτὸν ἐπιδέχεται λόγον τῆς οὐσίας · οἷον ἄνθρωπος
ἀνθρώπου οὐδὲν διαφέρει καθὸ ἄνθρωπός ἐστιν . . . οὕτω καὶ θεὸς θεοῦ
οὐδὲν διαφέρει ᾗ θεός ἐστιν.   [' *Homoousian* is that which has the same
ratio of being ; as one man differs not from another in the particular
of being a man . . . so God differs in nothing from God, in so far as
Godhead is concerned']. Every where one finds the same thing.

† Ego tibi Sabellium lego, anathema dicentem his qui Patrem et
Filium et Spiritum Sanctum ausi sunt denegare ; Biblioth. Max. Pat.
Lugd. VIII. p. 204.   [' I tell you of Sabellius, who pronounced an
anathema on those who dared to deny Father and Son and Holy
Spirit.']

‡ In proof of the first accusation, the following passages may be noticed, in addition to those already cited above. Ἰουδαϊσμός ἐστιν ὁ
Σαβελλισμὸς ἐν προσχήματι Χριστιανισμοῦ τῷ εὐαγγελικῷ κηρύγματι
ἐπεισαγόμενος · ὁ γὰρ ἓν πρᾶγμα πολυπρόσωπον λέγων πατέρα καὶ υἱὸν
καὶ ἅγιον πνεῦμα, κ. τ. λ. Bas. Ep. 210. 3.   [' Sabellianism is Judaism,
coming privily into the preaching of the gospel under the guise of
Christianity ; for it maintains, that Father and Son and Holy Spirit
are one and the same thing, although consisting of different persons.']

In proof of the second, the following passage may be cited from
Athanasius de Synod. 26 : καὶ τοὺς λέγοντας δὲ τὸν αὐτὸν πατέρα καὶ

ingly contradictory accusations be accounted for?] In some
such manner, I apprehend, as the following.

So far as the Trinity is related to Unity, in like manner as
God revealed is to God unrevealed; and so far as each member of the Trinity arises from a union of the Godhead with
something that is without it, [e. g. its union with the human nature, the church, etc.]; in like manner as the χαρίσματα of the
Spirit arise from his union with the rational faculties or powers
of men—in both respects each member of the Trinity stands
related to Unity, as that which is external stands related to that
which is internal.   This relation is expressed by the word πλατύνεσθαι.   For the *simple nature* of the Godhead, we can assume no symbol of which space can be predicated, except a
point.   Now if a point be developed, it must be by extent, i. e.
by a superficies that stands related to a point, and by which
only a point is presented to our notice; inasmuch as it cannot
be apprehended in its simple state as it is in itself.   The word
πλατύνεσθαι, employed to designate as it were the development
of a member of the Trinity, and the word πρόσωπον employed
to designate such member as developed, are connected *tropical*
expressions; for each signifies, as it were, *countenance or vis-
age* presented to our apprehension, of which the interior part or

---

υἱὸν καὶ ἅγιον πνεῦμα, καθ᾽ ἑνὸς καὶ τοῦ αὐτοῦ πράγματός τε καὶ προσώπου τὰ τρία ὀνόματα ἀσεβῶς ἐκλαμβάνοντος ... τοιοῦτοι γάρ εἰσιν οἱ
Πατροπασσιανοὶ μὲν παρὰ Ῥωμαίοις, Σαβελλιανοὶ δὲ καλούμενοι παρ᾽
ἡμῖν.   ['And those who affirm that Father and Son and Holy Spirit
are the same, impiously giving out three names for one and the same
thing and person ... these are called Patripassians among the Romans,
and Sabellians with us.'].   So again in his Πίστις διὰ πολλ. VII., he
says—μία ὑπόστασις, καὶ ἓν τριώνυμον πρόσωπον.   ['One hypostasis,
and one person with three names'].   So Theodoret (Fab. Haeret.) says :
καὶ τοὺς μὲν [τοῦ Σαβελλίου] Ἰουδαίων οὐδὲν ἄμεινον διακειμένους εὑρή-
σει, πλὴν ὅσον ὑπὲρ ὀνομάτων διαφέρονται μόνον.   ['He will find those
[of Sabellius' party] to be nothing better than Jews, except that they
differ merely in name].   In like manner Chrysostom : Σαβέλλιος γοῦν
ὁ Λιβὺς ... τὴν ἀπὸ τῶν ῥημάτων τούτων ἐγγύτητα πρὸς τὸν γεγεννηκό-
τα ἐμφαινομένην εἰς ἀσεβείας ὑπόθεσιν καὶ ἑνὸς προσώπου καὶ μιᾶς
ὑποστάσεως ὑπόνοιαν ἥρπασεν·   de Sacerdot. IV. Tom. I. p. 409. [Sa-
bellius the Libyan ... eagerly seized upon the proximity to him who
begat, manifested by such expressions, [i. e. proximity to the Father],
to make out an impious supposition, even the notion of one person and
one hypostasis.']   See also the same author, Hom. cont. Anom. VII.
4. Tom. I. p. 507.

central-point (if I may thus speak), must present itself to our
apprehension.

As a like instance, every χάρισμα is, as one may say, a kind
of πρόσωπον of the Spirit ; yet the πνεῦμα, which by necessary
supposition is discernible in each, is still but one πρόσωπον of
the Godhead.

Sabellius in this way admitted only *three* πρόσωπα, because
as a Christian he acknowledged only three ways in which God
had specially revealed himself; and these three he separated
definitely from each other. This definite separation was, in his
view, the τελεία τῶν προσώπων ἔννοια, [the perfect apprehension of the persons]. The Son was not, in his view, the same
as the Father, because he was united with something different
from that with which the Father was united, and acted in a different sphere ; and nothing but misunderstanding of his views,
and a failure to make a distinction between the *Μονάς* and the
Father, could accuse him of an opinion opposite to this. But the
real *Godhead* in the Father and in the Son was, in his view,
one and the same.

When the ancient fathers come out with their proofs, on the
other side, that the λόγος and σοφία must develope themselves
in a *substantial* way (οὐσιωδῶς), for otherwise God must be σύνθετος [composite] if this were not the case,* Sabellius justly
regarded this as a virtual undermining of the Christian *Τριάς*,
because one must, [in the same way of reasoning], make as
many γέννηματα [offspring, emanations] as there are divine attributes or perfections.   Moreover when his opponents represented the Godhead of the Logos as a different and *derived* one,
he must needs then say, that *in such a way and in such a sense*
he could not admit *persons* in the Godhead.†

That he even affirmed, however, that there is but one πρόσωπον in the Godhead, I do not believe; if we except what he
may have said respecting the period before the incarnation.
It would militate against the meaning of πρόσωπον, which his
adversaries not without bitterness attribute to him, viz. the part

---

* See Athanas. cont. Arian. Orat. IV. 1. 2.

† Ne ... duos nihilominus Deos separatim distinctos adserere con-
vincaris, aut ... nescio quam persouarum biformitatem portento alicui
similem ; Disput. Opp. Athanas. II. p. 644. ['Lest you be convicted
of putting together two who are nothing less than Gods separately
distinct; or ... I know not what kind of double-form of persons,
like to some monster.']

which the Godhead acts in respect to us ;* for he who acts *only one part*, does not in the proper sense act any part, [i. e. he sustains no *feigned* character]. More than this Sabellius surely meant, when he spoke of three persons ; for union with different objects leads to different offices, as we may say; and these must necessarily connect themselves with realities and not with mere pretences. Some glimmerings of such views as those in Sabellius, may even be found in the words of Basil respecting him. In all probability, however, the word πρόσωπον was not a peculiarity of Sabellius himself, but he borrowed it from his opponents ; while at the same time, the word πλατύνειν was probably not theirs appropriately, but a phrase borrowed from Sabellius.†

The effort to make out an antithesis between the opinion of Sabellius and the language of didactic theology among his opponents, was rendered very difficult by the oscillating sense of the terms employed for this purpose. We must notice in particular the words ουσία, ὑπόστασις, and πρόσωπον. Both parties were at that time agreed, that ουσία stands for that which is *Unity* in the Trinity. But Sabellius would not content himself with a loose and indefinite Unity of being. He was not satisfied with a community of essence in the three,‡ but he

---

* Καὶ νῦν μὲν τὰς πατρικὰς ἑαυτῷ περιτιθέναι φωνάς, ὅταν τούτου καιρὶς ᾖ τοῦ προσώπου· νῦν δὲ τὰς υἱῷ πρεπούσας, ὅταν πρὸς τὴν ἡμετέραν ἐπιμέλειαν ἢ πρὸς ἄλλας τινάς οἰκονομικὰς ἐνεργείας ὑποβαίνῃ· νῦν δὲ τὸ τοῦ πνεύματος ὑποδείνεσθαι προσωπεῖον, κ. τ. λ. Basil. Ep. 214. ['And now he takes to himself his Father's words, when the appropriate time comes for the appearance of this person; and then those of the Son, when he comes down to exercise his care over us, or to put forth any other of his energies in relation to the gospel dispensation ; and anon he puts on the personality of the Holy Spirit.'] To the like purpose Hilary, de Trinit. VII. 39; Non enim hic per demutationem nominum atque specierum Filius, qui via est et veritas et vita, mimis theatralibus ludit, etc. [' For this Son, who is the way and the truth and the life, does not act the part of mimic stage-players, by a change of names and appearances, etc.']

† Οὕτως μὲν ἡμεῖς εἰς τε τὴν Τριάδα τὴν Μονάδα πλατύνομεν ἀδιαίρετον, καὶ τὴν Τριάδα πάλιν ἀμείωτον εἰς τὴν Μονάδα συγκεφαλαιούμεθα. Dionysius, in Athanas. de Sent. Dionys. ['So we extend the Unity into a Trinity without any division ; and again we comprehend the Trinity in the Unity without diminution.']

‡ Ὥσπερ ὁ τὸ κοινὸν τῆς ουσίας μὴ ὁμολογῶν, εἰς πολυθεΐαν ἐκπίπτει·

acknowledged only one and the same essence in them ; and this one essence, according to him, was not in the three, merely in the way in which it belongs to things of the same species.* Consequently, as he contented himself with employing the word πρόσωπον, as above defined, in order to designate the members of the Τριάς, the principal contest turned upon the words ὑφεσ-τάναι and ὑπόστασις.

Sabellius maintained, that as the Godhead is only one being, so it must be only one substance. This involves the idea, that in the Godhead itself the antithesis between the general and particular [i. e. species and individual] has no place ; because those who made a distinction between οὐσία and ὑπόστασις, employed the latter word to designate separate and individual subsistence. His opponents avowed that whoever rejected the peculiar and several hypostases of the Godhead, the same could not acknowledge the Godhead of the Son, but *Judaized*.†
Sabellius on the contrary avowed, that whoever maintained the Godhead in the Son to be a different one from that of the Father, (and this they must do who supposed that as Godhead it had something ἰδιάζον in itself),‡ the same must suppose that there are many Gods, although partaking of the same essence.

Consequently Sabellius could admit three πρόσωπα, but not three *hypostatic* ones. His opponents, therefore, with whom the idea of *hypostatized* πρόσωπα was altogether predominant, represented him as holding to only one πρόσωπον, to which he gave several appellations.§   Some ground, however, there may

---

Basil. Ep. 210.   ['So that he who does not confess a community of substance, falls into polytheism.']

* Τριῶν γε κατὰ ἀλήθειαν ὑφεστώτων ἓν τὸ εἶδος ἐννοῶμεν · Athanas. cont. Sabell. Greg. 12.   ['We consider the kind as one, in the three truly existing substances.']

† Ὁ τὸ ἰδιάζον τῶν ὑποστάσεων μὴ διδούς, εἰς τὸν Ἰουδαισμὸν ὑποφέρεται · Basil. Ep. 210. 5. ['He who does not concede the peculiarity of the hypostases, i. e. persons, in the Godhead, is inclined to Judaism.']

‡ Indiscretae et indissimilis in Patre et Filio naturae, impie arripuit unionem ; Hilar. de Trinit. ['Who has impiously taken away the union of the undivided and not unlike nature which is in the Father and the Son.']

§ Εἰ δὲ τὸ ἓν διώνυμον, Σαβελλίου τὸ ἐπιτήδευμα · Athanas. cont. Arain. Orat. IV. 9. ['But if it is one thing with two names, this is the plan of Sabellius.']

have been for such an allegation. Sabellius may easily be imagined to have affirmed, that what is πρόσωπον to us, is only
ὄνομα in respect to the *Μονάς* itself, which does not admit of
real manifoldness.   By this he might appear strongly to deny
the original and eternal objectivity of separate members of the
Trinty, [i. e. personality in the Godhead as it is in itself or as
Μονάς] ; which his opponents affirmed by the assertion of peculiar hypostasis in the Godhead as it is in itself.   But Sabellius can never have employed ὄνομα and πρόσωπον in connection with each other, the one to indicate *manifoldness*, and the
other to designate *unity*.

Surveying now the contest from this central point which has
been brought to view, and to which every thing on all sides
converges, it would seem that Sabellius maintained the Trinity
to exist, as such, only in relation to the various methods and
spheres of action belonging to the Godhead.   In governing the
world in all its various operations on finite beings, the Godhead
is *Father*. As redeeming, by special operations in the person of
Christ and through him, it is *Son*. As sanctifying, and in all
its operations on the community of believers, and as a Unity in
the same, the Godhead is *Spirit*.

In opposition to this, now, the then dominant Symbols of the
church maintained, that there is a Trinity in the Godhead
which is purely internal; that there is something that was originally distinct and separate, independently of all the operations
of the Godhead ; that the Godhead was Father and Son and
Holy Ghost, in itself and from eternity, and would have been
such had there been no creation, or had it never united itself
with our nature, nor ever dwelt in the community of believers.

If now we ask the question : On the ground that this is all
the difference between the two systems, what means the accusation of irreligion which was brought against the doctrine of
Sabellius ?* Wherein now consists his blasphemy of the Father,

* Περὶ γὰρ τοῦ νῦν κινηθέντος ἐν τῇ Πτολεμαΐδι τῆς Πενταπόλεως
δόγματος ὄντος ἀσεβοῦς καὶ βλασφημίαν πόλλην ἔχοντος, περὶ τοῦ παν
τοκράτορος θεοῦ καὶ πατρὸς τοῦ κυρίου ἡμῶν Ι. Χριστοῦ, ἀπιστίαν τε
πόλλην ἔχοντος περὶ μονογενοῦς παιδὸς αὐτοῦ καὶ πρωτοτόκου πάσης
κτίσεως, τοῦ ἐνανθρωπήσαντος λόγου, ἀναισθησίαν δὲ τοῦ ἁγίου πνεύμα
τος · Dionys. Alex., in Euseb. Hist. Ecc. VII. 6.   [' In respect to the
doctrine which has been got up in Ptolemais of the Pentapolis, which
is impious, and contains much blasphemy respecting the almighty
God and Father of our Lord Jesus Christ, and much unbelief re

except that he did not regard him, whom he considered as one member of the Trinity, as being the *author* of the other two members ; for this his opponents maintained ?*

Here Sabellius might come in and with as good a right say, that the assertions of his opponents are blasphemy against the Son and Spirit ; yea, against the Trinity itself ; inasmuch as they make two members of the Trinity have a part in the divine Unity, only through the causality of the other member.

How can any one justly say, moreover, that he does not believe in the *only begotten Son* (παῖς μονογενής), who acknowledges that what is appropriately Son in him is the *only begotten;* since the Godhead exists in no other individual being in this peculiar way, but in him alone ; and who, with all this, still does not concede that the Godhead of the Son is in any respect inferior to that of the Father?

Or how can he be accused of want of feeling in respect to the honour of the Spirit, who beholds in his gifts and graces the purest resemblance of the *arcana* of the Godhead, and who looks on all these resemblances with the highest gratitude and joy?

But perhaps we may find the right key to unlock the secret of the accusations against Sabellius, and of his being rejected as a heretic, (although this did not take place by the act of any cotemporary Synod), in a passage of Basil ; who declares, that it is impossible for any one to accord in the usual *doxology,* who does not hold fast within his own mind the ideas of the

---

specting his only begotten Son, the first born of all creation, and much stupidity in regard to the Holy Spirit.']—Hilary (de Synod. 26) says : Idciro ne ... haeresis unionis irreperet, haec impietas damnatur, etc. ['Therefore, lest the heresy of the union (Sabellianism as he viewed it) should creep in, this impiety was condemned, etc.']   And again : Hinc et Sabellius, dum quod 'Ego et Pater unum sumus,' non intelligit, sine Deo Patre et sine Deo Filio est; Ibid.   ['Hence Sabellius, also, while he knows not the meaning of *I and my Father are one,* is without God the Father and God the Son.']   Again (ad Const. II. 9) he says that which reminds one of the manner in which Tertullian handles Praxeas.   And certainly Hilary would not have conceded that Sabellius believed in the Holy Ghost, if this passage had led him to speak of this subject.

* For example: ἀλλ' ἔστι μὲν ὁ πατήρ, τέλειον ἔχων τὸ εἶναι καὶ ἀνελλιπές, ῥίζα καὶ πηγὴ τοῦ υἱοῦ καὶ τοῦ πνεύματος · Athanas. cont. Sabel. Greg. II.   ['But the Father, who has perfect Being without any thing lacking, is the root and fountain of the Son and Spirit.']

peculiarities of each member of the Trinity without mixture or confusion of them.*

It is difficult to treat affirmations of such a nature in a serious way, yet it is worth the trouble of some attention. That the numerous Sabellian churches did not think with Basil, and omitted the doxology as at variance with their doctrine, is indeed certain; for this could not remain unobserved. But the ascription of glory and thanksgiving contained in the doxology, has always a relation to the beneficence and to the saving operations of the particular members of the Trinity; and as the appropriate authors of these, Sabellius definitely distinguished these members. With him it was a peculiar union of the Godhead with something else; easily and simply to be distinguished, which defined the province of each member of the Trinity. In accordance with this, the Unity might be glorified as Father, Son, and Spirit; and in this glorification the whole of Christian piety might be concentrated, as believed both in the μοναρχία and in the οἰκονομία.

If now a question be raised here, respecting limitations of a transcendental nature; then Sabellius might well have asked, how he who prayed to the Son, could pray to a Godhead that was begotten; and he who prayed to the Spirit, could pray to a divine nature proceeding in an indescribable manner from the Father; and yet the petitioner at the same time be able to separate the one from the other [as he was required to do], when at the very same time also he was required to consider the generation of the Son as *unlike* to any thing human, which of course made it inconceivable and indescribable to him?

The objection moreover made to Sabellius, he might disprove or reply to, if he chose; and no one can make it out, that any injury would have accrued to Christian piety in consequence of his doctrinal opinions.

Still less can he be accused of *Judaizing.* This could be said only of those who did not acknowledge the Godhead of Christ, from Artemon to Paul of Samosata, and to others still later and of the like sentiment. From these, now, Sabellius

---

* Ἀμήχανον γὰρ μὴ ἐν τοῖς ἑκάστου ἰδιώμασι τὴν διάνοιαν γενομένην ἀσύγχυτον, δυνηθῆναι πατρὶ καὶ υἱῷ καὶ ἁγίῳ πνεύματι τὴν δοξολογίαν ἀποπληρῶσαι · Ep. 210. 4. ['It is impossible that one, who has not his mind freed from confusion respecting the peculiarities of each person, should be able fully to accord with the doxology to Father, Son, and Spirit.']

was as far, or even further, removed than his opponents; although the latter, through ignorance, sometimes rank him with the aforesaid Paul.* Sabellius not only acknowledged the Godhead of Christ, but he did it in such a way, that in comparison with him even the Athanasians are Judaizers. For inasmuch as these maintain, that even under the Old Testament the Son was acknowledged, they do in a great measure remove the essential difference between Judaism and Christianity. Sabellius, however, denied that the Son was revealed under the Old Testament; and he avows his belief that this divine revelation commenced with the new dispensation. Consequently he must have regarded Judaism as less complete and satisfactory, than his opponents seem to have done.

The passage of Dionysius quoted above naturally gives occasion to conclude this essay, by a short sketch of some of the historical relations suggested in the view that has been taken. Before I make some remarks, as I intend in the sequel to do, on the manner in which this celebrated teacher opposed Sabellius, we must go back for a moment to the origin of Sabellian views, in order to render them more complete and explicit.

The whole form of the Sabellian doctrine, as we have traced it from its beginnings, might have arisen in and by itself, without having been evoked by doctrinal strife; for, in order to form such views, one needed only to take into consideration the views that are common to all Christians respecting a revelation through Christ and belief in Christ, and also what Scripture and history inform us respecting the gifts and graces of the Spirit. That such views as those of Sabellius, however, were from the outset formed in the way of antithesis to the Nazarean opinions respecting Christ, I trust is sufficiently clear; for those opinions, in themselves regarded and literally understood, cannot be viewed as consistent with Christianity. It is only when those who advocate them shew, by their lives, that they possess a

---

* Σαβέλλιος δὲ τοῦ Σαμοσατέως Παύλου καὶ τῶν κατ᾽ αὐτὸν ἐπιδέδεικ-ται τὴν γνώμην· Athanas. cont. Apollin. II. 4. ['Sabellius disclosed the same views as those of Paul of Samosata and his adherents.'] But the view which Athanasius here exhibits of Paul, does not accord with what we learn respecting him from other sources which are authentic. The only point of union between him and Sabellius was, that both denied the derivation of a hypostatical Logos out of the Godhead.

Christian spirit, i. e. when their lives are better than their doctrine, that they can be regarded as Christians.

That such an antithesis was a matter of design, may be concluded from the fact, that Noetus, as soon as he was attacked, alleged his opposition to the Nazaraean views in the way of defence, and put it to his own account as a matter of credit.* It would even seem, that he gave this turn to his explanation of the development of the Godhead in Christ, viz., that it was like the ancient *theophanies*, for the special purpose of making its credibility more striking than he could, if he assumed the incarnation of the Divinity as being a fact entirely unique in its kind. But of any influence of opposite doctrines upon their expressions and formulas, I can find no certain evidence in what is said of Noetus, Praxeas, or Beryll.

The further development of views like those of Sabellius, from the time of Beryll down to the period in which Sabellius himself flourished, proceeded without much hindrance, inasmuch as it took place in a region remote from the theatre of the earlier theological contests. Even in the case of Sabellius himself, so far as one can gather from the scanty notices we have of him, it is easy to separate those formulas and phrases which arose from the heat of contest, from those which did not; and such a process would undoubtedly result in the production of evidence, which would satisfactorily disclose the freedom and consistency of his views.

But whence came another polemic system of doctrine, opposed to all views like those of Sabellius, but which still did not originate from opposition to these views nor was directly occasioned by them? We can hardly give it any other name, than *the polemic system of the Alexandrine School;* for out of this, and as its advocates, came forth Origen against Beryll, and Dionysius against Sabellius. In regard to Hippolytus, the opponent of Noetus, we do not know from whence he was; and Tertullian, it must be conceded, was connected with the School in question only in an indirect way. Yet both of these last named writers were filled with Alexandrine views; and (what is of the greatest moment to our present purpose) with the apprehension that the Logos sprang *substantially* (ουσιωδως) from the Godhead, and that this derivation itself constituted the Godhead

* Tί οὖν κακόν ποιῶ, δοξάζων τὸν Χριστόν; Hippolytus, cont. Noetum, 1. ['What evil then do I commit, by glorifying Christ?']

of the Son, which was only an exact copy of the original. With these views the doctrine of Beryll, viz., that the appropriate Sonship of Christ commenced in time, did not at all harmonize. Origen therefore came out against it, as soon as he obtained a knowledge of it.

Still less did the more mature and more completely formed system of Sabellius agree with Alexandrine views. It threatened, moreover, to become a popular system. Against this Dionysius came forth, in defence of the common views of the Alexandrine School that had been cherished from the time of Clement ; with moderation, indeed, as to his *ecclesiastical acts*, inasmuch as he did not excommunicate the [Sabellian] Pentapolitan churches, nor their officers ; but still with great warmth of feeling, as the vehement passage above quoted (p. 70) fully evinces. This vehemence of feeling added to the difficulties that already had attached themselves to the Alexandrine system ; although what Dionysius says, is all of it much in the spirit of the School at Alexandria. In fact, the theory which Dionysius has presented to view and placed in a strong light, is in substance the same which Arius afterwards maintained against the formulas of the Sabellians.

One example may suffice to illustrate the difficulty that attends his views. He predicates ἀγεννησία only of the substance or essence of the Godhead. Now if the fact of being *unbegotten* is a matter essential to Godhead, (which Dionysius assumes), then the Godhead of the Son which is *begotten* of course cannot be a partaker in one essential attribute of Divinity.* Of course also, according to this view, the Son cannot be derived *substantially* (οὐσιωδῶς) from the Unity or Paternity, but must be formed in some other way, or created out of nothing ; and consequently his essence must be unlike that of the Unity, [i. e. he could not be truly and οὐσιωδῶς God.]

Even the friends of Dionysius concede that he has here exposed himself ; and they merely allege, in the way of reply, that what is said in the heat of contest must not be urged to the letter.† But after all, the views of Dionysius agree too well with

---

* Εἰ μὲν γὰρ αὐτὸ ἀγέννητόν ἐστι ὁ θεός, καὶ οὐσία ἐστὶν αὐτοῦ, ὡς ἂν εἴποι, τις ἡ ἀγεννησία κ. τ. λ. Dionysius, in Euseb. Praep. Evang. VII. 18. [' If now God is that which is unbegotten, and ἀγεννησία, as one may say, belongs *substantially* to him, etc.']

† Φασὶ τοῦτον ἐν ἐπιστολῇ τὸν μακαρίτην Διονύσιον εἰρηκέναι ποίημα καὶ γενητὸν εἶναι τὸν υἱὸν τοῦ θεοῦ, μήτε δὲ φύσει ἴδιον ἀλλὰ ξένον κατ'

the general tenor of the Alexandrine doctrine, to admit such an apology to have much currency. Arius himself says, plainly

οὐσίαν αὐτὸν εἶναι τοῦ πατρός . . . καὶ ἔγραψεν· ὁμολογοῦμεν καὶ ἡμεῖς εἶναι τοιαύτην ἐπιστολήν αὐτοῦ· Athanas. de Sentent. Dionys. 4. ['They say that the late Dionysius affirmed the Son of God to be created and produced, and that he was not by his nature the same in substance as the Father, but something different from him . . . and that he even wrote after this tenor. And we confess that there is such an epistle of his.'] The image from Dionysius, so often urged by others, respecting the vintner and the vine, I shall the less insist upon, because, confounding two different parables, he seems to have designed to express nothing more than a dissimilarity in general ; as sometimes represented by Christ himself.—Ἐπειδὴ γὰρ εἶρπεν ἡ Σαβελλίου αἵρεσις, ἠναγκάσθη . . . τὰ ἀνθρωπίνως καὶ εὐτελῶς περὶ τοῦ Σωτῆρος εἰρημένα ῥίψαι κατ' αὐτῶν· Ibid. 9. ['For when the Sabellian heresy crept in, he (Dionysius) was compelled to throw out, in opposition to them, the things which are spoken of the Saviour in an ordinary way and after the manner of men.']—Ibid. 6, οὐ δεῖ δὲ τὰ κατ' οἰκονομίαν γραφόμενα καὶ γινόμενα, ταῦτα κακοτρόπως δέχεσθαι, καὶ εἰς τὴν ἰδίαν ἕκαστον ἕλκειν βούλησιν. [' It is not becoming, moreover, to take those things in a bad way, which are written and said respecting the gospel-dispensation ; nor for each one to force them to conform to his own wishes.']—So Basil also says of him : σχεδὸν γὰρ ταυτησὶ τῆς νῦν περιθρυλλουμένης ἀσεβείας τῆς κατὰ τὸ ἀνόμοιον λέγω, οὗτός ἐστιν ὅσαγε ἡμεῖς ἴσμεν ὁ πρῶτος τὰ σπέρματα παράσχων· αἴτιον δὲ τὸ σφόδρα βούλεσθαι ἀνατείνειν τῷ Σαβελλίῳ . . . ᾧ γε τοσοῦτον ἐξαρκοῦν δεῖξαι, ὅτι οὐ ταυτὸν τῷ ὑποκειμένῳ πατήρ καὶ υἱός, καὶ ταῦτα ἔχειν κατὰ τοῦ βλασφημοῦντος τὰ νικητήρια. [' For this one (Dionysius) is almost of the same impious sect which is now so much talked of, that (I mean) which asserts dissimilarity. So far as we know, he first furnished the seed. The ground of this was, his earnest desire to restrain Sabellius . . . to do which it would have sufficed to shew, that Father and Son are not the same in substance ; and this would have ensured the victory over the blasphemer']. All this is flat enough ; for on the ground that ὑποκείμενον is made the subject of the sentence, Sabellius might easily admit it, because he would concede, that some things might be said of the Son, which could not be said of the Father.— Again, Ep. 92, ὁ δέ, ἵνα πάνυ ἐναργῶς καὶ ἐκ τοῦ περίοντος κατακρατῇ, οὐχ ἑτερότητα μόνον τῶν ὑποστάσεων τίθεται, ἀλλὰ καὶ οὐσίας διαφοράν, καὶ δυνάμεως ὕφεσιν, καὶ δόξης παραλλαγήν. [' But he (Dionysius) that he might certainly and superabundantly get the better of his opponent, not only maintained a diversity of hypostasis, but also a difference of substance, and a diminution of power, and a diversity of glory.'] But all this, not even οὐσίας διαφοράν excluded, is contained or implied in the passages of Origen and Clement above cited.

enough, that he only wishes to preserve fully and truly the doctrine for a long time held by the clergy at Alexandria; and in
later times, the Arians often make their appeal to the views of
Dionysius.

On the whole, one may truly say that the *Alexandrine* views,
so far as they were concerned with the contest against Sabellianism, were *Arian* views. Plainly the Alexandrine fathers
misunderstood Sabellius. They designed to avoid all appearance of dividing that which was homogeneous in the Godhead;
but Sabellius, in fact, never affirmed nor taught this. Arius,
however, could think of nothing but division in a corporeal sense,
as applied to the Godhead.* In order, moreover, to hold fast
the subordination-theory, the Arian party of the clergy went so
far as to give up the original and divine *hypostasis* of the Logos;
so that even the very appearance of *homoousian μέρος*, i. e. *division* or *partition* in the Godhead, should be avoided.

In process of time these views (like to those of the Gnostics,
although the persons who held them were not conscious of this
and were opposed to Gnosticism), so unfolded themselves, that
the doctrine of the Trinity lost its true ground, and a suspicion
began at length to arise in the church, that such views would
lead back to Hellenism, i. e. polytheism. This roused up some,
who had originally been in the same Alexandrine School to
make opposition to Arianism; and by such were the usual ecclesiastical formulas respecting the doctrine of the Trinity
brought to nearly their present state.

We must not omit here a distinct consideration of a very interesting period of time. A brief historical view of it may be
thus presented.

In the Alexandrine Christology there were two elements
brought into connection with each other, without ever being
consolidated into one; viz., the *subordination* of the Son to the
Father; and the *Godhead* of the Son as hypostatic Logos.
When the theory of Noetus respecting *God revealed*, had at

---

* *Εἰ δὲ τό, Ἐξ αὐτοῦ, καὶ τό, Ἐκ τοῦ πατρὸς ἐξῆλθον καὶ ἥκω, ὡς, μέρος αὐτοῦ ὁμοούσιον, καὶ ὡς προβολὴ ὑπό τινων νοεῖται· σύνθετος ἔσται
ὁ πατήρ, καὶ διαίρετος, καὶ τρεπτός, καὶ σῶμα κατ᾽ αὐτούς·* Arius, in
Athanas. de Synod. 16. ['But if these words : *I came out from him,*
and *I come from the Father,* are considered by some as meaning a homoousian part of him, or an emanation; then, according to them, the
Father must be composite, and divisible, and mutable, and have a
body.']

length become unfolded fully into a Trinitarian doctrine, as it
did in the hands of Sabellius; and this, before the Alexandrine
School had developed a specific and defined doctrine of the
Trinity (for such was the case); the views of Sabellius occasioned a controversy in the Alexandrine School, which finally
separated the two elements above named. The Arian party,
in order to hold fast to the *subordination-theory*, let go the theory respecting the divine hypostasis of the Logos, in order that
they might go to a still farther remove from Sabellian equality
or identity. The Athanasian party, however, fearing that, if
the Son should have *divine* honours paid him and yet be reputed as of a substance different from that of the Father, there
would be an appearance of polytheism, elevated the hypostatic
Logos or Godhead in the Son to a most exalted rank, (as appears from the writings of all this party), even so as to introduce a
kind of equality as to substance among the persons of the Trinity. In order to accomplish this end, they left out of view the
subordination-theory as much as they could; but still they held
fast to separate personality, inasmuch as, in common with the
Arians, they were opposed to the views of Sabellius.

As Sabellius was desirous of making out an entire antithesis
to the Nazaraean views, so the Arians and Athanasians, who were
both opposed to him, stood, almost unconsciously, between Sabellius and the Nazaraeans. Both Arians and Athanasians
maintained, each party in their own way, that Sabellius, in order
to oppose the Nazarenes, had on the one hand done too much,
and on the other too little. But both of these parties sought in
vain for some established stand-point between Sabellius and the
Nazaraean sect. The Arians, continually divided among themselves, could unite at last only in an assumption, which left
nothing that was properly divine to Christ; and still, in order
to avoid being Nazaraeans, they actually verged toward the views
of the Docetæ. On the other hand the Athanasians, in as much as
they were not willing to give up the subordination-theory of the
old Alexandrian School, were compelled in various ways to
approximate near to Arianism; especially so because they
sought to avoid what they called the Sabellian *confounding** of
persons. In so doing they made a distinction between οὐσία and
ὑπόστασις as applied to the supreme Being himself; and yet

---

* Σύγχυσις; and particularly in Epiphanius, by way of ridicule, it
is named συναλοιφή [besmearing.]

they could never establish any metes and bounds for this distinction.   Consequently they were continually oscillating between approach to Tritheism, or else to Sabellianism ; as Basil himself acknowledges.*   The more the predicates of κοινόν and ἴδιον, in respect to the Godhead, were insisted on, the more did they approach to Tritheism ; most of all when the κοινόν was treated much in the way of the Nominalists ; for by this mode of proceeding, nothing at last but a unity of power and will was left, and even this unity was infringed upon by their views of generation.   On the other hand, the more the *internal hypostatic* existence was insisted on, the nearer they approached to Sabellianism.   One may even say, that those who interpreted the relation of unity to Trinity in the former way in the Athanasian formulas, are farther removed from those who interpreted it in the latter way, than these are from the Sabellians.

On the contrary, such oscillation on the Sabellian side cannot be shewn by any facts from history.   Indeed it would be difficult to shew how it could ever have arisen from the simple elements of Sabellianism, had this continued to flourish.   Whereas it follows from the very mode in which the doctrine of the church Symbols originated, that this could never come to a pure systematical doctrine of the Trinity.   For, not to speak of the first person which according to these Symbols is not like the other two, still the second and third persons, according to them, are not like to each other.   The hypostasis of the Logos as a *divine perfection* lies at the basis of the theory respecting the second person ; but not so of the third.   Moreover the second person, according to the theory of the Symbols, is produced from the first only by generation ; which is left wholly undefined, when one merely avers that it is not like any human generation. But the third person is said to proceed from the first in an indescribable manner (ἀρρήτως) ; which again one attempts to explain by tropical expressions ; but these, on nearer inspection, prove to be wholly incapable of making any definite limitation.

Hence the third person, notwithstanding protestations to the contrary and against any unequality, is undeniably represented to be inferior to the others. Hence too arises the great multitude of formulas, which bear merely the *negative* stamp of caution against some error.   All this shews that the Athanasian form of doctrine

* Epist. 185. 2.

arose much less from any definite and positive basis, than from
the effort to avoid the force of other assertions made by an opposing party, and to wind one's way through them. To the
Sabellian views we cannot refuse at least to yield our testimony, that they are the result of originality of thought and independence of mind.

ADDITIONAL REMARKS BY THE TRANSLATOR.

It appears from the implied and express approbation which
Dr. Schleiermacher gives to the sentiments of Sabellius as
above ascertained, that he accords substantially with his views.
But when I say this, the reader must call to mind, in order that
I may not be misunderstood, nor Dr. S. misinterpreted, that the
common opinion respecting Sabellianism has been shewn by the
investigation of Dr. S., at least he is himself fully persuaded
that it has been shewn, to be quite erroneous. The common
opinion makes Sabellianism very little if any thing better than
the doctrine of the Patripassians, which abolishes all distinction
of person (πρόσωπον) in the Godhead, and represents the Father and the Μονάς as in all respects one and the same ; and
also maintains, that the names Father, Son, and Spirit, are merely names of various modes of action, or of various developments
of powers, belonging to that Being who is ever and only one
and the same.

If Dr. S. is right in his conclusions respecting Sabellius, (and
it would be difficult to shew that he is not), then does the system of Sabellius differ in a very important respect from the
scheme of doctrine just mentioned. Sabellius did not hold
that Father, Son, and Holy Ghost are the names of mere powers or attributes, or mere developments of them. God, acting
as hypostasis, i. e. (so to speak) in a *personal* manner, as Father and as Son and as Spirit, was what he strenuously maintained. God acting in reference to the scheme of redemption,
first as Father in preparing for it, secondly as Son in making
atonement, and thirdly as Spirit by sanctifying the heart and
thus carrying the whole plan into execution, was what he appears most strictly to have maintained. At any rate, such is the
view of Dr. S. himself.

The question is not, then, whether Sabellius, according to

this corrected view of his sentiment believed, nor whether Dr. S. with him, believed, in the real and proper divinity of Father, Son, and Holy Ghost. Higher Trinitarians, in *this* sense, can be found in no place nor in any age of the church, than these distinguished individuals. That there is really and truly Father, Son, and Holy Ghost in the Godhead, which are not mere names of powers or attributes, nor of simple developments of them, but names that correspond to real developments of the Godhead in a hypostatical sense, is fully maintained by them. That God has developed himself in these *three* different ways, is what they believe to be taught in the Scriptures, and to be commended to our spiritual consciousness by the nature of our wants, woes, and sins. Hence a *Trinity*, and not a Duality, or a Pentade, or a Heptade, etc. All accusations of *confounding* the persons in the Trinity, are mere deductions of opponents from the principles thus laid down ; they are altogether rejected by the authors themselves of this opinion.

· Sabellius and Dr. S. maintain indeed, that the *Μονάς* or divine Being simply and in himself considered, is not the subject of hypostatic distinctions. These they consider as having commenced in time; i. e. when God, or the *Μονάς* manifested himself as Creator, when the Logos became incarnate in Christ ; and at all times when the Spirit of Grace has operated on the hearts of men. In their view, it is the *Μονάς* simply in each of those cases, who has developed himself in these diverse ways ; and this diversity of personal or hypostatic developments, constitutes in their view the *personality*, i. e. the different *persons*, of the Godhead. But nothing is farther from their design, than to confound these different manifestations of the Godhead, or to reduce the Trinity merely to one person. The Father is Father, and not Son nor Spirit ; the Son is Son, and not Father nor Spirit ; and so of the third person.

Nor do they at all admit that this development of the Godhead is something that manifests itself in a merely temporary way, and then returns to its former state ; they do not hold to a mere *πλατυνισμός* of the Divinity, which is followed after a lapse of time by contraction again. This the opponents of Sabellius incorrectly charged him with maintaining. The relations of Father, Son and Holy Spirit, once constituted, are (as he viewed them) enduring, and never will cease to exist. They have such a relation to the church, that as long as the redeemed shall live and be happy, so long the most distinguished glory of the economy of redemption, that of Father, Son and Spirit, will not cease to shine. The Trinity once actually constituted, the persons of the Godhead once really and fully subsisting, this new relation of the divinity, will and can never be changed.

Here then is *Trinity;* here are three eternal persons in one Godhead, eternal *a parte post;* here is Father and Son and Spirit, each really and truly divine; here are all the offices that the works of creation and providence, the redemption and sanctification and glorification of the church require; and Dr. S. asks with deep emotion, What more is demanded? What more is necessary? What more can further the interests of *practical piety*?

An extensive examination of this theory of Trinity will easily lead us to see, that the great difference between it and the ancient patristical one, is, that it does not allow the *substantial* (οὐσιωδής) derivation of the second and third persons as divine; nor does it, as the ancient theory did, acknowledge distinctions of a so-named *personal* nature, antecedent to the time of the creation. It differs from the predominant modern view of the Trinity, inasmuch as it rejects the idea of *personality* being bestowed on the second and third persons by the first, and makes personality itself to consist in the different manifestations of the *Μονάς* and its different ways of union with, and action in, created things.

The first thought that naturally suggests itself to the mind, in reflecting upon this view, leads to the question: How can *personality* arise in time, and not belong essentially and originally to the Godhead itself? How can the Divinity, who is immutable, assume an attitude so new as would be the taking to himself a threefold personality, which did not originally and essentially belong to him?

It is easy to see, that these questions must be solved by determining what *personality* means. By one method of defining it, we may represent the theory of Dr. S. as nearly absurd; at least it will appear at once to be contradictory to the nature of the Godhead, which is essentially immutable. By another, no formidable difficulties will, on this score, be found to militate against the views of this acute and distinguished writer.

What then is PERSONALITY *as applied to the Godhead?*

The great problem among most Trinitarians has been, so to define and limit personality, that it will not interfere with the essential unity of the Divine Nature; a problem which does not seem to have been solved to the satisfaction of all, by any one of the current definitions which have prevailed in modern systems of Theology.

I will not, for the sake of illustration, dwell here on the ancient modes of representing this subject, which have been so fully presented to view, in the introductory part of this essay. *Specific* and not numeric unity, was what the ancient fathers mostly maintained ; as is evident from the whole tenor of their illustrations which are drawn from material objects, and especially disclosed by those which are drawn from different and individual men, such as Paul, Peter, and John. The theoretical inconsistency of this with the real unity of God, has so forced itself on the minds of most of the distinguished theologians of modern times, that they have tacitly, although not professedly, abandoned the real doctrine of the Nicene Creed ; as has already been shown in the former part of the present disquisition.

Let us come down to the modern writers, then, who hold to a numerical unity of essence or substance in the Godhead, and represent *personality* as the only thing communicated by the first to the second and third persons of the Trinity. Our first inquiry of course is : How have they defined *personality?*

The shortest method in which I can illustrate this, is to produce the definitions themselves.

Melancthon : Persona est substantia *individua,* intelligens, incommunicabilis, *non sustenta in alia natura.*

Buddaeus : *Personae* voce suppositum intelligens denotatur. Per suppositum, autem, substantia singularis completa, incommunicabilis, *non aliunde sustentata,* intelligitur. . . Tres personae in essentia divina . . . tres subsistentiae incommunicabiles, individuae naturae, hac ipsa manente indivisibili, indigitantur.

Baumgarten : Person means a *suppositum* which is the ground of certain actions peculiar to itself.

Morus : Persona significat ens per se, quod intelligit, et cum intellectu agit.

Reinhard : Persona est individuum subsistentiae incompletae, per se libere agens, et divinarum perfectionum particeps.

Gerhard : Persona est substantia individua, intelligens, incommunicabilis, quae non sustentatur in alio, vel ab alio...Non est modus subsistendi, sed est substantia certo charactere sive subsistendi modo insignita.

Sohnius and Keckermann : Hypostasis est τρόπος ὑπάρξεως.

Zanchius : Persona est ipsa essentia divina, proprio subsistendi modo distincta.

Turretin : Vox *personae* proprie concreta est non abstracta ; quae, praeter formam quae est personalitas, subjectum etiam notat cum forma a qua denominatur.

Calvin : Subsistentia in essentia Dei, qua ad alios relata, proprietate incommunicabili distinguitur, [following Justin and Damascenus of ancient times.]

Leibnitz, at the request of Loeffler, who wished to write in opposition to some English Antitrinitarians, sent him the following definition : "Several persons in one absolute substance numerically the same, signify several particular intelligent substances essentially related." Afterwards he changed the latter part of this by substituting : " relative incommunicable modes of subsistence." A third time he added, in the way of explanation : "We must say that there are *relations* in the divine substance which distinguish the PERSONS ; since these persons cannot be absolute substances. But we must aver, too, that these relations are *substantial*. . . . We must say moreover, that these three persons are not as absolute substances as the whole."

These are merely specimens of what might be gathered, on all sides, from the leading books in theology.

Of some of these definitions, i. e. those of Melancthon and Morus and some others, it might be said, that the word *person* as applied to three different men, could scarcely receive a more full and complete sense, than is given it in respect to the Godhead. Tritheism in *theory* seems to be the unavoidable deduction from such definitions. Of others it may be said, that they are no definitions, for they contain nothing positive or discretive. The definitions of Reinhard and Leibnitz represent the substance of the person in the Godhead as *incomplete*. But what idea can the human mind attach to such a definition of personality as this ? What is that which is a divine attribute or property, and yet is *incomplete ?*

Other definitions, and indeed most of all the definitions, represent personality as *incommunicable*. How then could the Son and Spirit have an *incommunicable* attribute *communicated* to them ?

The majority of those who undertake to define personality, represent person as a being or subsistence *who is not sustained or does not subsist in or by another*. Now if the Father, as most of these theologians hold, *communicates* personality to the Son and Spirit, how can the Son and Spirit be *persons* that do not subsist *in* or *by* another? If the Father is the *fons* or *principium*, the πηγή or αἰτία, of the personality of the Son and Spirit, then how is it that the persons of the Son and Spirit do not subsist *by* him? And if they depend on him for personality, (which is virtually maintained by the patristic and expressly by the modern theory of the Trinity), then how can their personality be conceived of as not existing *in* and *by* him? To avoid this difficulty we must say, that personality being once communicated to the Son and Spirit, it then becomes an independent attribute. But in this way the difficulty cannot be removed, for, first, the same writers do most of them declare, that personality is *incommunicable;* and secondly, it is not within the power of the human mind even to conceive of a being that is independent as to any attributes, so long as that attribute has been bestowed by another, and is not self-existent.

Much easier can I stop where Hilary does, and pour out my feelings in language like his, than I can adopt any of these definitions; with the exception that those of Baumgarten and Calvin in a *modified* sense, might be admitted without much danger, because they contain so little that is *positive.*

The truth once fully admitted (which all these theologians do admit), that there is a *numerical unity* of substance in the Godhead, and a numerical unity of all the attributes essential to Godhead in the *Μονάς*, it is beyond any intellectual power that I possess, to make out an intelligible and *consistent* proposition, from any of the more usual definitions of *person* in the Godhead.

Nothing can be more certain, than that *personality* cannot be applied to the Godhead in the same sense as it is to men, without verging towards Tritheism. In this, all intelligent Trinitarians of the present day, I believe, are agreed. Whatever personality is then, it is not such as that of three distinct and several persons among men who have merely a homogeneous nature, while they have distinct and individual substances, wills, affections, etc. A numerical unity of substance in the Godhead, is now almost universally conceded; and this necessarily excludes such personality as exists among different men.

But how is it with the divine *attributes,* the essential and moral attributes of the Godhead? I answer, that these also belong of course to the numerically one essence or substance of the Godhead. So says Turretin, expressly and fully, Quaest. XXVII. § 5; and so say most others. Infinite power, wisdom, justice, benevolence, etc., all belong to the *Μονάς*, i. e. to God in his simple unity. Indeed if this be not the case, then the *Μονάς* cannot be really and truly God; for how can there be a God without the attributes essential to Godhead?

In fact, the leading theologians, when they come to treat of the essential divine *attributes*, do not distinguish them from the divine *essence*. Thus Gerhard : " Those declarations in which God is called life itself, light, goodness, etc., prove the *entire identity* (omnimodam identitatem) of divine attributes with divine substance." Vol. I. p. 108. So Turretin : "The attributes of God *can not differ in reality* (non possunt realiter differre) from the essence ;" Tom. I. p. 206. It is only in our modes of conception, definition, and reasoning, that a separation is to be made between attribute and substance; at least this is so, if we are to listen to the declarations of leading theologians in respect to this subject.

If this statement be correct, or if it be substantially so, then we may draw from it what estimate we should put on the reasoning of those who make *personality* in the Godhead to involve the idea of three *separate* consciousnesses, wills, affections, etc. Can a *spiritual* being, i. e. can the *Μονάς*, be even supposed to exist without a consciousness, will, affections, etc. ? Does not his *moral* character, do not his moral attributes, consist essentially in these? And if these are not, as theologians aver, in reality to be distinguished from the *substance* or *essence* of the Godhead; and if this substance (as all agree) is *numerically one ;* then how are we to make out three separate wills, affections, etc. ? Or is it that the *Μονάς* is God, without any will or affections? Or if they belong to him, then does the Father as one person have a separate will, and the Son and Spirit as second and third persons have each a separate will? And are we, in this way of reasoning, to make out *four* separate consciousnesses, affections, etc., in the Godhead? What is all this in reality, but going back to an absolute *plurality* in the Godhead, and maintaining nothing in effect but mere *specific* unity?

To say that declarations like those in John and Paul, viz. that *the Logos created all things,* and that *God made the world by his Son,* must prove a *distinct* will of Son and Father, amounts to the same thing as to say, that they must prove the existence of distinct essential attributes. In the like way the Arians say, that the declaration of John, *and the Logos was* WITH *God,* proves that he could not be the same as God, but must be a distinct and different being; else how could he be *with* him? But here one is tempted to exclaim: When shall we come fully to learn, that in speaking of the Godhead as it is in itself, human language (as now formed, and indeed in any way in which it could be formed), must be altogether inadequate to a full and exact description? When distinctions in the Godhead itself are once admitted, and distinctions that pertain to an *intelligent rational* nature, in what other way can we speak and write respecting them, than the biblical writers have done? I know of none. The imperfection of human language forbids it. And it would seem to be quite as rational and scriptural to maintain that God is *limited in his presence* and is *local*, because the Scripture represents him as *ascending* and *descending*, as it would to maintain three *separate* wills, affections, etc., of the Trinity, because God is Father, Son, and Holy Ghost. There is a reason or ground in his very being, for his developments as Trinity; else they would not be made. These developments necessarily pre-suppose some distinctions belonging to his nature; but that these amount to *separate* consciousnesses, wills, affections, etc., would be a perilous position to assume. Perilous; because when once assumed, *theoretical* tritheism at least becomes logically inevitable. A man may contradict and disclaim this, I well know, in words; and he may sincerely and truly reject it in *intention;* but the inevitable *logical* result of his position, must be theoretical Tritheism? What more distinctive mark is there of three different persons among men, and in a human sense, than that they have separate consciousnesses, wills, and affections?

Perilous; because it assumes the position, that we know enough concerning the nature of the distinctions in the Godhead, thus to predicate of it what amounts to an essential part of distinctive individuality among men. Can we deliberately take and endeavour to maintain, such a position as this?

What God has done in developing himself we know from Scripture. That a distinction is necessarily implied by these developments, from the very structure of our minds we cannot avoid admitting. But to extend this in such a way as to make out a *metaphysical* definition of persons in the Godhead, (which of course must imply a definite knowledge of the particular and distinctive nature of *person* in it), seems to me to be treading on forbidden ground. Is it not advancing beyond the boundaries of human knowledge?

I can see no contradiction, no absurdity, nothing even incongruous, in the supposition, that the divine nature has manifested itself as Father, Son, and Holy Ghost, while its essence and essential attributes are and have always been numerically one and the same ; for that they are and have been so, all the leading Trinitarians agree. Nor is it within the compass of any effort that my mind can make, to conceive how numerical *sameness* of substance and attribute, is compatible with distinct consciousnesses, wills, and affections? What are these last but *essential* attributes of the *Μονάς* himself? And if so, how can these very same attributes be numerically three? If the Bible asserts this, then I will yield at once ; because I shall then take it for granted, that my darkened and feeble understanding is the source of my difficulty. But if the Bible (as I verily believe) does neither assert nor imply it ; then it must be shewn to be possible and consistent, before it can be entitled to our faith.

It would seem, that after all which has been done to shew the high and spiritual and incomprehensible nature of the divine Being, and the inadequacy of human language fully to describe him as he is ; we are yet called to argue in order to satisfy the minds of some, that such expressions as *the Logos being* WITH *God*, and *God's creating the worlds by his Son*, are not to be taken and reasoned from, just as if they had been employed in respect to known individual and entirely separate beings. If God communicates his *whole substance* to the Son, as the Nicenians, and most of the Trinitarians in modern times (who treat of and believe in eternal generation) actually maintain, how then can there be *separate* consciousnesses, wills, and affections? Or are we to suppose these to exist independently of the substance or essence of the Godhead?

In a word, it is only when we come adequately to learn the imperfection of human language, and the difficulties which attend communications by it respecting distinctions in the Godhead, that we shall be satisfied how inconclusive all reasoning must be, which is founded on deductions drawn from the language of Scripture, when we interpret that language just as if it had relation to finite intelligencies who are altogether distinct and separate beings. What cannot be proved, if we are to take such liberties as these? Surely the Anthropomorphites are not to be confuted, when such a position is taken. It seems to be quite as cogent an argument to say, that when hands, eyes, feet, heart, etc., are ascribed to the Godhead by the sacred

writers, they can mean nothing, unless we give to their language
a literal, or at least a *quasi*-literal, meaning; as it is to say that
the being with God, and *God's creating the worlds by his Son*
can mean nothing, unless it have a literal, or *quasi*-literal, meaning.   In the first case, we reject the exegesis of the Anthropomorphites, because we consider it absolutely certain that God
is a simple spiritual being.   In the second, then, the admitted
numerical unity and sameness of substance and essential attributes in the Godhead, would seem to stand arrayed with equal
strength against a supposition which would make three numerically distinct essential attributes ; for such must be three distinct
and separate consciousnesses, wills, and affections.   At least, it is
not in the power of my mind to conceive that these two things,
when put together, do not prove an absolute contradiction.   Still
if God's word asserts such a fact, I would admit its truth; not
because I can say with Tertullian : Credo quia impossibile est;
but because I can truly say, that God's word is rather to be
trusted than my own darkened reason.   I may commit mistakes;
that does not.

A *modified* sense then of such passages as John 1: 1 and
Heb. 1: 1, 2, is to be received; which indeed must be the case
in regard to nearly every possible assertion, that has respect to
the divine nature.   When I say *God knows*, I surely do not
mean that he studies, or makes effort to acquire knowledge;
that he tasks his memory to recal it, and his judgment to con-
solidate it.   When I say that *he is mighty*, I do not mean that
he has fully developed bones and muscles and sinews, and great
versatility of physical system, and robust health, and that he
taxes all these when he puts forth his strength.   And so of all
his other natural and intellectual attributes ; the *modus existendi* or *modus exercendi* must, in our conceptions, be abstracted
from all our declarations respecting them.   There is a real
truth at the bottom of all; but the *modal* part we must leave
undefined and unasserted.

Why is not this equally true now of the *distinction* in the
Godhead?   Granting the fact that there is one, (as the texts
under consideration and others like them seem necessarily to
imply), why should we reason from the *mode* of this distinction
just as if it concerned human or angelic persons, who are in all
essential respects entirely distinct and different beings?   Of
these we do not and cannot predicate *numerical* unity of sub-

stance, but merely *specific* unity. Of the Godhead we must all unite in predicating *numerical unity of substance and essential attribute.* We are foreclosed then against an exposition of such texts MORE HUMANO. And when this mode of exposition is given up, all the deductions from it which would make three separate consciousnesses, wills, and affections in the Trinity, are inapposite and incongruous. For more than this we could not deduce, if we interpreted these texts altogether in such a way as if they applied to *person* as it exists among men.

But we have further questions still to ask, in respect to the great subject before us. It is expedient that our views of *personality* should be still more fully developed. For this purpose, and in order that we may view the subject in another attitude, I would again ask:

What is *personality?* Is it *essence* or *attribute?* Not the first, one might answer; for essence in the Godhead is numerically one and the same. Not the second in an *essential* and *fundamental* sense; because, as we have seen, all the attributes that are of this description, belong to the one substance or essence of the Godhead. ' But if *personality* be neither substance nor attribute,' some one may exclaim, ' then can it be any thing, or have any existence at all?'

My answer is, that this last question is founded on some misconception, or at least imperfect conception, of the positions just laid down. God may have properties or attributes, which we do not consider as *exclusively* peculiar to Deity, and which do not of themselves distinguish him from created beings. Thus we may say, his nature is *spiritual;* and so is that of angels, and of that part of man which is made in his image. Such attributes, from their very nature, do hardly admit of *gradation* in the common sense. Other attributes he has, some of which are distinctive or peculiar to him principally in respect to degree; such as wisdom, justice, goodness, etc. Others he has, which are entirely and altogether peculiar and appropriate; such as self-existence, eternity absolute, immutability, etc. Now personality cannot be put among these two latter classes of attributes; because they belong, as nearly all agree, to the *Μονάς* or essential substance of the Godhead. If then personality belong to the Godhead, it must belong to it, as it would seem, not as *essential* to divinity, but as in some respect or other *modal,* or at least as an attribute which holds (in a logical arrangement) a secondary and not a primary place.

So Turretin himself concedes: Persona differre dicetur ab essentia, non *realiter*, id est *essentialiter*, ut res et res; sed *modaliter*, ut *modus a re;* Quaest. 27. § 3.

It is possible then, that there may be in the Godhead some distinctions which do not consist in a difference of substance; and which moreover do not consist in the high and peculiar and exclusive attributes of that substance which constitute Godhead, but which are, as Turretin avers, *modal;* or they may be of such a nature that we have no language to describe them, and no present ability even to comprehend them if they could be described. Can it be strange that the uncreated and self-existent Godhead should have some such properties as these? The impossibility or even the improbability of this, no man is able to prove.

There may then be distinctions in the Godhead, that lie beyond all our present logical and metaphysical conception or power of definition; distinctions which are co-eternal with the Godhead itself; and which, though neither essence or essential attribute in the highest sense, may still have an existence that is real and true.

Any theory which derives the essence of Godhead in the Son and Spirit from the first person, seems to strike at the root of *equal power and glory* among the three persons of the Godhead, and moreover virtually to deny the *self-existence* and *independence* of the second and third persons. Any theory which makes the *modus existendi,* i. e. the subsistence or personality, of the Son and Spirit to depend on the first person and to be bestowed by him, in like manner virtually denies the self-existence and independence of the second and third persons; for how can they be of that self-existent substance which is numerically one and the same with that of the Father, and yet this substance have no *modus subsistendi* of its own? How can substance exist without a mode of existing? Or if you say, that 'there are different and many modes of subsisting belonging to the same essence, and that personality is only one of them; or that other modes of existence may be necessarily attached to the divine substance which is one, but that *this* may be something which is *bestowed* on the second and third persons, or *imparted* to them;' then I have several difficulties to suggest which seem to lie in the way of such a supposition. (1) If the Father, Son, and Spirit are in *all* respects equal in power and glory, how can the Father have a power to bestow personality

181

on the Son and Spirit, when they have no such power in reference to him? (2) If the Father has a personality bestowed by none, this must be the result of the substance which he possesses, and a modification of it which is inseparably connected with its very nature ; but inasmuch as the Son and Spirit possess numerically the *same* substance, how is it that this same modification of personality, does not attach also to the divine substance which is in them?

Again ; we have already seen above, that the theory of personality, which represents three intelligent beings, distinct in such a full sense that each has his own individual consciousness, will, affections, purposes, etc., must amount to theoretical Tritheism ; for such are the principal distinctions that exist between three individual men. They are ὁμοούσιοι, *of a homogeneous nature*, i. e. of the same *generic*, or (if you prefer it) of the same *specific* nature. What then makes Peter, Paul, and John *three*, and not one? It is this very thing, viz., that the substance belonging to each, although homogeneous, is separate in its individual existence ; for the substance of Paul in no sense belongs appropriately to Peter or John, and so of the others. Now it is the connection of these three individual and separately existing substances with three distinct and separately existing souls or minds, wills, affections, sympathies, etc., each of which belongs in no appropriate sense to the other, that constitutes three distinct and different persons. But if one is disposed to turn off his mind from these circumstances of distinction or distinctiveness, and to fix his attention wholly upon the *homogeneousness* of Peter and Paul and John, either as to substance or essential attributes, then he may say that they are *one ;* and he may truly say, that logically and abstractedly considered, *they are of one and the same nature.* And so were the divinities of Greece and Rome. But when Jehovah proclaimed himself of old to be ONE JEHOVAH, in distinction from and in opposition to all the multitude of gods among the heathen ; and when in later times the one God, and the only living and true God, is proclaimed with equal solemnity, we seem to be no longer at liberty to form any theory of the divine Unity which will reduce the Godhead to a mere *unity of homogeneousness ;* for if this be all that is meant by *unity*, then there might be one God or thirty thousand gods, and the unity remain still the same.

To all that has been already said on this topic, we may add, that as the Godhead is not material, so its substance, (speaking

in the way of common parlance) is *spiritual*, and not material.
Spiritual substance then must in and of itself, by absolute necessity, be connected with or give rise to consciousness, will,
affections, etc., for these are the essential and inseparable properties of such substance. How then can the same identical
spiritual substance, with its same identical spiritual and essential properties, be the ground of three distinct and separate consciousnesses, affections, wills, etc., *more humano?* The supposition appears to be altogether subversive of the identity of spiritual substance and of numerical unity. Three distinct and
separately conscious intelligent beings, are not the less three because they are spiritual. In our own case, indeed, there is individuality or separate existence both of body and soul ; and so
the ground of separation or distinction is (as we may say) en-
larged. In the divine Being, *body* is out of question ; but while
his spiritual substance is numerically one and the same, how
what is numerically one and the same can yet have three distinct and separate sets (sit venia verbo) of attributes, all of
which again are identical in their nature, it would be difficult,
I believe, for any efforts of reason or philosophy to clear up.
And if it can be shewn that there are three such distinct wills,
etc., then does it follow with entire certainty, that personality in
the Godhead is like that in men, the material part of man only
being excepted. We must go back again of course, in such a
case, to the *specific* unity of the fathers ; a unity which in itself
does not forbid the existence of three or of three million persons
in the Godhead.

Person, then, cannot be such a division in the Godhead, as
makes separate and merely co-ordinate consciousnesses, wills,
affections, etc. ; for this brings us to admit a principle that would
consist with all the polytheism which we can imagine to exist,
or to be possible, among divine natures ; or else it reduces us
to make the impossible supposition, that one and the same identical spiritual substance has three distinct sets of attributes,
which in all respects are again one and the same with each
other, or at least exactly alike.

In fact, any definition of personality in the Godhead which
represents person to be *ens per se* or *substantia individua non
sustentata in alia natura*, as most of the definitions above given
do either assert or imply, seems plainly and substantially to infringe on the idea that there is but one and numerically the

183

same substance in the Godhead. I am not able to see why it does not clearly involve a logical contradiction.

One and all of these modes of Trinitarianism then, it would seem, must be abandoned by the considerate believer of the present day. Protestants have always professed themselves at liberty to pass in review Creeds and Confessions and Systems, venerable for antiquity, and long defended by eloquence and learning and even force. But let them not abuse this sacred privilege. Let them not reject any thing merely because it is old, or because it has been defended by arguments that will not abide the day of scrutiny; nor receive any thing merely because it is new and striking, and looks fair, and promises to relieve some of the difficulties that accompanied the older doctrine.

Must we come, then, if we abandon the idea of a derived Godhead, derived either as to substance or subsistence,—must we, in order to be Trinitarians at all, come to the theory of Dr. S. or substantially to that which Sabellius in reality embraced, but which in many important respects differed from what has usually been called Sabellianism? For myself at least I can freely say, that I do not feel compelled to do this; nor do I feel inclined to receive Sabellianism as the complete and proper representation of the Scripture doctrine.

Dr. S. makes the personality of the Trinity to consist in the hypostatic developments of the Godhead as Creator and Legislator, as Redeemer and as Sanctifier; and thus makes the doctrine of the Trinity to depend on the manifestations of God in respect to the great work of redemption. That God, as Father, Son, and Spirit, has thus manifested himself; and that this is the great and peculiar manifestation of the Trinity, and unspeakably the most glorious one, I have no doubt. So far as he goes in this direction, I can cheerfully accompany him. But I am not willing to stop where he does, nor to conclude that a distinction like that of Father and Son and Spirit in the Godhead, has commenced altogether in time, and has no foundation in the *Μονάς* itself of the divine being.

Let us examine and try the principles in question. God from eternity possessed those attributes which fitted him to be creator and governor of the universe. There was a foundation for this (so to speak) in the very nature of his being; or, in other words, the attributes of creatorship and lordship existed in him, before the creation of the world rational and irrational. Yet

God, before creation, was actually and in fact neither creator
nor lord. It was only when the world had been created and
was governed that he became actual creator and lord.

Now this fact argues no change in him; as Origen rashly
supposed, and therefore assumed the eternity of the world, and
the eternally and unceasingly continued generation of the Son.
It merely showed that the attributes which he possessed were
exercised in the way of development or action.

If now there had been no foundation in the divine nature itself for creatorship and lordship, then how is it possible to suppose that the divine Being would ever have been actually creator and lord? This would be to suppose an effect without an
adequate cause.

All this I take to be so plain, that it needs only to be presented to the mind in order to be admitted. But if this be so,
then we have something of the like nature to say as to distinctions in the Godhead, which were the ground of its manifestations as Father, Son, and Holy Ghost.

The fact that these manifestations have been made, Dr. S.
most amply and fully admits. I ask then, Were they made
without some corresponding *modus existendi* or property of the
Godhead, or in consequence of one? If the first, then is there
an effect without an adequate cause; if the second, then the
existence of the Trinity does not begin with the developments
themselves of *God revealed*.

We come by necessity, then, at least so it seems to me, to
the position, that there was in the Godhead, antecedent to creation and redemption, something which was the foundation of all
the developments made in the same. Was this in the substance
or in the attributes of the Godhead? It is easy to ask this question; but where can we apply for any satisfactory answer?
The Bible does not inform us. The definitions and distinctions
of the Schoolmen or of later Theologians, give us no adequate
information respecting it. According to what has been said
above, we may incline to say that *distinction* must be *attribute;*
yet as its specific nature lies beyond the boundaries of human
knowledge, how can we feel very certain respecting any conclusions relative to this point? If Dr. S.'s view of the doctrine
of the Trinity be correct and true, then what can be the meaning of the assertions, that "God made the worlds by his Son;"
that "the Logos was in the beginning with God, and was God;"
that "by him all things were created that are in heaven and on

earth?"   Or that."God created all things by Jesus Christ?" if
indeed this last reading be authentic.   Can a plain, sensible, un-
sophisticated reader of the Bible feel, when he reads such declarations, that there was no distinction in the Godhead before
the creation of the world, and therefore from eternity?   I am
unable to see how he can ; any more than he can believe that
the attributes of creatorship and lordship did not belong essentially to God, before the actual work of creation.

Instead then of making the personality of the Godhead to
arise in time, I would merely say, that *it was manifested or developed to creatures in time.*   It is true that the manifestation
is that with which faith and piety are most essentially concerned.
But it is equally true, that such is the case in regard to all the
divine attributes.   It would seem to be true, that he who hum-
bly and fully receives the doctrine, that the Trinity is *God revealed* only, does substantially admit the most *practical* part of
the doctrine.   But it seems to me equally true, that plain and
inevitable deduction, in the way of reasoning, leads us to the
belief, that God must be *in seipso* what he has revealed himself
to be.

Trinity, then, as it appears to my humble apprehension, does
not consist in or arise from the dependence of one person in the
Godhead upon another, or the communication of substance or
subsistence of one to the others, but in something which belongs
to the *Μονάς* itself, and which laid the foundation for all the
manifestations of the Father and Son and Spirit.   Who can disprove such a position?   That is impossible.   Who, that allows
numerical unity of substance in the Godhead and still believes
in Father and Son and Holy Ghost, can refuse to acknowledge
that either some modification or some property of the divine
nature, in respect to substance or attribute, led to manifestation
of the Godhead in what we call a *personal* manner?

Here then is TRINITY; and Trinity in its essential nature,
from eternity to eternity.   If you ask how this modification or
property or distinction can be described, as it originally existed
in the Godhead, my answer is, that we have no data by which
we can make out a description.   The fact of some distinction
in the divine nature, which laid the foundation for the manifestations of the Trinity in the economy of redemption, we may
and should fully admit.   But to describe this seems not to be
given to created intelligences who are of yesterday.   And if,
in like manner, a challenge should be made, to tell what is self-

existence, or independence, or ubiquity in the Godhead, all the answer we could make would be, to say *what they are not.* The attribute of *Trinity* does not stand alone, in regard to the *modus* being beyond our comprehension.

I content myself now with these plain and simple facts. I reject, therefore, all attempts to define personality in a metaphysical way; for they all imply the possession of a knowledge which we do not possess. I receive the simple fact and doctrine of a Trinity on the same ground that I do that respecting the incarnation, or God manifest in the flesh. The incarnation is a fact upon which my hopes of salvation are built; and yet I can make no approach to an explanation of the manner of it. Why then can we not, and should we not, treat the doctrine of the Trinity in the like way? When men come to believe that such is the best method of managing this difficult subject, the pious wish of Calvin may come nearer being realized : "Utinam sepulta essent *nomina*, constaret modo haec inter omnes fides, PATREM ET FILIUM ET SPIRITUM SANCTUM ESSE UNUM DEUM." Inst. I. 13, 5.

Entirely as I accord with the pious and liberal feeling which gave birth to this sentiment of Calvin, yet I cannot think it best, on the whole, that the use of the word *person* should be given up, in relation to the Godhead. Against attaching a merely human sense to the word, I have already protested at large.— Against nearly all the definitions that I have seen, I feel conclusive objections, because, when strictly examined, they appear to infringe upon numerical unity of substance or of essential attributes in the Godhead. But the failure to define in an unexceptionable manner; or misconception even as to the meaning of a word, by many individuals; will not always and of course prove that the word should be thrown away. I am fully aware; that the church has suffered a great deal of agitation in consequence of the word ὑπόστασις, *persona*, or *person*, being applied to the divine being. Thousands of times it has been assailed with the accusation that it makes a *plurality* in the Godhead ; and all the disclaimers in respect to this, which have been made by Trinitarians, have not seemed as yet to appease their antagonists. The accusation of *plurality* is still re-echoed down to the present hour ; and it ever will be so, until Trinitarians will cease to give metaphysical definitions of personality in the Godhead, which are merely copies taken from ideas respecting created, intelligent, separate beings. There is none of all such definitions, provided they contain any thing *positive*, to which an acute and distinguished mind may not make the objection, that, understood in their plain and obvious sense, they infringe upon the numerical unity of substance and attribute in the Godhead.

'Why not dismiss a word then, which has been so often abused by its friends, as well as its enemies?' Excellent brethren in the ministry I know, who are ready to say at once : 'Dismiss it ; for peace and conscience' sake, dismiss it altogether. The time never will come, when men will not cease to abuse it ; nor when a definition of it can be made out, which is intelligible and instructive, and at the same time consistent with the unity of the Godhead.'

I feel the full force of these considerations ; and I have sometimes almost been led strongly to wish, that the word had never come into use among Christians ; as it is a stranger (at least in the sense of modern usage) to the Scriptures. This being the case, the churches can never be held to the use of it, as a matter *essential* to sound sentiment or right faith. Yet after all the difficulties which lie in the way, I am not persuaded that the word can *now* be dismissed from our theological vocabulary. When the Father is represented as sending his Son into the world, in order to redeem it, and the Son as saying, 'Lo I come, my God, to do thy will ;' when God sends his Spirit, and pours out his Spirit ; when *I, thou, he,* are employed with verbs, etc., designating purposes, actions, feelings, etc., of Father, Son, and Spirit ; when we acknowledge that there are works or developments appropriate to each ; in what way are we to designate the distinctions which these things and modes of representation seem to imply, if not by the use of the word *person ?* Let any one who acknowledges the fact of such distinctions, make the effort to designate them conveniently, and yet avoid the use of the word *person,* and he will find himself embarrassed. This may be, and probably is, because he has been accustomed to think and speak in this way. Indeed this cannot be otherwise ; inasmuch as the Bible does not employ *person* at all in the modern sense, in reference to the Godhead. It was ecclesiastical dispute which first introduced the word.

Thus much, however, I would cheerfully concede to those respected brethren who feel difficulties about employing the word *person,* viz., that if it never had been used, and the question were now to be decided whether it should be *introduced,* I should feel altogether disposed to abide by simple *scriptural* usage, and not employ a term which the sacred writers did not think proper or omitted to employ.

Still, one may in like manner say, that the Bible no where employs the word *Trinity ;* and therefore we should reject it. But the rejection of it would occasion much circumlocution as matters now are in the church ; and the same would be the case, if the word *person* should he laid aside.

Those only are to be complained of, who speak of the God-head in a *polytheistic* manner, while they assert themselves to be *monotheists*. If I use the word *person*, yet tell my readers that I do not employ it merely *more humano*, but that I use it as a convenient term in order to designate a distinction in the God-head, which has been the ground of actions and words that seem to be represented in a personal manner—but still a distinc-tion beyond the reach of human power to comprehend or define as to its particular mode or specific properties—then the fault is their own if they abuse it, and accuse me of polytheism. If I tell them that I no more think of applying the word *person* to the Godhead, in its original and literal sense, than I think of literally interpreting the assertion that God has hands and feet and eyes and ears ; that he ascended and descended ; or that he is grieved, that he repents, that he laughs, or that he weeps ; then the fault is their own, if they insist on my polytheism. Did not the Anthropomorphites, and do not the Swedenborgians, make the like use of all tropical descriptions of the Godhead, contained in the Bible, and contend that they are to be *liter-ally* understood ? And must we demand that the use of them should be superseded on this account ?

Still, although for the reasons stated I would not drop the use of the word *person*, yet I would protest against the license which is often taken in speaking of the persons of the God-head. When authors speak of their eternal and mutual society and converse together ; of their taking counsel together and deliberating, just as if an effort were necessary in order to har-monize them, or to bring them to one and the same conclusion, or to be of one and the same mind, or in order to cast light upon what it may be proper for them to do ; when they tell us of one person entering into covenant with another simply as divine, and before the foundation of the world ; of one divine person com-manding, and another simply as divine obeying ; all this and much more of the same nature, so long as it is indulged in, will continue to bring upon Trinitarians the reproach of Polytheism ;

and I had almost said, that the reproach is not destitute of at least a semblance of justice. It is indeed steering fearfully close to the shoals of polytheism, familiarly to employ such language as this. I do not accuse the *design*. Let any one look around for a moment on the men who have indulged at great length in such modes of representation, and he will at once perceive the injustice of charging them with designed Tritheism. In heart and purpose they were strenuous advocates for the unity of God.

But let the considerate believer in the awful nature of the Godhead as revealed in the gospel, remember well that " Hear O Israel! Jehovah our God is ONE JEHOVAH," was the sublime and glorious truth that was the corner-stone and basis of the ancient church ; and that the Gospel has revealed nothing to shake or remove this foundation. To us still there is but one God ; although we know, what most of the ancient Jews do not appear to have well understood, that he exists in Father, Son, and Holy Ghost. But he is not the less one on this account. All representations of him, then, which are *extra-scriptural*, and which have a tendency to obscure, or render dubious or uncertain, the doctrine of the divine unity, however well intended, are greatly to be regretted. They are productive of two bad effects ; the one that they confuse the mind of the more simple and unenlightened believer ; the other, that they open wide the mouths of gainsayers. Where the Bible leads the way in teaching any truth, or in the use of any expressions which may seem to be obnoxious to the like objections, I would follow on after it, be the consequences what they may ; for God knows better than we do what ought to be taught, and how it should be taught. But if any one by his own gratuitous modes of representation, makes to stumble or misleads the more simple, and opens wide the mouth of adversaries, let him look well to the day of account for such a proceeding ; more especially when the Bible has actually treated of the same subject, and pointed out another method of speaking with respect to it.

I know well that the advocates for those unrestrained methods of speech, which naturally represent the distinction of persons in the Godhead as quite analogous to that which exists among men, appeal to the Bible in order to justify themselves. But so did Justin Martyr, Athenagoras, Tatian, Tertullian, and Hippolytus, who all held to a λόγος ἐνδιάθετος and προφορικός ; the first of which was God's internal reason or intelligence which

he possessed from eternity ; and the second was the Logos first
spoken into hypostatic or individual personal being, when God
said, Let there be light.   The Nicene Council and their advocates appealed to the Scripture, to confirm the *derived* nature
of the Son and Spirit.   The leading modern Trinitarians appeal to the Scripture in order to prove *derived personality ;*
although, on this particular point, I have rarely found them ven-
turing such an appeal, choosing rather, as it would seem, to sub-
mit the matter to the arbitrament of metaphysics.   The Arians appealed with great confidence to the Scriptures, in behalf
of their views; and so have Unitarians of all ages.   It is not the
appeal itself, then, which is to move us.   It is our duty to examine whether the appeal is well grounded in the laws and
principles of exegesis.

It is impossible for me, consistently with the limits prescribed
to this essay, to go at length into the examination of this subject.
A few hints are all that can now be submitted to the reader.

I regard it as a point *exegetically* certain, that all the representations in Scripture of the Father's commanding the Son,
covenanting with the Son [where is this?], sending the Son into the world, anointing him to be King, begetting him, giving
him to have life in himself, and all and singular of the like declarations, either refer to the Messiah, the θεάνθρωπος, the
Logos incarnate, in the way of prediction and anticipation, or
else in the way of history and as a statement of simple facts.
I am fully of the opinion that this can be made out in an unanswerable manner, if the laws of language, and not the assertions
of theological Symbols, are to be followed.   I appeal to one
simple consideration, which must go far in the mind of the sober and thinking reader, and ask : Why has not the Scripture
represented God the Father as addressing the Spirit or Holy
Ghost, as well as the Son; inasmuch as he sends the Spirit, and
the Spirit is said by the Creeds to proceed from him in a metaphysical or physiological manner ?   Is the third person in the
Trinity less important—less conspicuous even in the great work
of redemption—than the second ?   Is he less distinct as a person, so far as the divine nature is concerned?   Why then is not
the Father represented as conferring with him, and covenanting
with him, and consulting with him, and doing other things of the
like nature, which we are told he does in respect to the Son ?
Only one answer that will satisfy the mind, it seems to me, can
be given to this question; which is, that all those transactions

just referred to, concern the *theanthropic* person of the Son, and do not relate to him as Logos only. John, the only writer of the New Testament that gives us a view of the Logos or antecedent divine nature of the Son, does not even aver that he was *sent ;* but simply states that " he became flesh and dwelt among us ;" and then it was, that he ' beheld his glory, the glory of the only-begotten of the Father, full of grace and truth.'

And when the Son himself prays the Father that he may return to him and have that " glory which he had with him before the world was," although I think this and such passages fatal to the views of Dr. Schleiermacher, still I do not feel any embarrassment in my views as to the point before us. The composite *theanthropic* person of the Saviour could speak of itself, in respect to either nature. If one says that Abraham is *dead*, we understand him of course to mean, that his mortal part is dead. Again, if one says that Abraham is *alive*, we understand him to mean that his immortal part still lives. So when Jesus is said to have ' increased in wisdom, and stature, and in favour with God and man,' we understand this to be predicated of the human part of his person ; but when he says that he will ' have all the churches to know that he searches the hearts and tries the reins of the children of men,' and thus vindicates to himself the peculiar prerogatives of Godhead, we predicate this of his divine nature. And it is in the like way, that all those texts which speak of his state before the incarnation are to be construed. To assert that he was with God in the beginning, and that he had glory with the Father before the world was, is indeed to assert something which implies a distinction in the Godhead before the world began. So far as I am able to see, this stands full and direct against a part of the theory of Dr. S. and of Sabellius. But how such expressions can be construed as giving any liberty to speak of *society*, and *covenanting transactions*, and *deliberative counsel*, and the like, in the Godhead itself, which has one will, understanding, essence, etc., I am unable to see. Especially does this last idea of *deliberation* and *discussion* in the Godhead itself, seem to imply such a defect as to omniscience and infinite wisdom, as to be particularly repulsive.

Nor does the appeal to the *plural* forms of expression in the Old Testament justify the modes of representation in question ; such as, " Let us make man ; Let us go down and see ; The man is become like one of us ; Who will go for us ?" and the like. All these modes of expression seem naturally to spring from the almost continual use of the plural form אֱלֹהִים as the name of God. But he who has well studied the genius of the Hebrew language, must know that this often makes an *intensi-tive* signification of words by employing the *plural* number; and particularly that this is the fact in regard to words designating *dominion, lordship,* etc. Such is the case not only with אֱלֹהִים, but also with תְּרָפִים, אֲדֹנִים, בְּעָלִים, and many others, even when they designate single objects. *Elohim* is for the most part as much as to say, *supreme God.* But if any still insist on the argument to be drawn from this, as evincing of itself a *plurality* in the Godhead, what shall be said of its use in Ps. 45: 6, 7, where first the Son and then the Father is each respectively called *Elohim?* Is there then a plurality of persons in the Son and in the Father too?

It is then on the ground of this plurality as to form in the name of God, that we may most naturally account for such modes of expression as "Let *us* make man, etc." At all events, the subject of such plurality of names is encompassed with so many difficulties, when viewed in any other light, that nothing positive can safely be built upon it, in respect to *plurality* in the Godhead; an expression, by the way, against which the graver and more cautious writers on the subject of the Trinity are often warning us, because of its *polytheistic* aspect.

When moreover we are asked, with a kind of assurance which seems to be well persuaded that no satisfactory answer can be given, 'How could God make the worlds by his Son, if he had no Son until the incarnation?' We may answer in the first place, by asking, How could he "create all things by Jesus Christ," if Jesus Christ did not exist before the incarnation? In both cases the same answer is to be made, viz., that the *divine* nature that dwelt in Jesus did exist before all worlds, and created the worlds. *Son,* in such cases, is used as a proper name, descriptive of the whole person. In the second place we might say, that the question urged on us assumes, that we do not believe what we expressly profess to believe, viz., that there was a distinction in the Godhead, which laid the foundation for the development of Father, Son, and Holy Ghost, which distinction was prior to all time and absolutely eternal.

I have one more suggestion to make. This is, that the *names* themselves, *Father, Son,* and *Holy Ghost,* are names given not so much to characterize the original distinctions in the Godhead, as those by which the Godhead is disclosed to us in the scheme of redemption. These *appellations* may be said to spring from, and to be peculiarly characteristic of, redemption. If any one demands an illustration of the nature of this, let him ask whether God was actually *creator* and *governor* of the world before the world was made? The answer must be in the negative. To complete this relation, and to warrant the full and proper application of these names to the divine Being, the creation and government of the world must have first become matter of real fact. Why is not the same thing true now, in regard to the names *Father, Son,* and *Spirit?* Distinctions in his nature God always possessed. But these were not developed before the scheme of redemption began. The names could then, in their full and proper significancy, be applied only in anticipation of the accomplishment of this scheme, or else after its actual accomplishment. That the glorious Trinity in the Godhead has a special and peculiar relation to this greatest and best of all the works of God, the humble believer, I trust, will not be tempted to call in question.

If it be said that God's becoming creator and governor of the world depended merely on the *voluntary* exercise of the powers which he possessed of creatorship and lordship, and that therefore this case cannot be compared with the development of the distinctions in the Godhead; my answer is, that no essential or important distinction between the two cases, in respect to the *principle* concerned in them, can well be made out. God's original powers or attributes of creatorship and lordship were just as certain to lead to the development of them in the creation and government of the world, as the original distinctions in the Godhead were certain to lead to the development of them as Father, Son, and Holy Ghost. In both cases, the *causa primaria* was the nature of the Godhead itself which possessed such attributes and distinctions. The attribute of creatorship was not an effect of voluntary arbitrament; it was original and uncreated; and being such, it was certain to occasion the development of creative power. And so in the other case; the distinction in the Godhead was original and uncreated; and being such, it was certain to occasion the developments of Father, Son, and Holy Spirit. So far as merely the *developments themselves* are concerned, both are equally voluntary, and both depend on or arise from original nature.

But to proceed with the train of thought before introduced;

it is, I apprehend, principally because the Old Testament was
a revelation merely preparatory to the gospel in its full perfection, that it does but obscurely (if at all) reveal the doctrine of
a Trinity. I am aware, that this question has been often and
zealously disputed. But the proper subject of debate is not,
whether by a comparison of the declarations of the New Testament with certain things asserted respecting Jehovah or Elohim in the Old, and by the light which these declarations cast
on the whole subject, we can *now* find evidence in the Old
Testament of the doctrine of a Trinity. The appropriate question is, Whether the Old Testament in and by itself alone, reveals the doctrine of a Trinity? If it does so, and does it *clearly*, then how could the Saviour say, in reference to all that had
been revealed by Moses and the prophets, "No man hath
seen God at any time; the only begotten, who is in the bosom
of the Father, he hath revealed him?" Surely all the natural
and moral attributes of the Godhead, in the usual sense of these
terms, were clearly disclosed by the Old Testament writings.
What was there then for the Saviour to reveal, which neither
Moses nor any of the prophets saw or could see? I am not able
to answer this question in any satisfactory way, except by the
supposition that Jesus means to declare, that God, as exhibited
in the economy of the gospel, was never *fully* and *plainly* revealed until this economy was perfected by the incarnation.

If I should be asked: 'How could the New Testament writers
appeal to the Old Testament in order to prove the divine nature
of Christ, provided it be true that the Old Testament did not
clearly reveal that divine nature?' the answer is easy. In the
first place, I would say, that I know of no place in the New Testament where an appeal is made for such a purpose. Even in
Heb. i. the texts cited are designed by the writer to prove the
superiority of Christ over the angels, and not to prove his divinity; as John Owen himself explicitly confesses, in his commentary on this chapter. That the texts cited do establish
more than this, (for that they do I fully concede), results from the
nature of the case, and not from the particular *design* of the
writer. The sacred writer intimates, that Psalm XLV. and Psalm
102: 25 seq. relate to Christ; but if he had not told us this as
to the *latter* case, we should never have known and could not
have conjectured that Psalm 102: 25 seq. did refer to the
Saviour. It is only on his own authority, that we ground this reference. And as to the quotation of Ps. XLV., it seems to me to

be a clear case, that it does not fairly establish the truly divine nature of him to whom it is applied. *Elohim* appears to be here applied as designating an *official capacity*, which is high above that of all other kings.

The same is true of other like texts. When Isaiah VI. is quoted by John (12: 38 seq.), and this evangelist declares that the prophet saw the glory of Christ in the sublime and awful vision which he relates, it is on the authority of the apostle only, that we make the application of the passage to Christ; for no reader of it as it stands in the Old Testament, would ever suspect such an application. Not that there is any thing in the text of the prophet which forbids it, for I do not see how this can be truly alleged; but merely that there is nothing which *suggests* it, that is apparent in the original.

And the same will be found to be true of all the other appeals to the Old Testament. They are not appeals in argument with the Jews, made in relation to the question *whether the Saviour is divine;* they are applications to Christ, by the writers of the New Testament, of what was said simply of Jehovah in the Old Testament, and which establish the divinity of the Saviour *obiter* merely, and in the way of logical consequence. But the whole force of the proof rests on the credit we give to the writer of the New Testament, and the authority that we concede to him to expound the Old Testament Scriptures. I repeat it, however, in order that I may not be misapprehended, that no violence to the laws of exegesis is done in this case by the writers of the New Testament. There is, for example, a passage in the Old Testament which predicates something of Jehovah or of Elohim. The New Testament writer avers, that what is here affirmed belongs to Christ. We allow his authority to decide this; and if Christ be God, as Paul and John assert, then there is no reason why we should suppose that there is any violence done to the laws of interpretation. There is certainly nothing in the Hebrew text *against* such an interpretation; and in most cases of this nature it seems to be equally true, that there is nothing which would lead a simple reader of the Old Testament, who knew nothing of the New, to apply such passages to the Messiah.

But I must forbear; for the discussion of this topic, since the days of Calixtus, has been so often engaged in, and the subject is so fully and amply illustrated by later critics, that more need not be here said.

I have only one additional consideration here to suggest; which is, that if it be true, as some assert, that the Jews of our Saviour's time, before they became Christians, were accustomed to believe that their Messiah was to be a *divine* person, how can it be accounted for, that after the first generation of Christians among them, the great body of Jewish converts in Palestine, and many elsewhere, became Ebionites, the peculiarity of whose opinion was, a denial of the divine nature of that Saviour whom they professed to honour? If all the tendency of their education and traditional belief had been as stated above, this fact seems to be altogether unaccountable. It speaks more than volumes of mere reasoning from conjecture, or from the declarations of Rabbins living long after the Christian era had commenced; of which we find such striking examples in P. Allix's learned book on ancient Jewish opinions.

The reader will observe that I have only said, that the doctrine of the Trinity is at most but obscurely, and not fully and clearly revealed, in the Old Testament taken by itself alone. This of course is admitting, that there may be intimations and hints in it, from which the doctrine of more than one person in the Godhead might be deduced in the way of reasoning. Such are the prophecies which appear to ascribe a divine nature to the Messiah; and such some of the declarations, in which the Spirit of God seems to be set forth as a divine person. How much the pious Jews of ancient times actually deduced from such passages, we do not know; and we possess no adequate means of determining. But that the later Jews, and in particular those cotemporary with the apostles, knew nothing of the doctrine of a Trinity, seems to be rendered nearly certain from the fact, that neither Josephus, nor Philo in all his numerous speculations on the subject of religion, gives any intimation of this. Whatever there is in Philo, that seems to approach to this, is merely the *eclectic* philosophy intermingled with his religious views, and may be found in heathen writers almost or quite as fully as in him. At all events, the Nazaraean and Ebionitish sects so prevalent among early Christian Jews, incontestably prove what the usual and predominant state of the Jewish mind was.

On the supposition that has been made, viz., that the full development of Trinity was not made and could not be made, until the time of the Saviour's incarnation, it is easy to see why nothing more than preparatory hints should be found in the Old

Testament respecting it. He who finds more than these there, has reason, so far as I can see, to apprehend that his speculations in theology have stronger hold upon him than the principles of philology. But I must resume my more direct remarks.

So far as any views extend which I have been able to obtain in relation to this whole subject, the names *Father*, *Son*, and *Holy Ghost* seem to be given principally in reference to the revelation of God in these characters, in the economy of the gospel. In their full and appropriate sense, they could never be given, (unless in the way of hint and prophetic anticipation), before the incarnation took place. But let me not be misunderstood in saying this. I do not deny, but on the contrary firmly maintain, (as may be seen by what I have already said), that there was from all eternity such a distinction in the nature of the Godhead, as would certainly lead to the development of it as Father, Son, and Holy Ghost. But the characteristics designated by these significant names, were not fully developed, and could not in all respects fully exist, until the incarnation of the Son and the out-pouring of the Spirit had actually taken place. If you say that there is a difficulty in conceiving of this subject in such a way ; my reply is, that there is the same kind of difficulty, and no greater, as there is in conceiving, as has already been said above, that God was not in reality creator and governor, until the creation of the world and the government of it actually took place. The attributes of *creatorship* and *lordship*, i. e. those qualities which would lead the Godhead to develope himself as creator and lord, and which fitted him (if I may so express it) for this, he possessed from all eternity. In like manner, that distinction in his nature which would lead to his development as Father, Son, and Spirit, and which fitted him for this, existed from all eternity, and was an inseparable part of his very nature. But Father, Son, and Holy Ghost, *in the full sense of the economy of the gospel*, he *actually* was not, until the incarnation of the Logos and the out-pouring of the Spirit had been actually completed.

In other and fewer words ; the foundation, ground, or attribute (if we may or must so name it) of Trinity, is co-eternal with the Godhead itself. The distinction in the Godhead that would lead to the development of Father, Son, and Holy Ghost, always existed. But these adorable names always comprise within their *present* meaning, or at least as employed by us they always should comprise, *a reference to what has actually been done in the economy of redemption.* They can no more have their full and proper significancy without such a reference, than the name *creator* can have its *appropriate* sense, without any reference to actual creation.

In other words somewhat different still we may say, that the full sense of the words *Father, Son,* and *Spirit,* can be made out only by reference to *God revealed.* But the distinction in the Godhead itself, in which this revelation has its basis, is eternal; the development of it was made in time.

We have at last come then, unless I entirely misapprehend the whole nature of this subject, to the rock of offence on which so many have dashed with peril to themselves and others embarked with them. They have insisted that Father, Son, and Holy Spirit, are words that have a full and ample sense, in reference to the Godhead before the incarnation. In a word, they have maintained that God is the Father simply and fully in his divine nature, and in reference to the Godhead only of the Son and Spirit; while these second and third persons were all that their names as now given import, before the incarnation, and indeed before the creation of the world. The Symbol of the Nicene council, and all the long and animated defences of it made by its friends, take so much for granted. Hence the aim and effort to account for it, how God could be Father to the *divine* nature of Christ, and how he could breathe out or send forth from himself the Spirit. Hence too the efforts of the like nature among most of the leading Trinitarians of modern times, to shew that the *personality* of the Son and Spirit, as *divine,* proceeds from the Father. All—all reduces itself to the simple point, of believing and maintaining that Father, Son, and Spirit are names descriptive simply of the original nature of the Godhead as it is in and of itself, and not of the Godhead as manifested in the economy of the gospel.

We have seen what appalling difficulties lie in the way of the explanations which ancient or modern times have presented us, in respect to the subject as thus viewed ; explanations for the most part either contradictory to each other, or altogether wanting in perspicuity, or else at variance with the simple and numerical unity of substance in the Godhead, or absolutely subversive of the equal power and glory which should be attributed to each of the three persons in the Godhead. When one wanders through the immense regions of speculation in relation to this great topic as thus viewed, and sees here and there its precipices and its gulfs, he either becomes discouraged by the way, and gives over the pursuit of his journey, (which the more irresolute are prone to do), or else he turns his back on such a dangerous region, with wonder that any should love to traverse it, while a plain, simple, straight path lies open before them in another direction, in which they will be much more certain to reach the point of satisfaction and safety.

In a word, we may well ask : Why should it ever have any more been overlooked, that the names Father, Son, and Holy Ghost, are names that have a *relative* sense ; relative (I mean) to the developments of the Godhead as made in the economy of redemption, or as preparatory to it ; than that (such) names as *Creator, Governor, Redeemer, Sanctifier, Most High,* and others of the like kind have, and from their very nature must have, a *relative* sense, i. e. a sense which connects itself with the developments of the Godhead in relation to creatures ? The errors and difficulties in theology that have resulted from such an important oversight, are beyond the bounds of computation. Ages and generations have disputed, and been divided in affection, and refused co-operation or alliance, because of disagreement in explaining and defining that which was in itself indefinable and inexplicable, and which indeed was actually inconsistent (when sifted to the bottom) with real Unity or Trinity in the Godhead.

If the view now given of personality in the Godhead, i. e. of the meaning which we should attach to this term when employed in reference to the Godhead, be correct, then the question so often asked and urged, may be answered, viz., Are the names *Father, Son,* and *Spirit,* names of the simple and original nature of the Godhead, antecedent to all development ? Or are they names of merely the developments of the Godhead in various ways? The affirmative as to the first question was maintained by the great body of the fathers; especially after the Council of Nice. It has also been maintained with equal strenuousness by most Trinitarians in modern times, although on different grounds from that occupied by the Nicenians. On the other hand ; the Sabellians in ancient times, and a few in modern times who have approached near to or actually embraced their doctrines, have contended that *personality* is mere πρόσωπον, in the original sense of this word, i. e. merely the φάσις, or *species,* or *form* and *manner,* in which the Μονάς has revealed itself to men.

If now it be asked, after all which has been said above, which of these parties are in the right as to their mode of explanation, it seems to me that the proper answer is: Neither. Both of these views are extremes; into which parties warmly engaged in dispute are always prone to go. When Praxeas and Noetus and Beryll, and finally Sabellius, all within the latter part of the second century or during the third, declared themselves against the common *hypostatic* views of the churches at that period, the zeal of those theologians who felt it incumbent upon them to defend the *hypostatic* scheme of Trinity, was animated to an excessive degree, and the doctrine of personal *distinction* in the Godhead became a matter of much livelier belief and interest, than the doctrine of divine unity, which retreated quite to the back ground, and was principally brought forward only to repel charges of polytheism. A belief in the real divine nature of the persons in the Trinity was not abandoned; but to make out this and preserve hypostatical distinctions also, the Nicenians went back to the *original* state of the Godhead itself, and found there all the distinctions they made, just as fully and completely developed before time began, as after the plan of actual redemption had begun to be executed. This was one extreme to which the zeal of dispute carried the great body of the fathers, in their contention against Sabellius and others like to him.

On the other hand; the party of Praxeas, Noetus, Beryll, and Sabellius, not seeing any thing but *polytheism* as the logical result of their antagonists' premises, and strenuously contending for the strictest form of Monotheism that seemed in any way to be compatible with the gospel, came by the force of opposition and by party zeal to the conclusion, that there was in the Godhead itself no distinction, and that personality consists merely in the development of the Godhead as disclosed in the gospel. The amount of all was, that the parties separated as widely asunder as possible, without absolutely giving up the unity of God on the one hand, and all distinction in the Godhead in any way on the other.

Thus it is at all times and in all warm disputes, whether civil or religious. Parties being once fully formed, and marshalled before the world against each other, proceed to the utmost degree of separation that is possible, without renouncing all character and credit. The famous Synod of Dort affords an eminent example of this. Balcanqual, the deputy from Scotland to that Synod, tells us in his letters, that he and the English deputies, (all of whom were strict Calvinists), laboured very much to induce the Synod to express their disapprobation of the assertion, that "God moves the tongues of men to blaspheme." But the Synod refused to act in relation to the subject, because they knew that some of the members of it were accustomed to say this, out of opposition to what they supposed to be the lax sentiments of Arminius respecting the divine agency. A melancholy proof indeed of the tendency of party spirit to excess and extravagance !

The case which is now before us, I well know, is in many respects a different one ; but the principles or rather the passions of men in a warm dispute, operate in like way in all ages of the world, unless restrained by special interposition of divine grace.

Were the Nicenians in the right, and their advocates in the right, in construing the names Father, Son, and Holy Ghost, as names which had their *full* meaning as applied to the mere simple, original, and eternal state of the Godhead? Just as much in the right, I must answer, as we should now be, in saying that *Creator* and *Governor* are names of the eternal and original state of the Godhead ; and no more.

Were Sabellius and those like him as to opinion, and is Dr. S., in the right, in saying that the names of the Trinity have a simple reference to developments of the Godhead made in the economy of redemption ? To which I must repeat the same answer that has just been given. *In medio tutissimus ibis*, seems to be altogether applicable to the present case. Both parties have gone to the extreme. From eternity there existed that distinction in the Godhead, which was developed in the economy of redemption. The names of the persons in the Trinity I view as including and recognizing this fact. But the names themselves have also an express reference to the parts which the Godhead has actually sustained, and sustains, in the work of redemption. Their *full* significancy is and can be never given, without a reference to this. There is no more difficulty in this statement, than in the one that God was *actually* creator and lord only after the creation.

May we not indulge the hope that the time will come, as we approach nearer to the latter day of glory, and hold ourselves more and more free to canvass the opinions of uninspired men, and faster bound to the simple instructions of the Bible—may we not hope that the time is near, when men will see and feel, that the doctrine of the Trinity, when stated in a simple and scriptural way, contains nothing repulsive to sound reason, nothing that is more mysterious than what belongs to the other attributes of the Godhead, such as self-existence, ubiquity, etc. ? May we not especially hope, that Christians will cease to be agitated with such an undue zeal for the doctrine of *personality*, as will lead them to assert and maintain it in such a way, that the unity of the Godhead is put entirely at hazard by their mode of treating the subject ?   To what good purpose can it be, that they strenuously assert their belief in the Unity of God, while they continue to make representations, which, when strictly examined, prove to be altogether inconsistent, in a theoretical point of view, with numerical unity of substance and essential attributes ?   I am filled with unwelcome apprehension, whenever I perceive that a far greater proportion of zeal is maintained in any metaphysical school of theology, for the *personality* than for the *unity* of the Godhead.   Just as though, *Hear, O Israel! Jehovah our God is* ONE JEHOVAH, were expunged from the sacred record, or put in the back ground !   This should not be so.   It will be well for all the churches to remember, that the zeal of Origen, on this very same point, led him to a theory in no important respect better than that of Arius ; see p. 32 above.   Such was the case too with Eusebius, the church historian.   Arius himself, as we have good reason to believe, became what he was by his overflowing zeal against Sabellius. When the latter urged the truly divine nature of Christ, and the necessity of a simple divine nature and of unity in it, Arius, in order to parry the force of these considerations, betook himself to the fearful expedient of asserting not only the separate hypostatic, but (in order fully to make this out) even the *created* being of the Son of God.   So had Dionysius, bishop of Alexandria, already done before him ; for which he was rebuked by his brother of the same name at Rome, and drew back from his rash declarations, to a position within the covert of the dubious language of Origen ; which too often may mean, I had almost said, any thing or nothing in relation to this great topic.

    Can heated zeal on the subject of mere *scholastic* or *patristic* personality, ever be productive of any thing but hazard to the peace of the church and to the interests of true doctrine ? Or have we yet to learn, that zeal for the doctrines and commandments of men, and even those of theologians and councils, is not always a zeal for the simple decisions of the Bible?

I would hope, that due consideration of this subject may lead Christians to cherish more of that spirit which Calvin felt, when he uttered the sentiment that is quoted above (p. 97). We shall then be more likely to come at the truth, the whole truth (so far as we are permitted in our present state to know it), and nothing but the truth.

On the other hand, to give up the doctrine of the Trinity as exhibited in the gospel; to cease to maintain the true and proper divinity of the Son and of the Spirit, as well as of the Father; would in my apprehension, be to give up a distinguishing and *fundamental* part of the gospel. God as infinite in power, knowledge, holiness, justice, goodness, and truth; God as self-existent and every where present; the Jew, the Mohammedan, the Theist, believe in as well as the Christian. What then separates the Christian from them, unless it is the peculiar truths of the economy of the gospel? And what among all these can have pre-eminence over that which is expressed in "God manifest in the flesh," and making atonement — an all-sufficient atonement, for sin? I know of nothing to be set above this, so far as the peculiarities of a Christian system are concerned. If so, then let the Christian hold fast to this in life and death, in time and eternity. Why should he be required to be baptized into the name of the Father, and of the Son, and of the Holy Ghost, unless it is to teach him that his profession as a Christian must begin, continue, and end with the acknowledgment of this great truth? *God as manifested in the gospel*, is the God in which he believes; and this God is Father, Son, and Holy Ghost. *How much* that is signified by these venerable and adorable names, applies to the original state and condition of the Godhead, and how much to it as manifested in the economy of redemption, he need not solicitously seek to know. Enough that the names have a peculiar relation to *God revealed;* and that to suppose God to be revealed in this way necessarily implies a distinction in his nature which is eternal. For the rest, he contents himself to wait until he shall be introduced to that vision which is behind and beyond the veil, before he can expect to have a more definite knowledge. What he does know, he sincerely believes; and believing, he admires, he wonders, he adores. What he does not know by any express revelation, but which seems necessarily to result from what is revealed, he may well believe to be not the less real, because it is not in a direct way disclosed to him.   As to the *modus exis-tendi* of the Godhead, he is content to believe that it must of necessity involve more or less which is beyond the circle of his present knowledge or even conception.

And now I have only to entreat the reader, if he has doubts about the views that have been given, that before he comes to a final decision, he would traverse the *whole* ground of examina-tion.   He has no right to decide hastily, by merely a partial view of the subject.   If, when he has plunged deep into ancient and modern investigations respecting this great topic, and deliberately and often searched them out, he shall judge me to be erroneous and inconclusive in my reasonings, then I may hold him bound to give his reasons for such a judgment.   If I must stand condemned, he will suffer me to insist that the sentence of my judge shall be openly declared, in order that it may be ex-amined.   The days of the Nicene Council, who could bring the emperor of the world to publish their sentiments by the thunder of imperial edicts and of arms, is past.   The menacing tones of the Vatican too are echoing fainter and fainter every year.   The cry of *Dixerunt sancti Patres* is at last, almost every where, beginning to soften its high-raised notes.   The still small voice of reason and of eternal Wisdom in the book of God, we would fain hope, is beginning also to speak with more efficient power than in ages past, to the souls of men.   If any one will show that he has been a listener to this, and give satisfactory evidence to the world of the fact ; if his testimony shall convict me of error, I promise to be among the first who will listen to him, and among the most persevering in receiving his instructions.   Let him *discuss*, and he will be read.   Let him do it in the spirit of love, and he will find friends, even if they should deem him to be erroneous.   Discussion in the spirit of love and candor, will always promote the interests of truth ; zeal for tradition, and the fathers, and systems, and metaphysical definitions of things beyond the boundaries of human know-ledge, is never likely to achieve much that is useful or com-mendable.

It may be proper for me to say, that the results of this re-examination of the doctrine of the Trinity are, in their essential parts, the same as those which I some years since advocated in my letters addressed to the Rev. Dr. Channing, and the Rev. Dr. Miller, on the subject of the Trinity and Eternal Generation. Some of the detail which has respect to these views, in particular a few things of a *patristical* nature, I have found reason to regard in a somewhat different light from what I once did, inasmuch as I have now made a protracted and repeated examination; and accordingly I have not shrunk from representing such details according to my present convictions. If any industrious opponent should take the pains to point out some of these minor discrepancies, he is welcome to the task. My only reply is and will be: I never claimed perfection nor infallibility; and am well aware that I have never exhibited the one or the other. I have not yet, although somewhat more than half a century old, become too old to change opinions when I find reason for it; nor too assuming and haughty to proclaim my retractions; even if the reproach of those who think and feel that all truth and right and piety are theirs, should be incurred thereby.

I merely add, that for my own part I feel bound to say, at the close of this protracted effort to discuss and explain some of these very difficult subjects, that I rise from the discussion *a more thorough Trinitarian than ever. I do believe with all my heart, in God, the Father, Son, and Holy Ghost, as revealed in the Scripture; and my only hope of salvation hangs on what is connected with this belief.* But I have no zeal for the system of an *emanation*-Trinity, as taught in the Nicene school, nor for the *metaphysical* and *modal* one of more modern theologians. When it can be shown that either the one or the other of these is revealed in the Bible, then may we become disciples of those who show it. Until then, it is better for us to remain simple *scriptural* believers, and attached merely to the School of Christ.

www.ingramcontent.com/pod-product-compliance
Lightning Source LLC
La Vergne TN
LVHW051628080426
835511LV00016B/2236